No Trifling Matter

Taking the Sacraments Seriously Again

No Trifling Matter

Taking the Sacraments Seriously Again

✝

Msgr. Nicola Bux

Translated by
A Religious

Preface by
Vittorio Messori

Foreword by
Christopher J. Malloy

 Angelico Press

First published in Italian as
Con i sacramenti non si scherza
© 2016 Edizioni Cantagalli S.r.l.–Siena
First published in English by Angelico Press © 2018

For information, address:
Angelico Press
169 Monitor St.
Brooklyn, NY 11222
angelicopress.com

978-1-62138-351-2 (pbk)
978-1-62138-352-9 (cloth)
978-1-62138-353-6 (ebook)

Cover image: Raphael,
Disputation of the Holy Sacrament (detail)
Cover design: Michael Schrauzer

CONTENTS

ABBREVIATIONS

CCC *Catechism of the Catholic Church,* 1992.

CIC *Codex Iuris Canonici* [*Code of Canon Law*].

CCEO *Codex Canonum Ecclesiarum Orientalium* [*Code of Canons of the Eastern Churches*].

MD Pius XII, Encyclical Letter *Mediator Dei,* 1947.

GIRM *General Instruction on the Roman Missal,* 3rd Latin typical edition; English translation for the United States of America, 2003.

SC Second Vatican Ecumenical Council, Constitution on the Sacred Liturgy *Sacrosanctum Concilium,* 1963.

SC stands for the series *Sources Chrétiennes* whenever a patristic or ancient Christian writer is cited.

LF Francis, Encyclical Letter *Lumen Fidei,* June 29, 2013.

Abbreviations for books of the Bible and for patristic, papal, and conciliar sources are ones in common use.

To the memory of my beloved brother Andrea

Foreword

AN Italian priest and liturgical theologian, Msgr. Nicola Bux, has written a book on the sacraments quite popular in Italy, now available in English translation. This remarkable book is chock full of pithy insights, noble exhortations, and keen criticisms. Its unifying theme, the perennial sacramentality of the Church in the context of contemporary obstacles and difficulties, allows its scope to be quite vast and sprawling. *No Trifling Matter* is not intended as a textbook. Rather, its sundry edifying observations and notes of wisdom make for good reading in small portions. There is much food for thought here. The anonymous translator offers notes with helpful theological clarifications and background insight on Italian culture.

Fr. Bux presents a thoroughly Catholic view, touching on East and West, the spiritual and the physical, the Ancient and the New, the natural and the supernatural, sin and grace, predestination and free will, Church and world. Among the dominant sub-themes is the sacred and the profane. "Sacred" means holy, dedicated to God. "Profane" has several meanings. It first signifies what lies "before" or "outside" the temple. It also signifies what is natural, not *yet* consecrated. Finally, it can signify what is crass, tasteless, or even opposed to God. As Bux reminds the reader, what is earthly and ordinary, but not crass, is called to be taken up and ordered to God. The Church is called to consecrate the world to God.

This beautiful vision has been effaced from the Catholic imagination in the wake of an errant theology that obscures the distinction between sacred and profane. Under a semblance of mysticism, some (e.g., Karl Rahner, Vorgrimler, Martos) claim in various ways that the world is already sacred from the beginning. They mock a caricature of the Tradition, as though the Tradition denied that any grace exists outside of church buildings. The Tradition, including official Church doctrine, *never* made such a ridiculous claim. The Church teaches (a) that there are graces outside of her visible boundaries

1

and action, (b) that such grace objectively leads back *to* the Catholic Church, (c) that there is no salvation outside the Catholic Church, and (d) that only those who are invincibly ignorant of this truth are not condemned for not entering the Church (while even these are deprived of many helps). In short, the Tradition has by no means a simpleton's position.

Having dismissed the Tradition, the revolutionaries substitute errors in its stead. Claiming that grace is already in the world, they hold that the sacraments only *express* this fact with correct words and gestures. Understandably, some faithful Catholics too quickly critique this notion as reducing sacraments to merely indicative "signs." The revolutionaries have a ready response: They claim that the grace in the world "inclines" to become sacramental, "inclines" to express itself. In this way, they assert, the sacraments contain grace. They call the sacraments, thus understood, "Real Symbols."

In fact, the Real Symbol notion falls short of Catholic dogma. The revolutionaries are more straightforward when they describe their notion as a "Copernican revolution" in sacramental thinking. As they say, the Tradition (dogma) holds that sacraments are *causes of grace,* that sacraments convey grace otherwise not present. They reject this teaching. For them, the grace is already there but is in the sacramental act given the correct linguistic and gestural expression. Further, the revolutionaries have lost the sense of the supernatural and of sin and the need for repentance and sacramental grace to escape eternal damnation. If not many people are unfortunate enough to read this ruinous line of thought, many suffer in parishes because of its influence.

For those looking for a thoughtful antidote, Bux's book is a fine option. Bux recognizes the importance and necessity of catechesis, but he urges us to appreciate the noble work of the sacraments and not to let explanations dominate rationalistically. With the assistance of words, we should live and contemplate the signs, which point to and convey what is higher and deeper. To appreciate signs, Bux reminds us, is a basic human task. All of being is significant.

Hand-in-hand with the loss of the sacred goes loss of the sense of God, as Bux notes with Ratzinger. Many current celebrations of Mass fail to draw the mind to God. They fail to encourage us to lay aside earthly cares and attend to the heavenly banquet. His transcendent aim obscured, man becomes the center of attention. Although Vatican II did not ask for it, the tabernacle is often banished to the outskirts, making the Blessed Sacrament "homeless." The liturgy then becomes a field of human entertainment, not entry into the divine work.

In addition to this macroscopic view of things, Bux also hones in on particular, pressing issues. He points out, for instance, that Vatican II did not cast Latin into a dungeon. Sadly, Latin languishes despite having many reasons to be retained. In a globalized world, Latin offers an unexpected promise of unity not yoked to any current political regime. More importantly, Latin is a spiritual treasure of the Church, part of the living Tradition of handing on the faith. A simple return to Latin is not enough, however. Even the Latin of the Ordinary Form of the Mass, Bux notes, mutes expression of such elements of the faith as the existence of the devil, the darkness of sin, etc. The Ordinary Form of baptism retains no exorcisms, only prayers of liberation. This privation is a mark of discontinuity.

Bux also recalls the centrality of sacrifice in the Mass. Although also a banquet at the table of nourishment, the Mass is firstly a sacrifice of the altar, a sacrifice of right worship to God effective as propitiation for sins. We need to retain both aspects. Attention to the Real Presence also makes clear that the Mass is a divine work. The Eucharistic presence of Christ does not evolve gradually through the work of human hands but is achieved instantaneously by the power of Christ in heaven, working through the hierarchical priest on earth. How appropriate to ring the bells at this solemn moment!

In order to be fit to receive the Eucharist, one must be in the state of grace. Among today's great errors is flight from the Gospel's exhortation, echoed at the Council, to become holy. Not everyone may receive the Eucharist, for not everyone is in the state of grace. Many people today have left a marriage and attempted to become "remarried," without having received an official judgment from the Church that the first marriage was from its inception *null*. Those who have done this and are engaged in sexual relations are in a state of sin and may not receive the Eucharist. They must repent, which requires firm purpose of amendment, and receive absolution in

Confession. Only false mercy would attempt to override or reinterpret these life-giving elements of divine law.

Today's loss of the sense of sin goes hand-in-hand with the false notion that the world is already holy. Common sense tells us this notion is false. If it is holy, why are so many so spiritually sad, so misled, so confused, so distraught? Missionaries, who don't just think about loving others but do something about it, first exorcise new territories and then they lay their foundations. Similarly, church buildings are solemnly consecrated, set aside solely for divine use. The profane is not the sacred, although what had been profane can be consecrated and brought into the sacred. Alas, Bux cries, nowadays churches are treated as venues for mundane, even shameful events. How can the mind's eye rise to God when the house of the holy is just another theater?

Perhaps most timely is Bux's chapter on marriage. He nicely treats the differing theologies of the minister of marriage in East and West. He stresses the centrality of fecundity and the complementarity of male and female in the sacrament. As Bux relates, the homosexual ideology of its essence violates sexual difference, all the while pleading in legal contexts recognition of "difference." The argument is disingenuous because it (a) abolishes truth by demanding acceptance of error and (b) abolishes the loveliest of differences, male and female. Although respect is due to everyone as persons, human "rights" require reference to human nature and hence to God's law.

Not least, Bux reflects on the sacramentals. His narration of the organic development that led to building and consecrating churches is splendid. We are once again reminded of the sacred and the profane, of the natural and the supernatural. In reading, I was reminded of T. S. Eliot's line, "You are here to kneel, where prayer has been valid." Use of the sacred space for profane events, even if these be tolerable in themselves, is a "very serious phenomenon," even a "desolation." Similarly, the cavalier way priests carry on at Mass, with gym shoes and jokes, high fives, calling for applause, etc., represents "not a sacred order, but a profane and secularized disorder."

This book would make a fine gift for a priest who has an open mind to a call to return to the beauty and truth of Tradition. It might be seen as a bridge, inviting one to contemplate the disorders of today's liturgical experiences as reason to reconsider the timeless wisdom of the Church. Practicing lay Catholics without theological training will also enjoy it. May it be widely read!

CHRISTOPHER J. MALLOY
The University of Dallas

Preface

by Vittorio Messori

AS he is about to begin his exposition of the sacrament of holy orders, Fr. Nicola Bux writes: "The distinctive characteristics of the priesthood are found in the conferral and exercise of the three *munera*, that is, the tasks or offices of teaching, sanctifying, and governing." As regards "governing," I don't know if Fr. Bux has any particular ways and objectives in governing. As for "sanctifying," I have no doubt: I know how tirelessly he stays true to his call to be a mediator between the sacred and the profane, between God and man, his call to be the convinced and competent steward that he is of the sacraments. If we turn to "teaching," well, this very book of his, just published, is another confirmation of how seriously he takes the *munus* entrusted to him with the priestly consecration. In addition to his many other books, this is the third dedicated to the liturgy in the Church of all the ages, and above all, of today.

His great competence as a well-known and respected holder of a professor's chair in the subject matter is placed at the service of teaching, through these works as well: they are not for select groups of students, but for every Catholic, whether habitually practicing or occasionally. Or they can also simply be for a woman or a man who is searching, the kind of person we meet more and more frequently. Infiltrated by today's prevailing current in the West, which tends to create a sort of "liquid society" where everything seems to liquefy into everything else, the Church also appears to want to dissolve the clear edges of the faith in a sort of vague and mixed-up broth, typi-fied by the "my opinion is" that we hear from certain priests. Far from being held back, such priests are encouraged rather by the theologians whose names we need not mention. Well, the sacra-ments are the expression, the fruit, and the highest and most pre-cious gift of the faith. And so our liturgist Fr. Bux is here to dedicate himself to the topic, with his accustomed passionate enthusiasm,

7

following the helpful schema he already employed in his previous books. In the first place, he will clarify, for each of the seven "efficacious signs," its object, its significance, and its history. Then, the warning—necessary and more relevant than ever—the warning about the deformations, the equivocations, the additions, and the omissions that today threaten the sacrament under consideration. So we have a catechesis in a style at once learned and popular, followed by a sort of "user's guide." The efficacy of the approach is also confirmed by the great success the books have had not only in Italy but also in the countries into whose language they have been translated.

Fr. Bux can be severe with certain of his confreres and their "creative" itch that leads them to corrode a liturgical discipline that is not useless formalism, but rather the very substance of the sacrament. But his warnings do not have the scornful and imperious tone of the inquisitor or, worse, of the ideologue trying someone in the docket. With him the call back to order is expressed, fundamentally, with the understanding of someone who knows well the kind of deformed and deforming culture in which churchmen are also immersed. Moreover, he well knows how incomplete and maybe even suspect has been the formation (if it is still that) imparted too often to the haggard group of seminarians yet remaining to us. We seem to catch, in the professor who writes here, a sort of *pietas* for the poor priests, even in the background of the reproaches he formulates. For those priests, and as a confrere who is a specialist, but not for all that closed up in his academic ivory tower, he therefore points out not only a list of errors and misunderstandings, but also the direction in which to move in order to seek to remedy the situation.

At the bottom of everything that has been happening in the *Catholica* for decades now, there is all that the author denounced in his preceding books as well: that "anthropological turn that has brought into the Church a lot of the presence of man, but only a little of the presence of God." Sociology instead of theology, the World obscuring Heaven, the horizontal without the vertical, the profane that drives out the sacred. The Catholic synthesis—the kind of law that is *et-et*, the union of opposites that rules the entire edifice of the faith—has been too often abandoned in favor of an inadmissible one-sidedness.

As regards the sacraments in particular, as a layman I would be tempted to launch a kind of warning to the priests. Be careful!—it would occur to me to say—we have such an excess of sociologists, union leaders, political scientists, psychologists, ecologists, sexologists, and in general specialists of everything, that we can no longer manage! Be careful, because there is no need for priests, religious, and monks to exercise the occupations I mentioned, and as improbable amateurs, as they often do. It should never be forgotten that there is something only the consecrated person can do, a thing for which he does not and cannot have "competition": the function of go-between, of link between man and God. In the administration of the sacraments, precisely. To reduce it to the essential, "sanctifying" is the *munus* that justifies the existence and presence of consecrated ministers. If done well, a clerical commitment in social and cultural fields, in every field of human activity, is an excellent thing. Excellent but not indispensable: we laypeople also know how to engage in those commitments, and very often we do them better. As professionals and not dilettantes. But only a man on whom hands have been imposed, signifying the reality of those deep and awesome words *Tu es sacerdos in aeternum*—only a man such as that can assure us of the pardon of the Christ for whom he is a go-between; only he can transform, in faith, the bread and wine into the body and blood of the Redeemer. He alone. No one else in the world.

By a deep instinct, the crowds thronged around the altar and the confessional of Padre Pio, pushing and shoving to be as close as possible to his Mass and to have the privilege of confiding to him the sins that Jesus would judge. But we are not aware of crowds, except of students registered for that course, around the lecture platform of the clerical theologian who explains that it is childish to believe in a Eucharist that is even "materially" real, and that it is nothing but play-acting, unworthy of an adult Christian, to think that the pardon of sins passes through an instrument, a man like us. A man like us—of course! But at the same time, invisibly, he is something different. Different because consecrated.

Post scriptum

The very day I concluded my reflections above, I received the latest book by Hans Küng, *Morire felici?* [*To Die Happy*]. The Swiss theologian (who is offended if someone does not designate him as "Christian," "Catholic" even) is one of the promoters and activists of Exit, the best known and most active organization in Europe for "assisted death," that is, active assistance for euthanasia. With macabre hypocrisy, someone seeking to end it all is dealt with in something like a comfortable hotel, and when he so desires, he is made comfortable in an armchair in a silent and deserted lounge room. On the little table a nurse puts a glass of beverage that is pleasant tasting, but terrifyingly toxic, and leaves, closing the door. The door will be reopened shortly, so that she can verify the death and carry the corpse away. Macabre hypocrisy, I said. Exit limits itself to providing a quiet place and putting a deadly poison down on the table: what can they do if the gentleman, or the lady, decides to drink the mixture? They are free, by Jove, nobody is forcing them!

The "Catholic" Küng is a priest, and has never asked to abandon the priesthood, even if no one has ever seen him in a clerical suit, or worse, in church vestments, and he himself would be amazed if anyone called him "Fr. Hans." Already in the introductory chapter of this pamphlet of his, which means to demonstrate how "biblical" and even "evangelical" suicide and euthanasia are, he does not fail, as always, to rail against the *Catholica* that ordained him, and gave him the power to administer the sacraments. Saying that he desires the true good of man, unlike the inhuman Roman monsignors, he writes: "I would want a Church that helps man to die, instead of limiting itself to giving him Extreme Unction. The point is to help a person who wants to say good-bye to life to die well."

Social engagement to the farthest extreme, then: a Church-created and managed structure for welcoming aspirants to suicide, and helping them reach their end, quickly and painlessly. This is charity? This is the duty of the Christian community? Or is it charitable to be limited to that sacrament, the sacrament of Extreme Unction (or Anointing of the Sick, as it is called today), which only accompanies the dying with mumbled ancient words and anachronistic anointings, but is not concerned with the physical sufferings of the person dying? But Küng has not given and does not give the right example—illustrious pillar as he is of *Exit*, that "social" agency that, with Christian concern, welcomes the person who would otherwise be forced to throw himself into the river or out the window, or get himself ground up by a train.

It is with a bitter taste here that I have the unpleasant affirmative answer to the question I was asking myself above: forgetful as they are of their role of unfathomable value, a role that no one else in the world can exercise, what do we do with priests like that? Who would want to have beside his deathbed a theology professor of the prestigious university of Tübingen? Who would not willingly exchange him for the most unknown, and maybe unlearned of priests—yet one who is still conscious of the value, as mysterious as it is efficacious in the true sense, of the sacrament?

Aims of This Book

SOME years ago, after a Mass concelebrated for a medical convention, I was approached by one of the doctors, who asked me: Excuse me, Father, why did you put the tabernacle in a corner, with you the priests in the center? I responded: The priest also represents Christ. The calm reply: He represents Christ, but he isn't Christ. I answered back: You know, it's so we don't turn our backs to the people. Then a peremptory reminder for me: Father, do you know what the prophet says? "Instead of their face, they turned their backs on me" (cf. Jer. 7:23–24): in that way, you prefer the people to God! Excuse me, but you know, you've told us that the laity should study, so I'll ask this: Can one depose the Lord and put a man in his place, minister of the Lord though he be? I had no more arguments: if God is there in the sacrament, then today's liturgy is *de facto* turning its back on God. It hasn't much helped us to recover its eschatological dimension, as it is called—the Lord who comes to visit us, as we say in the *Benedictus*, in order to save us—and not even the ecclesiology of communion has helped, for communion descends from the gaze upon the Trinity, not from priest and people looking at each other.

The anthropological turn has brought into the Church a great deal of the presence of man, but little of God's presence. I'm helped here by a passage from Joseph Ratzinger's preface to the book by Alcuin Reid:

> If the Liturgy appears first of all as the workshop for our activity, then what is essential is being forgotten: God. For the Liturgy is not about us, but about God. Forgetting about God is the most imminent danger of our age. As against this, the Liturgy should be setting up a sign of God's presence. Yet what happens if the habit of forgetting about God makes itself at home in the Liturgy itself and if in the Liturgy we are thinking only of ourselves? In any and

13

every liturgical reform, and every liturgical celebration, the primacy of God should be kept in view first and foremost.[1]

In the face of today's abuses in the sacramental liturgy, the words of Jesus come back to us: "Isaiah prophesied well of you, hypocrites, when he wrote: This people honors me with their lips, but their heart is far from me and the worship they render to me is a pile of human ideas and commands" (Is. 29:13, in Mk. 7:6–7). Consequently we are confronted with a horizontal and sociological vision of Christianity, symbolized by the altar turned toward the people, a vision not seldom purchased at the price of unheard-of artistic devastations. A revolution in sacred space, disguised as "adaptation." The Church turns her back on the supernatural and ceases to consecrate the world. And so "Christianity's heaven is empty"—thus writes the philosopher Umberto Galimberti—since in his judgment Christianity not only "has lost the dimension of the sacred," but has even "desacralized the sacred."[2] This is also admitted by the encyclical *Lumen Fidei:* "Our culture has lost the perception of this concrete presence of God, of his action in the world. We think that God is found only in a beyond, in another dimension of reality, separated from our concrete relations to things" (n.17). Instead of this, the sacred for Christians is the presence of God and all that concerns him, and so: "The reawakening of faith is by way of the reawakening of a new sacramental sense of the life of man and of Christian existence, showing how the visible and the material open out upon the mystery of the eternal" (ibid., n.40). The sacraments are a special means for entering into communion with God.

In the crisis of meaning that runs through the whole world, here is the perspective appropriate for a book on the sacraments: to help the faithful rediscover the sacramental liturgy of the Church, in its fullness of life and truth, and reread the history and significance of the Christian sacraments, so that each one can make his own faith

1. Preface to Alcuin Reid, *The Organic Development of the Liturgy,* 2nd ed. (San Francisco: Ignatius Press, 2005), 13.

2. Cf. U. Galimberti, *Cristianesimo. La religione dal cielo vuoto* [*Christianity. Religion of the Empty Heaven*] (Milan: Feltrinelli, 2012).

into a life lived, able to ameliorate everyday human existence; but also to provide a means for satisfying the curiosity of all those interested by the problem of faith, from the standpoint of the evolution of culture and custom.

In the Church today, the "word" is exalted more than the sacrament. What St. Jerome says about Scripture, however, is forgotten: "it treats of mysteries that, as such, remain closed and incomprehensible for the uninitiated."[3] For the word also demands initiation into it. The Word was made flesh, which can be touched in the sacraments: through the sacraments we understand the written word as well, but without the sacraments the word stays on paper. Pope Francis has observed, in one of his morning homilies, that the people of God are always drawing near to ask for something from Jesus, and they are sometimes a bit insistent in this. But it is the insistence of people who believe. And he recounted:

> I remember one time, leaving the city of Salta on the patronal feast day, there was a humble lady who was asking a blessing from a priest. The priest was telling her: "That's fine, ma'am, but you were at Mass!" and he explained to her the whole theology of the blessing at Mass. He explained it well... "Ah, thank you, Father; yes, Father," the lady was saying. When the priest went away, the lady turned to another priest: "Give me a blessing!" All those words hadn't penetrated, because her need was of a different kind: the need to be touched by the Lord. That kind of faith we find always, and it is stirred up by the Holy Spirit. We have to facilitate it, make it grow, help it to grow.

But whereas Jesus instituted seven sacraments, we with our attitude institute an eighth: the sacrament of the "pastoral" customs inspection!

And thus we can confirm today's problem in the Church, a disagreement on the nature of the liturgy: is it a work of God, in which he has exclusive competence and his rights, or is it a human entertainment for doing what we want?[4] As drift and confusion, resulting

---

3. St. Jerome, *Prologue to the Commentary on the Prophet Isaiah*, n. 2; CCL 73:3.
4. Cf. D. Nigro, *I diritti di Dio. La liturgia dopo il Vaticano II* [*The Rights of God: The Liturgy After Vatican II*] (Milan: Sugarco, 2013), 71ff.

from the yearning for innovation, become more obvious, it also becomes evident that the best novelty is always the tradition, valued and lived appropriately. Ideology has not seldom taken hold of the bishops to the extent that they abhor whatever looks like tradition: but without the action of *tradere*, that is, without that movement of handing on what has been received, what is truly new does not arrive. The disagreement can be resolved only by understanding that the liturgy is sacred, that is, belongs to God, and he is present there and acts. Instead, the postconciliar tendency to reject the rights of God in the Church has also favored and encouraged anarchy and anomie in the liturgy, subjecting it to continual deformations in the name of creativity.

I concluded a previous essay with what J.R.R. Tolkien wrote to his son Michael:

> Beyond this dark life of mine, which has been so frustrated, I propose to you the only great thing to love on earth: the holy sacraments. Here you will find adventure, glory, honor, fidelity, and the true road for all your love on this earth, and more than that, for death itself, on account of the divine paradox that only the omen of death, which puts an end to life and claims everyone's surrender, can preserve and give reality and eternal duration to the relations which you seek on this earth (love, fidelity, joy), and which every man desires in his heart.[5]

All reality is the sign of a "beyond"; it is not exhausted in what is seen and touched, but refers us beyond itself. Eugenio Montale writes: "All images carry this written on them: 'go further.'"[6] The sacraments constitute a permanent reminder of that.

With aims such as these, and after trying the material out—which I did in the course of spiritual exercises with the Fraternity of the Most Holy Virgin Mary in Bagnoregio, who kindly gave me their attention, and to whom I am grateful—I present the sacraments in general, and in the order of topics in the *Catechism of the*

5. *The Letters of J.R.R. Tolkien,* ed. Humphrey Carpenter (Boston: Houghton Mifflin, 2000), letter 43.

6. E. Montale, *Maestrale* [*Northwest Wind*], in the collection *Ossi di Seppia* [*Cuttlefish Bones*] (Turin: Pietro Gobetti, 1925).

Catholic Church, that is, the sacraments of Christian initiation (baptism, confirmation, Eucharist), of healing (reconciliation, anointing of the sick), and of service (matrimony and order), not leaving out the extensive area of the sacramentals. I seek to respond to the questions most debated and most contentious in the media, in such a way as to widen interest in the topic, having no pretensions to exhaust it, but intending to touch on the thorniest questions in the way they are often formulated by the man in the street. There is in fact a cultural and generational change coming in the perception people have of the liturgy, but few are noticing it, despite so much talk about "the signs of the times."

I

Face to Face with Christ

At the school of the Fathers

HAS there remained anything visible of Jesus Christ so that we can touch him and be face to face with him? Ambrose and Leo respond: the sacraments. What are they?

The greatest of the sacraments, the "Sacrament Most Holy," is described by Dom Chautard, Trappist abbot of Sept-Fons, in an exchange with the French Prime Minister Clemenceau (the famous "Tiger"), as the divine sacrifice of Calvary brought forth again every day in our midst. Every day Christ offers to God his death, through the hands of the priest, exactly as in heaven, in the Mass of glory, he presents to his Father the glorious signs of his wounds, in order to perpetuate the redemptive efficacy of the Cross. Every day at Mass Christ renews the immense work of the redemption of the world.[1]

All the sacraments are a consequence of the Incarnation of the Word in Jesus. If he had not been made flesh, we would not have his presence, and his acts, his deeds, would not be possible: "Jesus has touched us, and through the sacraments, he touches us still today" (LF 31). He is present with his mysteries in the sacraments, and when these are celebrated, the events of Jesus's life are brought before us again, as they happened, and in the mystery they are brought before us today, here and now, for our salvation. The meaning of the sacraments, the essence of the sacraments, is this. They are certainly actions of Christ and of the Church, but they would not be the efficacious signs they are if he were not present. Theodoret of Cyr writes:

1. Cf. J.-B. Chautard, *Les cisterciens Trappistes, l'âme cistercienne* [*The Cistercian Trappists, the Cistercian Soul*] (Bégrolles: Bellefontaine, 1968).

By his wounds we have been healed. . . . From his opened side . . . there gushed forth the fountain of life that vivifies the world with its rivulets. His wounds renew us in the baptistery and give us an immortal life. The opened side serves to nourish us after our birth, and it does so at the very table of God, as milk sustains children and makes them grow.[2]

Vatican II speaks of sacraments of faith:

The sacraments are ordered to the sanctification of men, to the building up of the body of Christ, and, finally, to the rendering of worship to God; insofar as they are signs, they have in addition the function of instructing. They not only presuppose faith, but with their words and ritual elements nourish it, fortify it, and express it; for this reason they are called "sacraments of faith." (SC 59)

And "it is also necessary to say that faith has a sacramental structure" (LF 40).

The Christian is entrusted, says the Apostle, to a "form of teaching," to obey it; he is entrusted to an environment in which doctrine, worship, and morality are breathed in and lived: the Church.

What is communicated in the Church, what is transmitted in her living tradition, is the new light which is born from the encounter with the living God, a light which touches the person in his center, in the heart, involving his mind, his will, and his affectivity, opening it to living relations in the communion with God and with others. In order to transmit such a fullness, there exists a special means, which puts into play the whole person, body and spirit, interiority and relationships. The sacraments are this means, the sacraments celebrated in the liturgy of the Church. (LF 40)

But modern man thinks he cannot put up with repetition, because he does not understand that a sacred rite makes something new happen every time. It is the liturgy, in fact, that creates the bond—*religio*—between me and God. Antoine de Saint-Exupery speaks of rite as something that makes a day different from the other

---

2. Theodoret of Cyr, *Treatise on the Incarnation of the Lord*, n. 27, PG 75:1467.

days, and above all of the fact that man can see only with the heart, insofar as the essential is invisible to the eyes.[3] Stated summarily, I am told what the host is and what the chalice is by that which hides them: the veil. The liturgy must be beautiful, radiant, as Eastern Christians still attest today. Man has lost grace and must clothe himself anew with a new life that is not merely biological: that is the meaning of sacred vestments. And in this way the sacraments are that with which we oblige ourselves or others to something. The sacraments are thus a sacred pledge or oath, contracted by us with God, or vice versa: the faithful covenant.

The sacraments are not empty symbols that direct us away from themselves to the invisible, but a *reality*—from *res*, thing of some sort—of the invisible, made visible insofar as the sacraments contain what they signify: they contain the *virtus*, that is, the efficacious power that comes from the divine-human person of Jesus Christ; indeed the Eucharistic sacrament contains the reality of the person of Jesus in body, blood, soul and divinity. The power comes from his presence. And yet people believe so little in their efficacy, believe but little in their power to transform! Obviously there is a demand and a need today to understand the sacraments; however we also see the need to explain them again, because of the deformations that the sacraments suffer through ignorance on the part of priests, in the first place; consequently the faithful end up not understanding them. And yet priests are *sacred* ministers because, from the Latin etymology (*sacerdos*), they make things sacred and offer them to God. Nevertheless, for the past few decades and still today, there is a sense of boredom with the sacraments, and a preference for the Word, with the thinking that the efficacy of the latter can do without the former. Then there has been a priority given to pastoral, social, catechetical, or charitable activities, etc.—there's no time to hear confessions. But if the primary task of the Christian, and above all of the priest, is the *consecratio mundi*, or his conversion to the Lord and his salvation, this will not occur except through the sacraments. It is therefore a duty of all Christians to know what they are,

3. Cf. A. de Saint-Exupery, *The Little Prince*, trans. Katherine Woods (New York: Harcourt, Brace, and World, 1971), ch. 21, 68.

and above all a duty of priests, in order to be able to administer them and to sanctify themselves and all those who receive them.

Therefore we shall seek to better understand, in their sacred power, these sacraments that Eastern Christians—like the Latin Fathers in antiquity—still call mysteries, and to understand what kinds of deformations they are subject to.

In his treatise *De Mysteriis,* St. Ambrose writes: "Now has come the time to speak about the mysteries and to explain the nature of the sacraments. Had I done so to the uninitiated, before their baptism, I would have betrayed rather than explained this doctrine."[4] The great bishop considers that the mysteries are tied to the sacraments, in the sense that the latter are the divine mysteries communicated to man through the glorious actions that Jesus himself accomplished, and that the Church received, adapting them for reception by all those who would convert to the Gospel. Therefore, before all else, in the sacraments there are the mysteries of Christ; consequently it is not possible to speak about the nature of the sacraments, that is, about their inner reality, if the mysteries are not opened up: speaking about the sacraments is not something one should do with the uninitiated. St. Ambrose's method is coming to light, a method of not doing catechesis, as we would say today, with those who have not yet received the sacraments, but rather of postponing it till after. The holy Doctor is convinced that without the initiation it is not possible to explain the doctrine of the mysteries and of the sacraments; he would even end up betraying them. Rather, "one should add that the light of the mysteries comes out more penetratingly if it strikes the mind with surprise instead of coming after the first inklings of some prior summary treatment": here is a judgment that is timely today if one thinks about the TV host personality adopted by some priests in the celebration of the sacraments. It does happen that we are forced to witness sacraments transformed into long didascalias,[5] in which the priest—for example during the celebration of a baptism—starts out like this: "Now I'll explain to you what we are going to do"; or "now we take the oil;

---

4. St. Ambrose, *De Mysteriis,* n.2; SC 25bis:156.
5. The Greek term means "instructions."

now we give the white garment; this signifies that…" All of that is a sign of lack of trust in the efficacy of the rite. Since we fear that the persons attending will not understand, we put our words in place of the words of the sacred liturgy, of the words of Christ, the sacramental formulas. We forget that there is an invisible dimension of the mysteries, as St. Ambrose says, which penetrates the heart like a surprise, that is, without preparation in the natural or worldly sense of preparation. The truth is that we no longer believe in the efficacy of the sacraments. That is the reason why they are treated today either as didascalia or as symbolic rites useful only for evoking what they signify, but not containing it: they have neither efficacy nor salvific power. This explains why catechesis has become sterile. Without the sacraments, catechesis is like a gnostic doctrine apt for the learned and the intelligent.

With the sacraments we touch Christ, we listen to Christ, we are nourished on Christ, we taste Christ, that is, the one whom we have seen and touched, as the evangelist John tells us (cf. 1 Jn. 1). The sacraments should be understood in this way again, and not as a set of symbols to decipher and explain. When a person enters a church after many years and stands before a celebration according to the rite of the Church, he is impressed and understands better than if he had received instruction first. The reason is found in the fact that in the mysteries or sacraments there is the divine power, which is more important than human words. St. Ambrose asks the neophyte, the not yet baptized Christian:

> What did you see in the baptistery? Water certainly, but not that alone: there were also the Levites serving and the high priest asking the questions and consecrating. Before all else, the Apostle has taught you that we must not "fix our gaze on visible things, but on invisible things" (2 Cor. 4:18); . . . the invisible perfections of God can be contemplated with the intellect.

Therefore it is not seeing that is necessary, but *intelligere* (from *intus-legere*), that is, to read within, "in his works, his eternal power and divinity" (Rm. 1:20). Ambrose continues:

> For this reason the Lord himself says: Even if you do not want to believe me, at least believe the works (Jn. 10:38). And so believe

that the presence of the divinity is there. You wouldn't believe in his action and not believe in his presence, would you? How could you follow his action if his presence didn't come first?

Here Ambrose explains that the mysteries of Christ are his presence, on which his actions depend. It is like this for each one of us. A person is first present and then acts. So if one does not believe in his presence, how can one believe in the action? The sacraments are the actions of him who is present; but if one does not believe in him who is present, one does not believe in his actions either. Thus we see the need to affirm first of all that in the sacraments the Lord Jesus is present; in the second place that in the sacraments the Lord Jesus acts, with all his mysteries from the Incarnation to the ascension; but if the presence were not there, neither would there be the action. At this point we understand why all the sacraments depend on the great sacrament of the Eucharist, which is the sacrament of the presence. All the sacraments are therefore linked: they lead to, or lead back to, the Eucharist.

From Ambrose we learn the method of the sacraments: not to give too many explanations of them before they have illuminated those who believe, because explanations are not efficacious: to understand the sacraments, it is not necessary to open one's eyes, but to close them. In fact the word mystery comes from the Greek *muo,* which means to close the eyes, in the way that happens when we want to understand something better: *intelligere.* Therefore the mysteries are not understood through seeing with the eyes of the flesh, but through seeing the invisible perfections of God with the inner eyes. This should make us say that it is not with physical eyes that the liturgy needs to be seen, but rather with the eyes of the spirit: that is the beginning of mysticism. Here we have the reason why the Eastern Christians are not afraid to close the curtain of the iconostasis during the Eucharistic prayer, like the Latins of the Middle Ages who lowered the curtains between the little columns of the ciborium,[6] rendering the altar invisible, or else they placed the pres-

---

6. *Ciborium* in this context is the ensemble of columns surrounding the altar, with a solid canopy above.

byters' area together with the altar at the summit of a flight of steps going up from the level of the faithful. Today, instead, it is thought that with the altar in the middle of the nave the faithful have more success understanding what is happening. That is not the method of the Fathers. Furthermore, it could be asked whether it is fitting to celebrate in public, in the piazza, where uninitiated people are present, or passing by. The more we close our eyes before the mysteries, the more they descend into the heart and transform it.

In the *Apologia of the Prophet David,* Ambrose says: "You have shown yourself to me face to face, O Christ; I find you in your sacraments." Let us understand what the nature of sacramental celebrations is: they are not symbolic actions of the Church, but efficacious acts of the presence of Christ who, acting in this way, binds man to himself, and wishes to bind him in order to give him the life of the Spirit and carry him back to the Father from whom he has distanced himself on account of sin. This is the work of Jesus through the sacraments—a work whose meaning is fully contained in the expression "exercise of the priesthood." A priest, in fact, is one who intercedes between man and God. This Jesus has done, so he is a priest, and in a unique way. If the ministers of the Church can be called priests, it is because he gives them a participation in his mediating activity, which consists in bringing man to meet the Father, in order to bring him back to the Father. Consequently, priestly mediation is exercised under Christ, at his service, in which we do not fashion the sacraments according to our ways, since the work of redemption, the rescue or salvation of man, is *his.* The priest is minister also because he administers the mediation of Christ.

An *admirabile commercium* is actualized, a wonderful exchange between the life of God and the life of man: the Lord gives his life to us, and we give ours to him. The exchange of gifts began with the Incarnation of the Word; it was perfected with the resurrection, and it culminated with the ascension, when, St. Leo the Great says, "that which was visible of our Savior has passed into his sacraments,"[7] while the invisible has remained hidden with him: in fact, the Lord's

7. St. Leo the Great, *Sermo* 74, 2; CCL 138A:457; PL 54:398.

ascension is not a putting at a distance, but a new way of being present, even more closely.[8]

Jesus said to the woman with the flow of blood: "Your faith has saved you." Then, to the ruler of the synagogue whose daughter had died: "The girl is asleep, not dead" (cf. Mt. 9:18–26). Is it possible for faith to be so powerful that it may heal, and even raise from the dead? Faith is the recognition of God in the world. To me, this definition seems to enjoy the most truth. If God is present, we are not alone. Faith is a discreet light that permits us to grasp a reality beyond the appearance; one kind of faith makes you believe that in order to be healed we need a doctor, the other kind makes us practically touch the fact that we need a doctor quite Other; one kind makes you think a dead man is inert, the other kind makes you believe that he is only sleeping: for this reason Christians call the place of burial a "cemetery": a place where they sleep, while in reality the departed are living in another manner.[9] Therefore, reality also comprises the invisible, and God has created things visible and invisible, but they are always things that are real.

Through the hem of his mantle Jesus healed her who had faith, and laying on his hand, he raised her who was dead: a presence, his own, operating. We call it a sacrament, a presence that speaks and does what it is saying: that's what operating or acting means here. Faith without actions is dead. A presence: the sacrament is that invisible *res* or reality that makes itself visible thanks to the sacrament, for which reason the reality of a sacrament is holy because he is *the Holy One*. The hem of his mantle and the extended hand of Christ transmit the power of the Holy Spirit that makes all things new. Certainly there were and there are those who deride, because they are prisoners of visible reality, when on the contrary visible reality is only a part of the whole reality, which is invisible. Blessed is he who has faith, the light of faith, to understand this and recognize its presence. Jacob recognized its presence in the dream of the ladder extended between heaven and earth (cf. Gn. 28:10–22). Heaven is

---

8. Faith in Christ's sharing the one divine nature with his Father overcomes, as it were, the distance from earth to heaven. (Translator's note)

9. The Greek word *koimētērion* means a dormitory.

open on earth and the angels come down bearing the divine presence: "The Lord stood in front of him and said: I am the Lord, the God of Abraham your father and the God of Isaac." My God, the God of each one of us, is there before us. He "gives us the land" because he is our heredity, our fecundity, our blessing, our protection, and he will not abandon us without doing what he has promised. In the sacred liturgy, that is, in the sacraments, the angels make heaven come down to earth, as the Christian East says.

Jacob understood, once awakened from sleep: "Indeed, the Lord is in this place." He became conscious of the fact, he was afraid, and said: "How awe-inspiring is this place! This is none other than the house of God, this is the gate of heaven." The divine presence pushes the patriarch to fashion the stone, on which he had slept and received the dream, into a stele, the primitive altar, and to anoint it on top. We would say: to consecrate it. God, in fact, had established his abode, his house; for this reason he changed the name and called that place Bethel, in Hebrew, house of God. That stone founded the house of God. Consecration renders the Lord always present in a place made by human hands, and increases reverent fear and devotion for the abode and house of God. Consecration changes the designated use of the place: it cannot be used for profane purposes. But unfortunately today things are not always like that! And so God leaves us, is not with us, does not protect and accompany us in the journey of life, does not feed us, does not make us return safe and sound to our home. Here is why faith is necessary in order to recognize the divine presence in the sacraments, welcome it and make it part of the content of evangelization. The sacraments are like the "nets" of evangelization.[10]

The sacramental sense of life

All the sacraments have the Eucharist as their end or goal, St. Thomas Aquinas affirms. Baptism is for receiving it; confirmation for perfecting us so as not to be deprived of it; Penance and the anoint-

---

10. Cf. N. Bux, *Il Signore dei misteri. Eucaristia e relativismo* [*The Lord of the Mysteries. The Eucharist and Relativism*] (Siena: Cantagalli, 2005), 130–32.

ing of the sick prepare us to receive it worthily; Order confers the power to celebrate it, and matrimony is for expressing the union between Christ and the Church, which is actualized precisely in the Eucharist.[11] From the Eucharist the sacraments draw the grace that they give; in fact, only the Eucharist has the force and power to confer grace. St. Bonaventure says:

> Through a divine disposition it was permitted to a soldier to transfix and open that sacred side. There came forth blood and water, the price of our salvation. The gushing forth from a similar font, that is, from the secret of the heart, gives to the Church's sacraments the capacity to confer eternal life, and it is for those who already live in Christ a drink from the living water that gushes up for eternal life (Jn. 4:14).[12]

All the other sacraments give grace insofar as those who receive them desire to receive the Eucharist. The sacraments would not give the grace proper to them if they were not in a certain sense caused by and ordered to the Eucharist as their goal. Therefore, what Vatican II says about the sacred liturgy as the *font and apex* of the life of the Church concerns the sacraments, because the liturgy is formed essentially from the sacraments.

After the Eucharist in order of greatness, the other great sacrament is baptism, although not on the same plane, because one comes to the Eucharist "alive," whereas one comes "dead" to baptism: it is he who is dead through sin who must be reborn with baptism, and to the Eucharist one cannot come if one has not first been reborn with baptism or with Penance. From this we have the difference between the "sacraments of the living" and the "sacraments of the dead," definitions from classical theology, still valid.

The novelty of placing the baptistery near the altar has been established. Such a custom could be explained by the fact that this sacrament, together with the Eucharist, sprang forth from the heart of Christ transfixed on the Cross; but from the point of view of the meaning to be transmitted, the two sacraments are not on the same

---

11. Cf. St. Thomas Aquinas, *Summa theologiae* III, q. 65, a. 3.
12. St. Bonaventure, *Opusc. 3, Il legno della vita,* 29; *Opera omnia,* vol. 8, 79.

plane, insofar as baptism is a sacrament for those not yet converted, while the Eucharist is a sacrament for the converted. The baptistery, from the beginning, has been placed outside the church or at most at the entrance, in order to signify the journey of initiation from baptism to the Eucharist; this is also the reason why the tabernacle for reserving the Eucharist was not placed outside the church, as tends to happen in our days; in fact, to arrive at the Eucharist, one needed to be baptized, that is, one needed to enter the mystery of the Church.[13]

In baptism and in the Eucharist, the Lord, through his death and resurrection, passes among us, accomplishes his Pasch (in Hebrew *pesaq*) in the power of the Holy Spirit, and exchanges our life with his. With baptism we come to be joined to the Son's economy of salvation, becoming members of his body, receiving uncreated grace, that is, God himself, through his divinized human nature: in this way man comes to be sanctified, God enters into communication with him, and communicates himself to him, above all through the Eucharistic celebration. In every sacrament the Holy Spirit is invoked with a specific supplication (*epiclesis*) and he descends, distributing one of his gifts.

The sacraments have the Eucharist for their center. For this reason they can be administered even within a Mass; the sacrament of Penance, too, can be received individually while a Mass is being celebrated in the church. From the beginning, penance is the principal condition for preparing oneself for the Eucharist. St. Thomas considers that the relation of the sacraments with the Eucharist is maximally expressed in the character, or indelible seal, which three sacraments—baptism, confirmation, and holy orders—confer on the believer once and for all, so that, consequently, they cannot be repeated. The character has to do with receiving (in baptism and confirmation) or handing on (in holy orders) the holy things of the liturgy.[14]

The "seven" are also called the *greater sacraments*, in order to dis-

13. Cf. N. Bux, *Come andare a Messa e non perdere la fede* [*How to Go to Mass and Not Lose Your Faith*] (Siena: Cantagalli, 2010), 79–81.

14. St. Thomas Aquinas, *Summa theologiae* III, q. 63, a. 3.

tinguish them from the *lesser sacraments,* known as "sacramentals": specifically, blessings and exorcisms, which nevertheless draw their signification from the grace of the Eucharist.

After Vatican II, the verb "celebrate" became the preferred usage for the sacraments, instead of "administer." *Sacrosanctum Concilium* says that "liturgical actions are not private actions, but celebrations of the Church, which is the sacrament of unity" (n. 26); nevertheless, it also speaks of administration of the sacraments (cf. n. 63). The Latin word *celeber* means "frequented, populous"; when the term "celebrate" is used, it signifies that many are rushing to join in, but beyond that the term means that in the sacrament a public action, an ecclesial action takes place, even when there are only a few people. To administer a sacrament means to interpret a concrete situation of life in the light of faith, and to proclaim it, through the liturgical-sacramental prayer, as a salvific action of God. The verb "to administer," from the Latin *ministrare,* "to serve," considers the sacrament from the standpoint of the priest who is its minister; however the administrator must be faithful, Jesus says;[15] he must not add anything of his own, and even less should he take away something that has been entrusted to him. Administration of something involves being very attentive to guard that which has been received. The sacraments must be administered and celebrated according to the norms of the liturgical books, not only in the presence of a great assembly of the faithful, but also of a few, and even when there is only one person (confession and communion for example, but also other sacraments in a time of persecution), because we are members of the Mystical Body. When at the baptism of a single baby the whole family is present, there is a little church evidently present. It is right to celebrate, when possible, with a great number of people, but equally so with a single person, because that is one of the rights of the faithful. And in every sacrament celebrated, there is one who administers it and one who receives it.

Every sacramental action, even one done for a single member of the faithful, helps to build up the Mystical Body: it is a fundamental act of the Church, through which divine power is carried over to

---

15. Mt. 24:45, 25:21, Lk. 12:42, 16:10–12; cf. 1 Cor. 4:2.

man, personally, in order to transform him; man receives the strong force of the Incarnation of the divine Word that is communicated to him. Let us comprehend the reason for which St. Augustine says that the sacraments are *for* the Church, since they build it up (cf. CCC 1118).

The divine word—it is said to be performative and not only communicative or informative—creates the reality of the sacrament, which includes the sign and the one who receives it; as St. Augustine, once again, explains: "Take away the word, and what will the water be, except merely water? But instead, the word is added and a sacrament comes into being."[16] He is not referring to a human word, but to the Word incarnate, the *Logos*, the *Word*, that is, Christ himself, who with his presence gives the sacraments their form. The signs, which also go to make up the sacraments, would not be efficacious without the power of the word, whose force derives from Christ. Earlier I was saying that the sacrament cannot be separated from the mystery: to speak of a sacrament is to speak of a mystery, of a present mystery of Christ, of his Incarnation, of his baptism, of his nativity, of his Passion, of his resurrection, and of his ascension. And so the divine word is folded around the sacramental matter, the sacramental words, the sacramental rites, and renders them efficacious. With the uncreated grace that is God himself, the profane world comes to be shot through and consecrated by the sacraments, which, as the *Catechism* explains, "are efficacious because Christ himself acts in them"; "in this way the Holy Spirit transforms into divine life that which is brought under his power" (CCC 1127). When, therefore, one speaks about the action of the Spirit—and often it is put in opposition to the action of Christ—it must not be forgotten that what he accomplishes in the world and in the hearts of men is the action of transformation, and that it comes principally through the sacraments. The action of the Holy Spirit continues the mission of the Son through the working of the sacraments. In such a way, with uncreated grace (God himself), the Holy Spirit brings it about that the profane character of the world, that is, the world that has distanced itself from God, is led back to him.

16. St. Augustine, *Hom.* 80, 3 *in Joan.*; PL 35:1840.

Today the sacred is considered a problem. Certain theologians consider that there no longer exists a distinction between the sacred and the profane, ever since God became flesh. In principle, it can be considered true that the Lord by entering into the world, that is, into the profane (from the Latin *pro-fanum*, in front of and outside the temple), oriented it to himself; but the profane is in fact often opposed to God and in subjection to the devil, and if it is not liberated, it remains far from God. Here is why one can never *eliminate* the distinction between sacred and profane until the end of the world, when, as the Apostle says, God will be all in all (cf. 1 Cor. 15:28); but it is first necessary that Christ be all in all (cf. Col. 3:11). The sacraments cause us to meet Christ, and they lead to God.

Faith in the sacraments and the unity of the Roman Rite

The sacramental rites are gathered together in the Ritual and in the Pontifical (the book used by the bishop), corresponding, respectively, to the Eastern Christian *ieraticon* and *archieraticon*: the Latin books provide essentially the same things as the liturgical order of the *Apostolic Tradition*[17] of Hippolytus and of the sacramentary of the early Middle Ages. The sacraments administered by the bishop, such as confirmation and holy orders, are found in the Pontifical, while the other five, administered by a priest, are in the Ritual. The *Rituale Romanum*—which was put together in 1614 by Paul V to carry out the deliberation and decision of the Council of Trent of December 4, 1563—was expected to serve as a model for the ritual books in the various dioceses; in reality, it imposed itself on account of the demand for a unified liturgy, to the point that it was not reviewed until Vatican I, since it was desired that priests administer the sacraments according to the *ius divinum*, and not according to local customs.

In conformity with Catholic doctrine, the sacraments are validly

17. A collection of instructions and models for the life and worship of the Church, probably compiled for the most part in the third century. (Translator's note)

and efficaciously administered, that is, they transmit the divine power of Christ (*ex opere operato* is the expression of classical theology) if he who administers them has the intention to accomplish the act entrusted by Jesus Christ to the Church, on the basis of the four prescribed requisites: the matter, the form, the intention of the minister, and the right disposition of the subject. According to the principle of CIC can. 845, section 1, the sacraments of baptism, confirmation, and holy orders, insofar as they impress the character, cannot be repeated if they have been duly conferred without doubts of any kind arising about their validity (for which the matter, the form, and the intention are all necessary). In the contrary case, it will be necessary to prudently check the matter and form used, if, for example, the words of the sacramental formula were changed; the intention of the candidate, if he was an adult; the faith and intention of the baptizing minister; and possibly administer such sacraments anew, but conditionally (cf. can. 869, sec. 1 and can. 845, sec. 2).[18] If doubts should persist, they will have to be administered *ex novo.*

The Second Vatican Council, with its Constitution on the Liturgy *Sacrosanctum Concilium*, confirmed the possibility of adaptations of the general Roman Ritual, but subject to the review and confirmation of the Apostolic See (SC 63b). Now the coexistence of the general Roman Ritual and of particular ritual books—with adaptations to the local customs and customs in accord with the demands of mission—is possible if it does not lead to substantial differences in the celebration of the sacraments or the outright denaturing of them, distorting the sacramental formula that constitutes the essence of the sacrament. It is true that in antiquity the sacraments, especially those of Christian initiation, knew diversity within their celebration, but it is likewise true that in the same period the necessity of safeguarding the celebration's structure in its essential passages was respected, as the Church gradually took consciousness of its unity and catholicity.

---

18. A minister's errors in faith concerning the sacrament he administers do not normally render it invalid if his errors leave intact the intention "to do what the Church does, or what Christ instituted."

The liturgical Constitution of Vatican II, as we indicated at first, dedicates an entire chapter to the sacraments and the sacramentals, and points out their purposes: "The sacraments are ordered to the sanctification of men" (n.59); this is the first point: men are not holy, they must become so. Next "they are ordered to the building up of the body of Christ" (ibid.): they must give life to its members with baptism, strengthen them with confirmation, and nourish them with the Eucharist. Tertullian establishes that there is a correspondence between the sacramental action on the body and the effect on the soul: the body is washed in order for the soul to be purified; the body is anointed in order for the soul to be strengthened; the body is fed in order for the soul to be vivified. Therefore the sacraments sanctify men; they build up the body of Christ; they are acts of worship; they instruct insofar as they are signs.

The sacraments presuppose faith, but at the same time they nourish it, with the words and with the rites; they strengthen it, and they express it with words and objects; therefore they are called "sacraments of faith": as we have said, St Ambrose explains them only *after* they have been celebrated. "They confer grace, but their celebration itself disposes the faithful very well to receive them fruitfully" (SC 59). At the end of this paragraph the Council says: "therefore it is very important that the faithful easily understand the signs of the sacraments." Note well: it says "understand the signs," because understanding the sacraments is not possible without that wonder at the mystery of which we have spoken; but the signs must be accessible and not enigmatic. Therefore "let them approach with great diligence those sacraments that are ordered to nourishing the Christian life" (ibid.).

In addition to the sacraments instituted by the Lord, "Holy Mother Church has instituted sacramentals, sacred signs that bear a resemblance to the sacraments; they signify effects, particularly of a spiritual kind, which are obtained through the Church's intercession," and dispose people to receiving the principal effect of the sacraments (cf. SC 60). The Constitution adds: "Thus the liturgy of the sacraments and the sacramentals offers to the faithful who are well disposed the possibility of sanctifying nearly all the events of life" (SC 61). If the facts of the life of Christ are represented in the sacraments, the events of the life of the faithful are sanctified through the sacramental mysteries. All the stages of human life are sanctified "by means of the divine grace that flows from the Paschal mystery" (ibid.), which, in a manner of speaking, reaches our capillaries by means of the sacramentals. "And thus every right use of material things can be directed to the sanctification of man and the praise of God" (ibid.). Here we see the purpose of blessings, holy water, exorcisms, funerals: the right use of material things, to direct man to God through them. We will treat of the sacramentals in the last chapter.

St. Ambrose brings to mind the fact that the sacraments themselves come before catechesis. So the question arises: doesn't faith come from hearing? Is it not adherence to an instruction that is heard? In reality, initiation comes about through three sacraments, because the Lord introduces us into his life. It does not come about in the very first place through the *Catechism*: the latter prepares and re-echoes (in Greek *katechein*), that is, helps to instruct, but the sacraments, from baptism to the Eucharist, make us progressively enter the mystery, or "initiate" us into it. The sacraments also serve to instruct and illustrate—think about the complementary rites, as they are called, in baptism and holy orders—although, for instruction, the Church has developed the catechumenate, that is, the propaedeutic preparation for the sacraments.

Faith is a gift for which a proclaimed and announced word is needed. In fact, the Apostle says: how will they believe if they have not heard? But the call to faith does not come, obviously, from an instruction: it comes from an announcing that communicates the divine power of the word and calls man. From the time we are children, the sacraments are received in their essence. The catechesis that precedes them helps for receiving them in a knowing way; but if we did not receive the sacraments, catechesis would be reduced to something theoretical. We need what is essential, that is, to receive the power of the Spirit that, through the sacraments, leads us gradually to an understanding of the truth in its fullness. Therefore the efficacious power of the sacraments cannot be replaced by the catechism. We must first of all believe in sacramental power or *virtus*, and thus we will arrive at the need for catechetical instruction from the sacraments themselves.

We are asked: if for the purposes of the salvation that God wills for man, the sacraments are the ordinary and not the exclusive means of grace, can one maintain a certain communion and friendship with the Church and with God even without them? How then can we meet the desire of the person, divorced and remarried for example, who does not relinquish the intention to be in communion with the Church and with God, knowing however that he cannot approach the ordinary way of grace that is the sacramental life? In actions concerning the soul, it is necessary for the soul to be fully awake: such acts are not an automatic reflex, any more than they are for the body; rather we pay attention to what we are ingesting. Now in the spiritual life it would also be necessary to identify the cause of standstill (if one is not actually going backward). In the question of the divorced and remarried—who participate at Mass but cannot receive communion—people leave out of consideration the causes of the failure of the preceding marriage, as well as the fact that they themselves, perhaps, could be at fault for the situation in which they have come to find themselves. In such a case, should one not do penance? How can one claim to be in a relation of communion without expiating the sin that has been committed against it? The man of today is in fact exonerated of his responsibilities, as if it has become impossible to ever impute any sin to him; consequently people do not want to expiate the sin and do penance, and this is also because the ministers of the Church speak little about it. To live in a state of separation and not be able to be united with another person is a penance. But is it necessary to be paying all one's life? Only God knows that. Isn't the person confined to bed by serious illness paying his whole life long? The attitude of the publican in the temple, who says, "Lord, I am not worthy, because I am a sinner," seems to have disappeared. The Fathers of the Church were compassionate toward sinners, but they readmitted them to communion after years of penance, and after having examined the fruits. It is common doctrine that the Lord works in some extraordinary fashion outside the Church as well, but he does it in order to bring people over to the Church, outside of which there is no salvation, and in which he acts, ordinarily, by means of the sacraments instituted by him.

Concerning post-baptismal catechesis, we are asked if conceiving the Christian life as a permanent catechumenate should be considered a point in favor of the ways proposed by Neocatechumenals. He who has already received the sacraments is not on the same level with someone who has not received them; that would be like affirming that the grace of God was useless. So Neocatechumenal practice is weak on this point, and that favors a Judaic-gnostic conception of the sacraments, because they suppose it necessary to come to the sacraments through an almost esoteric knowledge. It is known that the Neocatechumenals have official catechisms, and others off the record, if we may put it that way, in which they teach things different from Catholic doctrine: this is very serious. The "re-evangelization" of those who are already baptized cannot be confused with a catechumenate, because it is a question of reawakening faith, not of making it known for the first time; remaking the path of the ancient catechumenate is a very good thing, provided it is made clear that he who is already baptized has already received divine grace. Therefore one cannot treat the baptized person who does not adhere to the Neocatechumenal path as if he were a pagan. Above all, it should be said, along with Vatican II, that the sacraments are acts of the Church, not of a group.

In this work, we will present the sacramental rites in the form of celebration found in the Tridentine liturgical books—insofar as that is now granted as an Extraordinary Form to those who request it—as well as in the Ordinary Form prepared after the Second Vatican Council in order to implement the Constitution on the Liturgy as regards reform of the sacraments: adaptations, simplifications, use of the vernacular language, etc. (cf. nn. 62–82). Today's manuals of sacramental theology skim in a rushed manner over the old form, since it is deemed incomplete or defective. Perhaps that is due as well to this affirmation cited from the Constitution on the Liturgy:

> With the passage of time, however, there have crept into the rites of the sacraments and sacramentals certain features that have rendered their nature and purpose far from clear to the people of today; hence some changes have become necessary to adapt them to the needs of our own times. For this reason the sacred Council decrees as follows concerning their revision. (n. 62)

37

Fifty years have passed since 1963, when the liturgical Constitution was promulgated. It is legitimate to ask whether the adaptations brought in—which were considered necessary to make the nature and end of the sacraments more clear—were really necessary.

For our last topic in this introductory chapter, we touch on the question of the language of the sacramental liturgy (cf. SC 63). Already before the Council, the sacraments were being celebrated in Latin with parts in the vernacular. For this the Constitution on the one hand prescribes that "the use of the Latin language . . . is to be preserved in the Latin rites" (n. 36, 1; see also n. 54), on the other hand it regulates the use of the vernacular (n. 36, 2–3): in the Mass and in the sacraments "a more ample use can be granted to the vernacular." Readings, admonitions, some prayers and songs are mentioned, but not the strictly sacramental parts such as the epicletic or consecratory formulas and prayers, which, in a way analogous to the Canon of the Mass and presidential prayers, were considered as obviously having to be kept in Latin.

On July 13, 1967, Paul VI had written through the Secretariat of State to the *Consilium ad exequendam constitutionem de sacra liturgia* (the office instituted for the precise purpose of implementing the Conciliar text) that Missals were to be bilingual: Latin and the vernacular. Thus on August 10, 1967 the *Consilium* issued a communication to the presidents of national episcopal conferences, affirming in it:

> It is the desire of the Holy Father that Missals, in both daily and festive, complete and partial editions, always carry the Latin text beside the vernacular version, in a second column or on facing pages, rather than in separate folders or books, according to the norm contained in the Instruction *Inter Oecumenici* of September 26, 1964 of the Decree of the Sacred Congregation of Rites *De editionibus librorum liturgicorum* of January 27, 1966.

In 1969 Paul VI asked the same thing again from the Italian national liturgical commission as well, regarding the translation to be undertaken, since they were entering into the august, austere, sacred, venerated, and tremendous precinct of the Eucharistic prayers—constituting the heart of the Mass, the moment of the consecration of the bread and wine—where he exhorted them to "proceed with patience, without haste, and above all with some humility" (n. 11). The phrases will be taken literally into the third Instruction, *Liturgicae Institutiones* of 1970—minus the reference to humility! But the pope was not listened to, whether in regard to the bilingual format or in regard to the translations. So, as Manzoni would say, the "shouts" were given, but they were not observed.[19]

In the face of the unstoppable proliferation of translations-interpretations, the Congregation for the Doctrine of the Faith had to intervene in 1974, to establish that "the meaning to be understood through these translations is, according to the mind of the Church, that meaning expressed by the original Latin text." Result: the Latin original disappeared, thus preventing priests and students of the liturgy from understanding the authentic meaning of the translated text.[20]

In fact, if one makes a comparative study of the vocabulary and syntax of the Tridentine Missal promulgated by St. Pius V, and even the Latin typical edition of the Missal of Paul VI, there are not a few surprises to be had. For example, an oration of the ancient missal reads: *Deus, qui nocentis mundi crimina per aquas abluens, regenerationis speciem in ipsa diluvii effusione signasti:* "God, who by washing away the crimes of a sinful world with water, didst prefigure its regeneration in the very inundation of the flood." In the present-day missal, it is rendered like this: *Deus, qui regenerationis speciem in ipsa diluvii effusione signasti:* "God, who in the very inundation of the flood didst prefigure regeneration." Thus the expressions having to do with the human condition of sin, the dangers, and the tricks of the devil and the world have disappeared. Why? Perhaps so as not to shock contemporary Christian sensibilities (cf. the Instruction of the *Consilium* of 1969).

---

19. "Shouts": certain legal proclamations in northern Italy in the 16th and 17th centuries, which often had no real effect; the ironic term was immortalized by Alessandro Manzoni's novel *I Promessi Sposi*. (Translator's note)

20. This was particularly problematic in view of the often loose translations, more in the nature of paraphrase, that were approved for use in many territories, thus removing the clergy and the faithful even further from the Latin *editio typica*. (Editor's note)

The examples just given are symptomatic of the ideological optimism stigmatized in 1985 by Joseph Ratzinger in *The Ratzinger Report*; that was an optimism which today finds itself confronting the drama of relativism. What should one think and do? Uwe M. Lang notes:

> The conciliar Fathers did not imagine that the sacred language of the Western Church would be totally replaced with the vernacular. The linguistic fragmentation of Catholic worship has been pushed to such a point that many of the faithful today can barely recite a *Pater noster* together with others, as can be noted in international meetings in Rome and elsewhere. In an age marked by great mobility and globalization, a common liturgical language could serve as a bond of unity between peoples and cultures, aside from the fact that the Latin liturgy is a unique spiritual treasure which has nourished the life of the Church for many centuries.... Finally, it is necessary to preserve the sacred character of the liturgical language in the vernacular translation, as noted with exemplary clarity in the Instruction of the Congregation for Divine Worship and the Discipline of the Sacraments on translation of the liturgical books, *Liturgiam Authenticam,* of 2001.[21]
>
> Finally, what should be said to someone who objects that the Latin language does not permit communication and participation at the liturgy? The response is that Latin, as a "sacred" language, has a communicative power insofar as it is employed within a sacred act. Furthermore, the characteristics of being the inheritance of a tradition, its universality and immutability, which parallel the characteristics of the core of the faith, render it particularly suited to the liturgy, which treats of the *res sacrae aeternae*: Latin corresponds to the mission of the Church of Rome. The young Churches of Africa and Asia need a unifying and universal language in particularly significant moments of their life, such as the liturgy. Therefore Latin

---

21. Uwe Michael Lang, *Il latino vincolo di unità fra popoli e culture* [*Latin, bond of unity between peoples and cultures*]. Contribution to the First Conference on the Motu Proprio *Summorum Pontificum—Una ricchezza spirituale per tutta la Chiesa* [*Summorum Pontificum—A Spiritual Treasure for the Whole Church*], Rome, Sept. 16–18, 2008, cited in *L'Osservatore Romano,* Nov. 15, 2007, 5.

answers to the demand of a globalized world. As is known, the vernacular languages evolve, and this is not insignificant for the meaning of the terms, which with linguistic mutation slips into other meanings.

It is necessary to ask ourselves serious questions about disobedience to the Second Vatican Ecumenical Council, found in the *de facto* and total abolition of Latin in the liturgy and the sacraments, accompanied by a misunderstanding of the meaning of *participatio actuosa* and a reduction of the liturgy's cosmic range to the local level. Furthermore, in comparison with fifty years ago the situation is much more serious: the faith itself is in question, together with the unity of the Roman Rite that expresses it (cf. SC 37–38).

II

The "Ticket" for Paradise

Jesus willed it

ONE Sunday evening, upon entering a church with some historical and artistic value, though not spared the so-called postconciliar adjustments, I was faced with a performance: the parish priest had placed as many chairs as possible in the sanctuary, to seat relatives and invited guests for the baptism of some newborn children. With arms leaning on the altar, by way of a balcony, on which he had placed a basin, he was haranguing the people there about what he was preparing to do, that is, baptize some little ones, when inadvertently he plunged his elbow in the basin, knocking it over. Bursts of laughter, naturally. His talk was long, notwithstanding the witticisms he put in to lighten it up, and thus most people were distracted and bored, while only a few had the energy to pay attention to it. The baptismal rite was difficult to catch, diluted as it was with comments on the various gestures and prayers, because there was no conviction that the sacrament could speak for itself—even though from the beginning, comprehension of the liturgy has come *per preces et ritus* (through prayers and rites, if that needs to be clarified)—as the liturgical Constitution also reaffirmed. At the end, in the midst of prayers, gestures, and witty remarks, came the baptisms, with the water poured over the heads of the little ones in the basin on the altar, followed by the inevitable applause of the people standing around, laughing and talking. I asked one of them whether he had prayed, and what he had caught of the object of the "celebration"—despite the fact that there wasn't even the shadow of a true celebration—and its effects, but he had no answer. During the rite itself, the priest had done what he should have done as a part of the preparation for the baptism: explain the signs of the cross, the lay-

43

ing on of hands, the exorcism, the blessing of the oils, the water, the light, the white garment, etc. But the behavior of the priest was worrisome: he seemed to be doing street theater rather than administering a sacrament. Something from a TV comedy show.

It is only one episode among many, representing as it does the "deformation at the limit of what can be endured" that confronts us in our days, on account of the boundless desire to adapt the liturgy, presuming that the faithful will better comprehend it as a result. The impression left is that the liturgy has been abandoned to each one's own invention. But let us take a step backward, in order to understand the origins of the rites of Christian initiation: from baptism to confirmation and communion, which conclude the journey.

The requirement to prepare or "initiate" someone in the Christian faith takes its origin in the ancient Church from the ritual bath practiced by the Jews in order to indicate the washing, that is, the purification necessary for man to be pleasing to God. Therefore it should not be amazing to us that Jesus himself baptized, even more than John the Baptist (cf. Jn. 3:22; 4:2), and then sent the apostles to baptize, instituting the sacrament with this command: "Go, and make all peoples disciples for me, baptizing them in the name of the Father, and of the Son, and of the Holy Spirit" (Mt. 28:28).

This purifying function of baptism is today rather neglected, because the fact, revealed by Scripture, that from birth man enters the world having in his hereditary DNA the sin originating in the progenitors of our race, original sin, has been relegated to second place; furthermore it is thought that a child has no need for purification. Also the lack of belief in the existence of the devil or evil one results in the reality of creation and of creatures being conceived as free from any harmful subjection, and in an entirely good condition. In contrast with this, the Eastern and Western Christian liturgical tradition attests to the existence of original sin, of a fragile nature, and of the devil. In fact, before the baptism exorcisms are done. Therefore to hide the fact that he who comes to baptism is under the influence of Satan means hiding the truth and forgetting that the washing, just as in the Jewish tradition, serves in the first place to purify, to destroy the impurity of the evil one. This is the first effect of baptism. Next there is the effect of regeneration.

If one were to accept the theory according to which the succeeding parts of Christian initiation (bath in water, invigorating anointing, refreshing table) come from the Hellenistic tradition of hospitality (as in the myth of Odysseus when he was welcomed by Nausica), one would also have to agree on the need to free oneself from impurity in order to be regenerated in it. The symbols of initiation also draw from the signs present in nature.

In AD 150, in the first book of the *Apologia* (chapters 61 and 65), St. Justin provides a glimpse of the apostolic practice of the celebration of baptisms throughout the year and not only at Easter (even if he himself has a predilection for Sunday). Moreover in Justin's *Apologia* the renunciation of Satan does not appear before the Profession of Faith. St. Leo the Great will be the one to mention it explicitly as an immediate preparation for baptism; in the future, it will be received into the Gelasian Sacramentary.

What distinguishes the sacrament is the immersion in water (or pouring of water) accompanied by the invocation of the name of the most holy Trinity, according to the already mentioned command of the Lord, motivated by his affirmation "Unless a man be born again of water and the Holy Spirit, he cannot enter the kingdom of God" (Jn. 3:5). In the patristic age, baptisms that did not contain the explicit invocation of the three divine Persons, but were administered "in the name of the Lord" or "in the name of the Lord Jesus," were considered as invalid and needing to be redone.

Thus in the Christian tradition, initiation, even with variations between Rome, Milan, and the East, has its initial "negative" phase, insofar as no one can come to God if he is not pure. The washing, therefore, must destroy something. Water destroys: the Flood destroyed, the Red Sea destroyed, and John immersed sinners in the Jordan in such a way that they manifested repentance. Water, with its double signification, destroys and regenerates, causes to perish and saves, submerges and renews.

Now the entire process is set up in order to come prepared to the moment of the true *baptism*, that is, the immersion: from the writing down of the candidate's name to the verifying of his intention, from the inquiries about the preparation up to certain points—the so-called scrutinies—to the *traditio* or handing on of the common

Profession of Faith and the Our Father, which had to be memorized and handed on or rendered back (*redditio*).[1] That is what happens in the older form of the Roman Rite of confirmation, when the person to be confirmed is brought before the bishop, who asks him some catechetical questions to which he must respond. It is an element that goes back to the ancient catechumenate: putting to memory serves to conserve well the contents of the faith, so that over time they are not forgotten or transformed into something else. Therefore this mnemonic method, which is attributed to the *Catechism of St. Pius X*, is a method from the Fathers of the Church. Some rites, such as those for the *traditio* or *redditio*, whether of the common Profession of Faith or Creed, or of the Our Father (*Oratio Dominica*), are symptomatic of the importance of the catechumenate: an apprenticeship or training in preparation for the baptismal immersion.

The practice of the baptism of infants would become ever stronger in the social order of Christendom, so that the Roman Ritual of 1614 treats it as the ordinary form of baptism. In the older rite, now in force as the Extraordinary Form, there are three prayers of exorcism, as in the Byzantine rite. After the making of the sign of the cross on the forehead and breast, and the reading of a passage from Scripture, the first deprecatory prayer begins: "I exorcize you, unclean spirit," while the priest places the violet stole on the baby, who is in the arms of the godfather, and has him brought into the church. There follows the Profession of Faith; next, before the baptistery, the second prayer of exorcism takes place, again saying: "I exorcize you, unclean spirit"; and finally, in the rite of the *ephpheta*—an Aramaic word uttered by Jesus to make the deaf hear and speak—the priest, touching the nostrils, says: "Be gone, demon, for the judgment of God is near." The devil is not easily driven away; it is necessary to insist. (These prayers seemed not relevant for the times, and so in the new rite, they have been reduced to only one, followed by the anointing with the oil of catechumens. The force needed for the effect of driving out Satan has been reduced, accord-

---

1. The creed is rendered or returned when it is recited back. (Translator's note)

ing to some scholars of exorcism; but the Latin language, consecrated by use and therefore a bearer of efficaciousness, has also been
reduced in practice.) The exorcisms are done with a breath on the
face, to indicate the wind that represents the Spirit, as the bishop
still does *ad libitum* in the Ordinary Form of the Chrism Mass on
Holy Thursday, when he blows on the chrism to indicate the out-
pouring of the Holy Spirit.

Next there is the blessing and imposition of the salt, which goes
back to North African customs, in order to conserve, not to corrupt,
and thus to signify that the catechumen's intention of faith must be
maintained, must endure; there are also those who see in the salt a
sign of hospitality, since at one time a guest was welcomed to a banquet by giving him a little salt. Certainly the rite is there to indicate
that the life received after baptism is freely given, abundantly dispensed. There is still the rest of the ritual to come, complementary
to the baptism, such as the *ephpheta*, which consists in touching
with saliva the ears and lips of the person baptized. The fullness of
the rite attracts the heart and brings it to be open to the mystery that
is being accomplished.

But what is happening that is mysterious? The driving out of the
devil from the catechumen and Jesus Christ's coming to dwell in
him, symbolized in the Eastern rites by the renunciation of the
devil, made while looking toward the west (in Greek *Europe* resembles a pre-Greek word for darkness), and by the Profession of Faith
looking toward the east (*anatolè*, where the light, Christ, rises). Is
this not an extraordinary symbol? The comparison of the rites helps
one to understand the things that would otherwise escape notice. I
don't understand why in Italy, in the new rite of marriage, the
crowning of the spouses, of Byzantine usage, was introduced *ad libitum*, while for baptism the rite of the salt, of North African usage,
was abolished.

Finally, baptism. Some consider that originally it was done only
through immersion in flowing water, or at a spring or fountain of
water; in the absence of that, the *Didaché*—one of the most ancient
Christian documents—prescribes baptism by infusion, pouring the
water on the head three times, in the name of the Father and the
Son and the Holy Spirit (cf. 7:2–3). We can also suppose that there

could be a combination of immersion and infusion: the person being baptized went down halfway into a pool of water, while from above other water was poured.

What baptism means

St. Ambrose explains:

> As Moses, that is to say, the prophet, cast a piece of wood into that spring of water, in the same way the priest pronounces upon this font a form of words exalting the Cross of the Lord, and the water turns sweet in order to confer grace. Therefore don't believe only the eyes of the body. What is invisible is better seen, because what is seen with the eyes of the body is temporal, but what is not seen is eternal. And what is eternal is perceived better with the spirit and with the intellect than with the eyes.[2]

Baptism is the gateway to eternal life: it places in our souls a "seed" of God, which is sanctifying grace. This seed of divine life is destined to fully develop, to produce sanctity. We are all called to reach it, although in diverse grades, according to the measure of our predestination in Christ.

All religions have rites of purification, since they set out from the observation that we are soiled, or have fallen low and need to be washed, that is, pulled out and saved. Precisely this "going down," this submersion and reemergence is what baptism is. Here, we descend into the sepulcher with Jesus who was dead, and rise up again with him resurrected and living. Precisely this co-burial saves us. But why water to indicate the sepulcher? Jesus, when he immersed himself with his body in the Jordan, sanctified forever all waters, transferring to them a spiritual force: since then, the consecrated waters from the Spirit wash man from every sin, beginning with the sin of the origin inherited from our progenitors Adam and Eve, and baptism remits all the penalties consequent upon sin. The water, consecrated at the time of the baptism or at the Paschal Vigil,

2. St. Ambrose, *De Mysteriis*, n. 14–15; *Sources Chrétiennes* 25bis:162–64.

thus possesses a power (*virtus*), thanks to the divine mystery of Christ, the Word Incarnate, and gives the grace, that "seed of God," which sanctifies man and makes him become a saint, if he cultivates it. In fact grace renders him capable of accomplishing, through free choice, works good and meritorious for obtaining paradise.

The matter of baptism is the water to be poured or used to immerse the person being baptized; the form is constituted by the words: "N., I baptize you in the name of the Father +, and of the Son +, and of the Holy Spirit +," accompanied with the threefold sign of the cross. This is the sacramental formula. The intention of the celebrating minister is to do what the Catholic Church does when she confers baptism, that is, to do what Christ willed to do, when he instituted and commanded the sacrament of baptism. Furthermore, according to the Catholic Church, baptism cancels not only personal sins but also original sin: consequently infants, too, are baptized for the remission of sins. Whoever has been baptized without those requisite elements or without the requisite intention, as happens in the so-called churches and communities like the Mormons (the "Church of Jesus Christ of Latter Day Saints"), must be baptized, for the first "baptism" is not valid. The right disposition, finally, of the subject to be baptized derives from the fact that he (or the parents and/or godparents) has the use of reason; the subject (or his sponsors) needs to have been instructed according to the doctrine and faith of the Catholic Church.

Who can receive baptism

Whoever believes that Jesus is true God and true man, risen from the dead and living, can receive it. This believing is an immediate illumination, deep and total, and is not the result of catechetical preparation, necessary though that is for putting order into the doctrinal content. The term "catechumen" indicates those preparing for baptism; it is a Greek middle voice participle, indicating a condition which in reality is almost permanent, insofar as we are all "teachable" or needing to be catechized by God. When the baptized are children or infants, they receive the same gift, since they are born with a fallen human nature contaminated by original sin (CCC

1250): previous merits are not required, precisely because baptism is a gift, like the natural life received from the parents, or the school to which they will be sent without their prior agreement. Consequently there is no good sense in wanting to leave children to a future free choice, so as not to impose a religion on them—an attitude that in Europe today induces not a few parents to not baptize their children. By the same reasoning, they should not have brought them into the world, since they didn't consult them first, nor should they have sent them to school, again for the same reason. And if they retain all of this as they grow up, they will also be able to refuse it: by not going to school or to church, or by simply taking their own lives. Unfortunately we are here confronted with the new religion of self-determination. In reality, Christian parents who baptize their children—and who should be helped to rediscover the importance of the Catholic faith given in baptism—are showing their willingness to transmit what they are and what they have, as is natural in all relations between adults and children, thereby valuing as well the faith of the grandparents, who should be involved in the Christian education of the grandchildren.

Because of this, the Church has baptized children from the beginning. Jesus reveals that the Father loves the children even before they know him: "Let the children come to me, for to them belongs the kingdom of heaven" (Mt. 19:14). With the baptism of their children, parents decide to entrust them to an eternal love, greater and more stable than their own: even if parents should abandon us, God will never abandon us (cf. Is. 49:15). All of this already constitutes an educative commitment to the growth of faith, by speaking of Jesus and sending the children to catechism to receive the other sacraments of Christian initiation. That is how it is for godparents, catechists, and grandparents. Godparents must be at least 16 years old, Catholic, baptized and confirmed. The parents cannot be godparents (cf. CIC, can. 874); neither can cohabiting couples, the divorced (unless the divorce was against their will), divorced and remarried, and those who have contracted civil marriage. What kind of witness would they give? Nevertheless, if the two parents are merely cohabiting, the child can receive baptism like anyone else, provided there is someone who will see to his

Christian formation. Once again in regard to the godparents, who guarantee this formation, they cannot be amoral or immoral persons, but must be witnesses of the faith: otherwise there would be a self-contradiction. In fact, if someone is in an irregular state as regards moral principles, he cannot be a godparent. This too should first be explained.

Can the baptism be done without a godparent? In the new rite, the godparents do not have the same importance as the parents; nevertheless they are present. So they cannot be considered secondary in view of the testimony they give, even though, sometimes, they are chosen by the parents for reasons of friendship, exchange of courtesies, etc.: reasons that obviously cannot be ruled out, but are not primary. Above all in the case of children baptized with the consent of the parents, but without their having personal convictions about it, the figure of the godparent has a high profile as regards testimony to the faith and to moral conduct.

For the children of non-believing parents, which is a widespread case, and for whom baptism is requested by relatives and friends, while the parents are not opposed to it, the correct appreciation of the situation is not for the priest to go ahead with the baptism because "that's good enough," nor should it be a simple refusal. Even in the case of adults who freely assent, baptism comes in the faith of the Church, which is always there before we are, with the tradition of her faith; it is into this that the child is welcomed through baptism, as likewise the adult.

These things should be explained in the preparation of the parents.

Why it is necessary to receive baptism, and who can administer it

The last words of Jesus, before visibly leaving this world, are: "He who believes and is baptized will be saved; he who does not believe will be condemned" (Mk. 16:16). So it is necessary to receive baptism in order to enter eternal life. Since we enter a world under the dominion of the evil one, we must therefore be liberated from his power and become sons of God, having been orphans from the

Father ever since Adam, the first man, rebelled against him. God has bound salvation to the sacrament of baptism; nevertheless he is not bound to the sacraments (cf. CCC 1257). For example, he who dies for the faith without yet having been baptized receives salvation with a "baptism of blood" like that of Jesus, or a "baptism of desire," if he dies having only desired a baptism never actually received.

It is asked: Are infants who die without baptism saved all the same? Pope Innocent III, in 1201, sent a letter to the bishop of Arles, Imbert of Eyguières (1130–1202), in which he confirmed that the baptism of infants is useful and reasonable, because it avoids the danger of damnation, causes rebirth in water and the Spirit, and obtains entrance into the kingdom of heaven; while still hoping that infants who die without baptism might be saved by the divine mercy that prepares some remedy for them. This is still today the thinking of the Church.[3]

Baptism is ordinarily administered by the ministers consecrated with the sacrament of holy orders: bishop, priest, and, in the Latin Church, deacon (as an extraordinary means, anyone who has the intention to do what the Church does can do it, as said before), with the threefold immersion or sprinkling with water, and reciting the sacramental formula.

How baptism is celebrated

The account of the baptism of the Ethiopian official by the deacon Philip (Acts 8:25–39), and that of the pagan centurion Cornelius with his family—therefore also the children—by Peter (cf. Acts 10), attests that at the beginning the sacrament was administered immediately after an instruction on the essentials. Therefore baptism can

---

3. Cf. H. Denzinger, *Enchiridion Symbolorum,* 43rd ed., ed. P. Hünermann, Eng. ed. R. Fastiggi and A. E. Nash (San Francisco: Ignatius Press, 2012), n. 780. It was to justify infant baptism, apparently questioned by some, that Innocent III replied, "Let it simply not be that all little ones, of whom so great a multitude dies every day, should perish without the merciful God, who wishes no one to perish, having provided them also with some means of salvation." (Translator's note; Ignatius Press translation modified)

be received as soon as possible after birth or, in the case of adults, after conversion. The first way, as we have seen, is in order to escape from the influence of the evil one as soon as possible and receive the precious grace of God. The condition for that is a beginning of sincere faith, which must develop, and not a perfect and mature faith (cf. CCC 1253), and so at the Paschal vigil, every year, the promises are renewed.[4] The second way foresees the preaching of the gospel and its having been welcomed by the catechumen in a Profession of Faith. At any rate, the catechumenate precedes—or, in the case of children, follows—the baptism; on the other hand, explanation of the mysteries present in baptism, or *mystagogy*, comes after the reception of baptism.

The Roman rite of baptism, in the Ordinary Form, begins with the salutation, the sign of the cross, and the dialogue with the parents and godparents concerning the name given or to be given, as well as the Profession of Faith, which should preferably be done at the entrance of the church, to signify a true "entering." It is recommended that the name of a saint be assigned, at least as the second name, so that the baptized person will have a model to imitate and someone from whom to ask intercession on his behalf.[5] Theorctically, a child who had a pagan name, once he has become Christian, could become a saint. The ancient saints, and not only they, became saints, even without having Christian names. If one wanted to suggest to the parents the name of a patron, perhaps alongside the name chosen by them, this should be said in the preparatory phase before baptism, explaining to them the significance of the name. This also expresses the firm wish that the child be able to imitate and appropriate the meaning, the significance of such a name. At the ambo there follows the Liturgy of the Word, which concludes with a single prayer of exorcism, followed in its turn by the anointing with the oil of catechumens, which renders the exorcism efficacious. The celebrant addresses himself directly to the parents and

---

4. This renewal of baptismal promises was inserted in the Easter liturgy in 1955 by Pius XII. (Translator's note)

5. *Compendium of the Catechism of the Catholic Church*, 264.

godparents rather than the newborns, as is done in the ancient rite (Extraordinary Form), for the newborns are in no condition to understand, but are carried by the godparents, either because the mother is not in the physical condition to participate, or because she does not have the catechetical preparation needed for responding. And so the godparents, better instructed, take on themselves the responsibility to do this. It has been deemed necessary to attribute an important role to the parents, as the first ones responsible for the upbringing of their child. What is dramatic today, however, is the fact that many parents do not baptize their children, or even if they are not opposed to the baptism, they have no intention of fostering a Christian education; so the parish priest must choose the godparents who will be the guarantors of that.

It is necessary that the catechetical explanation of the words and gestures of baptism, and its *mystagogia* or more mysterious content, especially, be given beforehand to the parents and godparents, at home or at the parish. In such a way the adults are evangelized and the premises are laid for catechesis of the family and of the young. It is not good for that to happen during the rite, since it risks transforming the rite into an unbearable and inefficacious didascalia, preventing those present from drawing near to the sacrament with faith and devotion. During the rite, it is possible, in a brief introduction and in the homily or at the end (or even better, the following week), to insert a mystagogical illustration, and likewise a concise synthesis is opportune, reaching the parents, but never indulging in the banality of anecdote. The gifts of the sacrament that make us pass from sin to grace, and the effects and obligations assumed, must be placed in high relief.

When to receive baptism

The new rite says that it should be received sometime during the first weeks after birth, at any rate no later than the end of three months, so as to be freed from the power of the evil one, and not be deprived for long of the Lord's salvation. This applies to children and adults alike. Whoever asks for baptism has the right to receive it. Any reservations there may be, or outright refusal by the priest, must be motivated by grave reasons, and the assent of the bishop is also necessary.[6]

With this sacrament one enters the Church and becomes part of it. Furthermore, the baptismal or common priesthood can now be exercised, thanks to the indelible spiritual sign (character) that baptism produces. The sign of faith, as the Roman Canon attests, cannot be wiped out by sin, and for this reason baptism is received only once, for one's whole life. With this seal on our forehead we shall be recognized by the Lord, the judge, as one of his own on the day of universal judgment (cf. Eph. 4:30).

To make this understood, the communal celebration of baptism has been encouraged since the Second Vatican Council. But it has gotten to the point where it is practically no longer possible to baptize one child, even though the ritual provides for this. What should be said? If the number of newborns were truly quite large, that would be understandable, but in these times of a demographic rate close to zero, certain priests' refusal, with pastoral motivations or justifications, is ideological. In reality these priests, by forcing families to wait, instill the idea that there is no need to baptize as soon as possible. And in fact the rite for several children, the so-called communitarian baptism, does not cancel the fact that the sacrament is administered one by one. Catholic baptism is not a collective immersion. The rite for several infants can be celebrated during the Paschal Vigil and a few times a year at Sunday Masses, in order to revive in the faithful the memory of baptism. Beyond that, it should not be inserted too often into the celebration of Mass, insofar as the outlines and the very identity of the sacrament end up unperceived. It happens not rarely that people no longer know how the rite of baptism is carried out, precisely because it is "diluted" within Mass.

Where it is received

Ordinarily, baptism is received in the parish church where the baptized person lives, so as to develop the sense of belonging to the

6. Presumably in a case where appeal would be made to the bishop by the person denied. (Translator's note)

Christian community in which he will grow in the faith while con-tinuing with the other sacraments; in extraordinary cases, with the required permissions, anywhere, in view of increased territorial mobility, not only from one neighborhood to another, but from one city to another and from one nation to another, especially among the young. Although belonging to the universal Church must take place through belonging to a local community—even though the former as an effect of baptism precedes the latter—still, one's belonging to the Church cannot be totally identified with that local community.

Baptism should be done in the proper place, called the baptistery, which constitutes a self-standing environment: it is either a chapel of the church or, as a minimum, it should be found near the entry doors to the church, so as to recall that the sacrament is just that: *ianua ecclesiae.*[7] As it is the beginning of the path that concludes with first communion, the baptistery or its "replacement," such as a small basin, cannot be on the altar. How is it possible for someone who is still subject to the devil to draw near to where the Eucharist is celebrated? Or, how is it possible to do the rite of exorcism against the spirit of evil next to the altar of the Lord? What is expected from liturgists is the truth of the sign: precisely for this reason the baptis-tery cannot be in the sanctuary. Unfortunately the practice of doing the baptismal rites outside the baptistery has become established, because of the preoccupation with participation—which has been reduced to having the people comfortably seated—rather than with a fully visible pool of immersion, which gives the idea of Christ's tomb in which we descend in order to rise up again, resurrected. Would it not be more visibly participatory if everyone, celebrant and people or family members, processed to the baptistery? This is the way it was done, following the patristic tradition, until Vatican II; and this is still set forth by the new rite, the same as the ancient rite, now the Extraordinary Form of the Roman Rite.

Therefore, the entrance rite can begin at the entrance of the church, then go by the ambo where Holy Scripture is read, or equally

7. Door of the church.

by the baptistery itself, and at the end, after the baptism, draw near to the altar for the praying of the *Pater*, not without first carrying out at the baptistery the so-called explicating rites: the anointing with chrism, the giving of the baptismal garment, and of the candle signifying the illumination that happens to the believer, and the rite of *ephpheta*, which, in the Extraordinary Form, is accomplished by the celebrant anointing ears and lips of the person now baptized with his index finger touched with saliva.

Innovations

The liturgical Constitution of Vatican II had ordered the revision of the rites of Christian initiation, in particular: to re-establish the catechumenate of adults consisting of several steps (n. 64); to welcome, alongside the elements proper to the Christian tradition, elements as well from initiation rites of indigenous peoples—those rites, obviously, which would be compatible with the Christian tradition; to revise the rites of baptism of adults, both the short and the solemn one, and then to insert a proper Mass connected with the conferral of baptism (n.66); to revise the rite of baptism of infants or small children, adapting it to their real condition and placing in higher relief the role and duties of the godparents (n.67); to provide adequately for the case of a large number of people to be baptized (n.68); to revise "the rite of confirmation so its intimate connection with the whole of Christian initiation may appear," and for this reason the Council determines that baptismal promises should be renewed before confirmation, and that confirmation should be celebrated during Mass (n.71).

The work of revision of the sacramental rites began after the closing of the Council, and led to the promulgation of the Rite of Baptism of Children in 1969, and then of the Rite of Mass in 1970 and the Rite of Confirmation in 1971.

The rite of Christian initiation of adults (*ordo initiationis christianae adultorum*), restored by the liturgical Constitution, though *grosso modo* present in the *Rituale* of 1614, provides for the consecutive celebration of the sacraments of baptism, confirmation, and communion. The catechumenate begins with the welcoming of the catechumen at the entrance of the church. The candidates must express the motivations pushing them to want to undertake the catechumenate, and then the choice is made of those who will guarantee, or godparents, who must vouch for the path of conversion, accompanying the aspirants to baptism. There is an exorcism in the *ordo,* presented as optional; next a renunciation of pagan rites; the sign of the cross on the forehead—but it can also be made on the senses: ears, eyes, mouth, chest, shoulders; and the readings and homily. The celebrant delivers the book of the gospels to the candidates, who are then dismissed from the Eucharistic celebration. These are the rites of welcome.

The second phase coincides with the remote preparation, which is done a few years before. It is expressed by way of small exorcisms, recited with the hands extended over the catechumens: man, when he is not Christian, is under subjection to the evil one, and must therefore be liberated from his influence. The gesture can also be done by a lay catechist. A document of the third century, the *Apostolic Tradition,* says: "After the prayer the teacher imposes his hand over the catechumens, prays, and then dismisses them. Regardless of whether he is a cleric or layman, the teacher must in every case do that." Therefore this exorcism can be done by a layman deputed for it.

The third phase is the proximate preparation, which begins with the recording of the name, after the hearing of the testimony of the godparents and the catechists concerning the candidate's assiduity in his formation. In this way, the candidates are elected, chosen by way of the scrutiny; their preparation is examined.

Finally, the proximate preparation, the last phase, a time of purification and illumination. This is generally done in the third, fourth, and fifth weeks of Lent, and the readings used are those found in cycle A of the lectionary proper to the new rite (the Samaritan woman, the man born blind, Lazarus). At the end of the homily, the candidates are presented by the celebrant, together with the godfathers and godmothers. The rite follows as for the baptism of children.

The "mysticism" of initiation: a "water grave"

Christian initiation is for the insertion of believing man into the Mystical Body of Christ, in order to receive the divinizing grace, an idea dear to the Christian East. In initiation God acts upon man, brings him into an exchange, a synergy. This action helps man to enter into the divine life, above all in the life Christ has rendered accessible with his death and with his resurrection. He is born a new creature, a new I, who will allow him to believe, to hope in God, and to love God; to live and act under the action of the Holy Spirit, to grow in the moral virtues.

St. Ambrose asks himself: "Indeed what is water without the Cross of Christ, except an ordinary thing without sacramental efficacy?"[8] With baptism, therefore, we enter into the mystery of Christ dead and risen, and we receive his salvation, thanks to the efficacy of his Passion and the power of his resurrection. If baptism joins the neophyte directly to Jesus Christ, then chrismation or confirmation, in a certain sense, places him under the conjoined action of the Holy Spirit. Indeed the "economy" of the two divine Persons is only one. In the Eucharist, the third sacrament of initiation, the believer is inserted completely into the mystery of the Church. This distinction of Christ, the Spirit, and the Church should not lead us to understand the action of Christ as something separated from or other than that of the Spirit; on the contrary, they act in unity, although operating in distinct ways, insofar as they lead to the origin, which is the Father. Consequently the economy is only one, the Trinitarian economy, within which the believer is inserted in the forward movement of baptism, of the water that destroys sin and regenerates to eternal life; of the anointing of the Holy Spirit that confirms and reinforces it; and finally, of the mystical nourishment of the Eucharist, through which the Lord gives himself to the believer as food, making him completely into a member of his body, which is the Church. He belongs no longer to himself, but to Christ (1 Cor. 6:19). Thus is born the sacramental bond of the unity of

8. St. Ambrose, *De Mysteriis*, n. 20: SC 25bis.

Christians, with the overcoming of every limit of language, culture, people, and nation.

Baptism reminds us that faith is not a work of the isolated individual, it is not an act that man can accomplish counting only on his own powers; rather it must be *received*, entering into the ecclesial communion that transmits the gift of God: no one baptizes himself, just as no one is born into existence through himself. We have been baptized (LF 41).

Only in this way is Christian initiation completed.[9]

9. Baptism is sufficient Christian initiation for salvation, but the phrase "Christian initiation" today usually refers to baptism, confirmation, and the first reception of the Eucharist together. (Translator's note)

III

Training for the
Battle in the World

What confirmation is, and the reason for receiving it

TO a mother who asked the parish priest if her son could be confirmed in the year following his first communion (as is customary in Italy), the answer was: (1) that at least two years of catechism were necessary, since confirmation is the sacrament that is received when one is mature; (2) in this way the son would not stop going to church. The mother's reply was at the ready: "If he has already received communion, which is the greatest of the sacraments, then my son is already mature!" To these words the parish priest did not know what answer to give. Delaying confirmation keeps the boys for a few years more in the parish, after which it becomes—as the sociologists of religion tell us—the sacrament of farewell to the Church: in that case, isn't delaying it an instrumentalizing of the sacrament? If the sacrament is a means of divine grace, would it not be needful to receive it as soon as possible, fixing the aim as essentially the blossoming of the faith? St. Thomas, referring to confirmation, speaks of maturity of faith and not psychological maturity. Furthermore, are not confirmation and the other sacraments also administered to the mentally handicapped? Consequently, let us either affirm the primacy of grace over nature, or else schizophrenically say: Oh no, the boy is not yet mature! In that case, it is reasonable to respond: How can that be, he's received communion! Communion is the sacrament that completes the itinerary of initiation, and consequently of Christian maturity: otherwise we would be faced with the paradox that the Christian faithful, who have become mature through communion, are not mature for confirmation. Consequently, to present confirmation as the sacrament of maturity is debatable and generates confusion (cf. CCC 1308). Confirmation must remain united on the one hand to baptism, and on the other hand to communion. Scripture says that thanks to the Holy Spirit, we come to recognize Jesus as the Lord and consequently to perfect our faith and charity: for this reason, it would be better to receive the Holy Spirit before communion. Nevertheless the Holy Spirit enters us already with baptism and communion; in confirmation he comes to equip us for the battle in the world, that is, to equip us for the mission of truth to which we are to testify. St. Cyril of Jerusalem writes: "participation of the Holy Spirit is granted in proportion to the faith of each one."[1]

Whether confirmation takes place before or after first communion, the effect produced is the same, because the Persons of the Trinity operate together, although with different contributions.

Without entering into the debate on direct or indirect institution of some sacraments—confirmation would be one of them—and noting carefully that confirmation should be considered in tight unity with baptism, it is worth recalling that after his baptism by John, the Holy Spirit descended on Jesus Christ coming up from the waters of the Jordan, to guide him in his public mission. On the evening of Easter the risen Lord poured him out for the first time on the disciples, in the upper room, for the remission of sins (cf. Jn. 20:22), while he asked them to prepare to receive him as the principle of interiorizing and of missionary expansion of the Church, which happened at Pentecost. The institution of the sacrament of confirmation by Jesus Christ is traced back to this sequence of events.

A "double sacrament" is what St. Cyprian calls it.[2] St. Paul says: "It is God himself who confirms us, together with you, in Christ, and has conferred the anointing, has impressed the seal upon us and has given us the pledge of the Spirit in our hearts" (2 Cor. 1:21–22). In the Bible, the anointings, which in a special way the Latin church

1. St. Cyril of Jerusalem, *Catechesis* I, 6; PG 33:378.
2. St. Cyprian, *Ep.* 73, 21: CSEL 3/2:795; PL 3:1169.

distinguishes into three types—with chrism, with the oil of catechumens and of exorcism, and with the oil of the sick—are for indicating abundance, joy, the purification before and after the bath, the
invigorating or strengthening of athletes and wrestlers, the healing
of bruises and wounds, beauty, health, and strength. The anointing
with chrism steeps the recipient in oil and fragrance, and so it
impresses a *character* or *seal*: an indelible spiritual mark in the baptized person who has received, with the laying on of the bishop's
hand, the seven gifts of the Holy Spirit, seven being a biblical number that symbolizes fullness. Once impressed, the seal always
remains; for this reason, confirmation—like baptism—is received
only once in a person's lifetime. In short, it is the indelible imprint
of the Spirit in us. In this way, from "chrism," we have the explanation of the names Christ and Christian, which mean "anointed" or
consecrated, by the Spirit, to be exact, sent to fulfil a mission: the
salvation of man.

This "double sacrament"—reinforcement of baptism—gives us
over entirely to Jesus Christ, places us in his service for all time. We
shall in this way be protected, in view of the final test of the Apocalypse (cf. 7:2–3; 9:4); for the Antiochene liturgy it is the shield of
faith and the invincible helmet against all the machinations of the
adversary.[3]

The sacrament serves to reinforce—that is the true meaning of
confirmatio and of the attached symbolism of the oil of chrism
(from the Greek *chriein*, to anoint)—the grace and faith of baptism,
and so it is better to have it done as soon as possible and not put it
off till later. The sooner one is joined to the Church—confirmation
impresses a character of belonging that goes further than that of
baptism—the sooner we shall be able to spread the faith by word
and deed, thanks to the *virtus* or further strength from the Holy
Spirit, as the balsam and fragrance mixed with the oil of chrism (cf.
CCC 1285) signify the spreading abroad of the good odor of Christ
to whom testimony is to be given.

3. *Pontificale iuxta ritum Ecclesiae Syrorum Occidentalium id est Antiochiae*, Pars
I, Versio latina (Libreria Editrice Vaticana, 1941), 37.

How it is administered

In the Ordinary Form, when confirmation is received at a distance of years from baptism and communion, the baptismal promises are renewed first of all, to indicate the tight connection with the first sacrament, and then the Profession of Faith is made; next, the bishop performs the imposition of hands on those to be confirmed: "Almighty God, Father of our Lord Jesus Christ, who has regenerated these sons of yours by water and the Holy Spirit, freeing them from sin, pour into them your Holy Spirit, the Paraclete: spirit of wisdom and understanding, spirit of counsel and strength, spirit of knowledge and piety, and fill them with the spirit of holy fear of you. Through Christ our Lord." Then the sacramental formula is pronounced: "N., receive the seal of the Holy Spirit, which is given to you as a gift." This formula, changed from the previous formula by decision of Paul VI, is intended as an inspiration from the Byzantine formula. In the Extraordinary Form, on the other hand, the ancient formula: "*N., signo te signo crucis, et confirmo te chrismate salutis* (N., I seal you with the sign of the Cross, and I confirm you with the chrism of salvation)" remains and is said while the gesture of the imposition of the hand, or likewise the anointing, is done.

In fact, a question was stirring theological debate after Vatican II: whether confirmation happens through the imposition of the hands or through the anointing with chrism. Regarding this, the Apostolic Constitution of Paul VI *Divinae consortium naturae* says it is conferred with both of these, because at the beginning the anointing was added. So the bishop places his hand on the forehead of the person to be confirmed and, with his thumb anointed in chrism, anoints the forehead while reciting the formula. The imposition of the hand is the gesture of conferral of the Holy Spirit, through ancient tradition (cf. Heb. 6:2). This imposition of hands is rightly considered by Catholic tradition as the first origin of the sacrament of Confirmation, which in a certain way makes the grace of Pentecost perennial in the Church (CCC 1288).

Nevertheless, we ought not to fall into archeologism: the liturgy has an organic development that should be respected. If, in the sub-apostolic era, the anointing with scented oil or chrism was introduced into the rite, together with the imposition of the hand, it means that the Church had deepened her understanding of it. The Eastern Christians call this sacrament *myron* (chrismation), and they practically anoint the whole body, from head to foot, pronouncing in Greek the words "*Sphragís doreás pneúmatos hagíou*," that is: "Seal of the gift of the Holy Spirit." The term *sphragís* stands out: in Italian, the assonant word for it is scar or gash (*sfregio*), an indelible sign. Confirmation concludes with the kiss of peace or, in the Extraordinary Form, recalling medieval knighthood, with a little smack to express the firm communion of the bishop and all the faithful.[4] Consequently it still meaningful to say that confirmation makes one a soldier of Christ, since life is a struggle with the evil one, until the end.

Some zealous priest, in order to keep the sacrament received present in everyone's mind, dressed the boys in cardboard head-coverings in the shape of flames. Wasn't the fascia, which until Vatican II bound the forehead just anointed with chrism, more decorous?

When to receive it

On confirmation, canon 890 of the CIC reads: "The faithful are obligated to receive this sacrament in timely fashion," because without confirmation and the Eucharist initiation is not complete. When should it be received? "About the age of reason" (ibid.), save in exceptional cases, like "danger of death" or grave reasons (cf. CCC 1307). In the dioceses, however, certain "paths" of Christian initiation are offered, or more often imposed, in the context of not inconsiderable resistance and desertions: anyhow the flight from the Church after confirmation is not stopped in this way.[5] Where such paths are implemented, it seems they have not produced the expected miracles; neither have the socio-pastoral strategies pre-

---

4. This gesture is also explained as a gentle reminder of the persecution the Christian should expect to suffer in the world as he bears witness to the true faith. (Editor's note)

5. As mentioned above, it is common in Italy to require some years of catechesis before conferring the sacrament, itself considered by many as little more than a family or social custom. (Translator's note)

vented the spiritual desertification of Europe; in fact just the opposite is happening. Fortunately there are many parish priests who resist such planned programs, preferring to meet with persons, from young people to adults, as the Lord brings it about. Only in this way does "faith happen," as the encounters with Jesus in the Gospels show.

Unfortunately, this sacrament is suffering from a kind of pastoral action separated from doctrine, which, in pushing the idea that confirmation is the "sacrament of maturity," seeks to put it off to a more adult age. The fact that confirmation reinforces the baptized person and renders him mature for the battle of faith has led to an assimilation of maturity in faith with a psychological maturity that would grow with age; but growth in age and growth in grace do not necessarily proceed together. Most unfortunately, that leads to misunderstanding confirmation, which instead of being the strengthening (Latin *confirmatio*, Greek *bebaiosis*) of the profession of faith, turns into the maturity exam.[6]

Who can receive the sacrament, and who can administer it

The necessity that baptism be received as soon as possible resulted in its being conferred in the absence of the bishop, and in confirmation being deferred. However, there was no desire to do the same for communion. Consequently, in the majority of dioceses in Italy and not a few European countries, confirmation is received by children and adults after communion. Now it is communion, as the greatest sacrament, which brings about Christian maturity. And so, as we said before, can a Christian who has been considered mature enough to receive communion, be immature for the reception of confirmation, which is not the greatest sacrament? That is the first contradiction, together with the other concerning the ordinary minister of the sacrament, which we will see shortly.

6. Italy's equivalent of high school graduation or diploma exams. (Translator's note)

To receive confirmation after reaching the age of reason, as a child or an adult, it is necessary to be in the state of grace. For the person who has just been baptized the state of grace is there, but for the person who receives the sacrament as an adolescent or adult, it may not be assumed. If confirmation is received as a grown-up, it is necessary to confess, with first communion having taken place earlier and, as is obvious, confession before that. This is the reason confirmation is usually made to follow communion.

With regard to the sponsors, it is good for them to be the same people as the godparents in baptism, in order to indicate the continuity between the two sacraments and through all of Christian education. Many ask why cohabiting couples cannot be godfathers or godmothers: it is because those who must guarantee the faith of the one being confirmed must give evidence of their own moral integrity.

The Constitution *Lumen gentium* of Vatican II calls the bishop the "original minister" of confirmation (cf. n.26), in order to make room for the priest as an ordinary minister; instead of that, in the East the priest normally does confirmation in the same celebration right after the baptism, with chrism consecrated by the patriarch or bishop in order to signify the apostolic link. It is done in the same way in the West with baptized adults. However if baptism is received by little children—since it is not followed by confirmation—one immediately receives from the priest another anointing with chrism: this signifies that the baptized person can exercise priestly, prophetic, and royal functions, that is to say, participate in the sacred liturgy, give testimony to Christ in the world, carry the judgment of faith into the temporal realities. Adult catechumens do not receive this post-baptismal anointing, but immediately they receive the anointing of confirmation, always with chrism, which signifies the conferral of the "seal" or distinctive mark of belonging to the Church. Consequently we can understand that if the East underlines the unity of initiation, the West takes note of communion with the bishop, who guarantees the state of belonging to the Church, one, holy, catholic, and apostolic, and, as a consequence, with the apostolic origin of the Church (cf. CCC 1292).

And in the Latin rite the bishop is the "ordinary minister" of confirmation. In case of necessity, especially at the point of death for a person not yet confirmed, it is the priest who would be "extraordinary minister."[7] The fact is that in our day it has become ordinary to see priests administer confirmation, and given that they have already administered the anointing with chrism to the child immediately after the baptism, it becomes hard to explain the difference between two anointings with chrism done by the same minister. Besides, this practice leads to a forgetting that confirmation had been separated in time from baptism, and thus *de facto* deferred until after first communion, precisely in order to ensure contact between the baptized person and the bishop, at least once in a lifetime (cf. CCC 1313). Thus it is happening that bishops no longer do confirmation, but delegate it to the priests.

Since the fourth century, confirmation has been displaced until after communion, because the bishop could not be present at the baptisms no longer celebrated exclusively in the cathedral but in the various parishes and their churches into which the dioceses were being distinguished, given the expansion of Christendom. Since, as was just said, in the Roman rite of baptism there is already an anointing with chrism done by the priest, the anointing that follows, which bishops used to do, since it is final and conclusive (the seal, *sphragis*), came to be put off until the bishop was available. He recognizes the person to be confirmed and inserts him into that portion of the flock of which he is himself the pastor. Delegating the chrism anointing of confirmation to a priest causes us to lose the significance of the seal, which is the chrism anointing made by the bishop, he who admits the person being baptized into the Church. In which case the Eastern Christians would be right to have confirmation administered by the same priest right after the baptism, considering that the bishop is present in this initiation through the chrism, insofar as the bishop himself consecrated it.

---

7. A priest does not receive a more ample sacramental character when he receives the faculty to confirm; he will be an "extraordinary" minister insofar as he cannot confirm without the faculty from the bishop, who is a "high priest" in the Church. (Translator's note)

At any rate, in the new rite of confirmation, found in the Roman Pontifical, it was said at first that the bishop is the *minister ordinarius,* and then once it was being done by priests habitually (and no longer if and when necessary), the bishop became *minister originarius.* But, I repeat, the chrism anointing is a seal, impressed by the bishop: without him, the anointing to a certain extent loses its significance, insofar as the priest has already done the anointing with chrism after baptism (cf. CCC 1313). In fact, it had been separated from baptism for this very reason. If the priest is going to do the chrism anointing of confirmation, it would be much more worthwhile for him to do it after the baptism!

At this point, it serves no purpose to put confirmation off until after communion. It is worthwhile to have it administered by the priest right at the time of baptism, or a few years later, or before communion. Doing it otherwise causes an obscuring of the Western Catholic tradition, according to which confirmation is the anointing-sealing concluding the various anointings that come earlier and are done by the priests: the catechumenal anointing of exorcism, and the immediate post-baptismal anointing. It is a problem we can't solve here, because to a certain extent it touches, I believe, on the functionalism that has entered into pastoral ministry in these last decades, and which has ended up bending the liturgy to itself. Undoubtedly the theology and liturgy of the East can help in a way to recover what has been lost, but we shouldn't necessarily copy either, since ritual traditions should be preserved: for example, the tradition of confirmation after communion has existed in Milan since the fourth century, precisely because of the will to maintain a meeting of the baptized person with the bishop.

It should once again be the bishops who ordinarily administer confirmation, because it is their task as the supreme pastors, who introduce the sheep into the Church and sign them with the seal, as if to say: you are of Jesus Christ, you belong to him, he will recognize you on the last day. This is the meaning of the sign. The anointing as a seal has great significance ecclesiologically. If confirmation is the Pentecost of the Christian, and if Pentecost marked the birth of the Church, then shouldn't we conclude that the bishop is the one who authenticates entrance into the Church and recognizes his

sheep one by one and brings them in? To progressively make the figure of the bishop disappear from confirmation, as is happening in
the West, makes it useless to shift confirmation to after communion, because, as we have said, that shift occurred historically in
order to permit the baptized person to meet the bishop for the first
time and to receive from him the episcopal seal of chrism. If statis-
tics tell us that the majority of the baptized do not even know the
name of the bishop, then at least once in their lifetime, the baptized
person should personally meet the bishop. In what other moment,
if not, above all, in confirmation? If the bishop doesn't have time to
administer confirmations, what becomes of his episcopal function
as supreme administrator of the sacraments?

Where

The ancient rite, now restored in the Extraordinary Form, shows
the difference precisely in the fact that the person is confirmed
receiving the anointing from the bishop and not from the priest.
Since antiquity, the practice was that, upon their arising from the
baptismal pool, the baptized were anointed with chrism by the
priests, who were in a way the crown of their bishop. From the baptistery the baptized then went up to where the bishop was, in the
consignatorium, and here they received the last anointing, the seal.
By its nature, confirmation should be celebrated after renewing the
baptismal promises, by going in procession with the bishop to the
baptistery or, better, near the place where the holy oils are kept and
stored, since this recalls the ancient *consignatorium*. Precisely
because confirmation is a distinct sacrament and prepares for the
Eucharist, it should not be celebrated in the sanctuary, by the altar,
but in front of it, at least. It would be better to outfit a chapel distinct from the baptistery, or some point within the baptistery, for
keeping the holy oils and celebrating the sacrament. The difference
between the two places can be marked out by the image of the baptism of the Lord at the Jordan and by the image of the descent of the
Holy Spirit in the cenacle.

Beyond the distinction, we must also rediscover the interdependence of the sacraments of initiation, because only he who has been

fully initiated through baptism, confirmation, and communion can most fully participate in the redemption and consequently be inserted in this way into the work of the Son and the Spirit, who are, as St. Irenaeus says, the hands of the Father.

Effects

It is the special pouring out of the Spirit, as in the apostolic Pentecost: what is received is the grace of spreading and defending the faith with courage, never becoming embarrassed on account of Christ. St. Ambrose explains: "God the Father has placed a sign on you, Christ the Lord has confirmed you and placed the Spirit in your heart as a pledge."[8] St. Thomas recalls that the person confirmed receives the power to publicly profess the Christian faith, as if it were an official task.[9] Confirmation is the sacrament for the spiritual battle and not the decoration after the battle. Perhaps some modern theologian will tear his garments, because the image of the spiritual battle, of the soldier of Christ, has been considered a development from the Middle Ages, historically late in coming, so much so that the knightly symbol of that would be found in the *alapa* or smack, or the kiss of peace received from the bishop. Removing the image of battle would be a diminution of the objective reality of the sacrament.

The sacrament of confirmation empowers one for the *militia Christi*, certainly, but united with baptism and the Eucharist: together they are for the battle, because, as St. Ambrose says, life is a battle: *ubi certamen, ibi corona*. The Christian life as combat is a patristic image that well befits the theology of the sacraments, especially those of initiation. It is not a piece of theology that arrives late on the scene. And even if it was, the development of doctrine does not send everything not born in the first five centuries up to the attic, considering it useless or downright harmful.

Christ began his public life with the temptations in the desert, then he affirmed on the vigil of his Passion, "I consecrate myself"

8. St. Ambrose, *De Mysteriis*, 7, 42: CSEL 73:106; PL 16:403.
9. St. Thomas Aquinas, *Summa theologiae* III, q. 72, a. 5, ad 2.

(Jn. 17:19). If the devil after trying all temptations withdrew, then we cannot conquer him without having the mystery of Christ upon us: the sacraments of initiation constitute our fundamental consecration to the Lord.

"The Lord Jesus said: 'Where two or three are, there too am I' (Mt 18:20). Therefore I believe that when he is invoked by the prayers of the priests, He is present. How much more will he not deign to grant his presence where the Church is, where his mysteries are?"[10] The point is to understand the sacraments as the presence of the mystery of Christ, as the following of Christ, today. The Christian follows Christ in his mysteries, in his salvific comings through the sacraments, from birth to death; in this way, from his birth until his death, we pass to our birth and our death, because everything that happened to Christ happens also to me. This is the meaning of "the life in Christ," as Nicolas Cabasilas, the celebrated Byzantine commentator says, or as the *Imitation of Christ* says. Seeing the Christian life as *militia Christi*, or as *sequela Christi* or *vita in Christo*, means retracing his mysteries.

---

10. St. Ambrose, *De Mysteriis*, n. 37; SC 25 bis:170.

IV

In His Presence

Who is there in the "Most Blessed" Sacrament

A MISSIONARY friend in Uganda told me this experience of his: "One day a lady who was very ill passed by the mission and asked for the possibility of baptism. And thus I baptized her with the name Catherine. After two years she called me: she was going to die. She had never come to catechism during those years, and so I was at a loss. I asked her: 'What is the Eucharist?' She answered me: 'The heart of God!' I had never heard such a definition. Returning to the mission, Father Bresciani asked me why I had given communion to Catherine, who had never attended catechism. I reported her response. Father Penso, doctor of theology with a thesis on the Sacred Heart, exclaimed: 'But that's the definition St. Albert the Great gave for the Eucharist!' So turning back to Father Bresciani, I exclaimed, 'And you wanted me to refuse communion to St. Albert the Great?' The heart of Christ is truly the human form of the heart of God, of God who is love."

St. Pio of Pietrelcina used to prepare himself for Mass thinking about Jesus Christ, who in his earthly life—the *Imitation of Christ* says—was never for a single hour without crosses and sufferings. The sacrifice of the Lord is not an act, more or less long, but a state, from the first moment of the Incarnation until the "It is accomplished," pronounced at Calvary. The state of victimhood reaches its sacrificial apex with the immolation on the Cross. Consequently St. Pio prepared for Mass with the greatest care and attention. To the question "Why, Father, do you suffer so much at the consecration?" he used to respond: "Because it is precisely there that a new and awesome destruction and creation takes place." In a line, short and succinct, Padre Pio this time says something more. The utterly unique miracle of the Eucharistic conversion is affirmed with absolute clarity. The tremendous mystery of the consecration holds in itself the last hours passed by Christ on the Cross.

We come to the communion, which was the culminating part of his Mass, the supreme moment of the Passion of Jesus. To the question: "Would you like to celebrate more than one Mass a day?" he used to respond: "If it were in my power I would never come down from the altar." Not being able to stay always nailed to the altar, this most exceptional liturgist transformed himself into an altar with the intention of making the Passion of Christ visible at all times.

It was asked of Padre Pio: "How should we hear Holy Mass?" He answered: "As the most holy Virgin and the devout women attended it. Like St. John at the Eucharistic sacrifice, and at the bloody one on the Cross." And again: "What benefits do we receive hearing Mass?" "They cannot be counted. You will see them in paradise."

I can hear the accusation of "devotionalism" coming on. But in the Fathers of the Church, like the above-mentioned Theodoret of Cyr, we read the same things. With the Mass we enter the heart of the mystery of Christ the Redeemer, who became altar, victim, and priest.[1] How irreverent the widespread liturgists' slogan "More Mass, fewer Masses!" appears in comparison. We understand that Christ frees us from the devil and from sin, frees us from injustices and poverty, but never completely: as long as there will be sin on earth, we will have the poor always with us (cf. Jn. 12:8). It is the heart of man that must be freed and redeemed. How many priests, instead of collaborating in the work of eternal redemption and salvation, follow after earthly utopias!

With the Holy Eucharist, or Holy Mass, Jesus Christ is rendered present, he who on the Cross transformed the act of violence done against him by human beings into an act of self-donation and love. What men did to Christ is the culmination of the evil committed in all times: a greater evil than that one will never be committed. Jesus, Son of God, offered himself to the Father as the innocent lamb, victim of expiation for the salvation of mankind from sin. He accomplished the sacrifice of his body and his blood, that is, his person and

1. *Paschal Preface V,* Roman Missal of 1970.

his life. He is, therefore, the Savior and Redeemer of all men, that is, "he who pays the ransom"; the Eternal High Priest, the "sacred gift," the one mediator between man and God.

How to define this sacrament

Christ instituted this sacrament in order to make present on altars his Passion and death, his sacrifice. In fact he says: "The bread I will give is my flesh for the life of the world" (Jn. 6:51). He did it in order to remain with men for the whole time of their life: "I am with you all days until the end of the world" (Mt. 28:20). He did it in order to make himself food and drink of the soul, saying: "I am the bread of life, he who comes to me will hunger no more" (Jn. 6:35). He did it in order to visit man in the moment of death and to carry him to paradise. In fact he said: "He who eats my flesh and drinks my blood has life eternal" (Jn. 6:54)

I have already treated of the Eucharist and its institution by Jesus in the context of the Paschal supper and, above all, on the Cross.[2] Here I present again a primary question about the character of the Eucharistic sacrament: is it a supper or a sacrifice? This is how the *Catechism* responds:

> The Mass is at the same time, and inseparably, the sacrificial memorial in which the sacrifice of the Cross is perpetuated and the sacred banquet of communion with the Lord's body and blood. But the celebration of the Eucharistic sacrifice is wholly directed toward the intimate union of the faithful with Christ through communion. To receive communion is to receive Christ himself who has offered himself for us. (CCC 1382).

Certainly the term *memorial* can be understood as the recalling of a past fact. That is not the case here, thanks to the Holy Spirit who reminds us of everything (cf. Jn. 14:26). The Eucharist done by the Church makes present and effective the Passover of Christ and his sacrifice offered once for all (cf. CCC 1364). Does it also make the resurrection present? With baptism and above all with the Eucha-

2. Cf. N. Bux, *Come andare a Messa*, 102–59.

rist, the Christian suffers and dies with Christ, while receiving the seed of the resurrection that will develop in fullness at the end of time, according to the word of the Lord: "I will raise him up on the last day" (Jn. 6:40). But as long as we are in the flesh, we participate in his Passion and await, in faith and hope, the day of glorification.

Furthermore, we have to do here with "a *sacred* banquet or feast, in which Jesus Christ is received, the memory of his Passion is recalled, the heart is filled with grace and the pledge of future glory is given" (St. Thomas Aquinas). "Sacred" means that his divine presence is there, and so it is necessary to draw near with the fear of God that is one of the seven gifts of the Holy Spirit.

The sacramental sacrifice is defined as "Eucharist," a Greek term signifying the giving of thanks or blessing, a memorial and presence of him brought about by the power of his word and by the Holy Spirit; the whole of it culminates in communion. It is a *feast* in the spiritual sense, not the worldly one: it isn't something that lives on account of attractive new ideas, it is not to be an expression of ephemeral current events, it is not an entertainment that has to succeed, but a strengthening of the awareness that the mystery is present among us. It is a feast of faith in which to "lay aside every worldly attitude," as the Byzantine liturgy says, because mystically we represent the cherubim.[3]

Now in songs, prayers, and prayer guides for Eucharistic adoration the expression "Jesus Christ is present in the consecrated bread" is the fashion today. Even Luther maintained that Christ was in the bread. In approximate language lacking in doctrine, he adds: but it is a mystery. However, Christ did not say he is present in the bread, nor that this bread is my body, but he said "this is my body," where *this* indicates the passage from bread, which he took in his hands, to his body, because it is consecrated in that moment: the substance of the bread is converted, as the Council of Trent says, into the substance of his body. Under—in the ontological and not spatial sense—the appearances or characteristic features or *species* of the bread (today

---

3. Liturgy of St. John Chrysostom, offertory troparion. In English this is usually rendered "Let us who mystically represent the cherubim and sing the thrice-holy hymn to the life-creating Trinity now set aside all earthly cares."

we would say the phenomenality) stands the body of Christ. It is no longer bread but Christ. The species over which the "thanksgiving," from the Greek *eucharistò*, was made, have become Eucharistic. Consequently one must speak of the "presence of Christ under the Eucharistic species."

The expression "consecrated bread" should also be explained. Even when Jesus, and later Paul use expressions like: "he who eats this bread" (Jn. 6:51), and "the bread which we break" (1 Cor. 10:16), they are to be understood in a transferred sense;[4] in any case, when Jesus affirms that he is the bread of life (Jn. 6:26–71), he means to speak of his person and his life, his body and his blood, in the concrete Semitic way of speaking. Is this difficult? Here we see the need for catechesis, even in the songs.

Jesus instituted this sacrament when he took the bread, saying "this is my body offered in sacrifice," and, next, the chalice of wine, saying "this is the chalice of my blood, poured out . . . ," and ordering, "Do this in my memory." The consecratory words declare the purpose: the body is offered in sacrifice for us and the blood is poured out for the remission of sins. Consequently, in relation to the Passion of Christ, in which the blood was separated from the body, the Council of Trent defines the Holy Mass as the true and proper sacrifice of Jesus Christ. He makes himself present on the altar—*alta-res*, the high place for the sacrifice—in obedience to the consecratory words of the priest, and because of the sacramental separation of the body from the blood, he is in the condition of an immolated victim.[5] For this reason, the altar is *also* the table of the Lamb who was slain (cf. Rev. 5:6), the table made to receive the bread as sacrament of the body, and the wine as sacrament of the blood.[6]

And so, what kind of body of Christ is present in the sacrament? The body assumed of Mary in the Incarnation and transfigured with the resurrection and the ascension. Some would say that it is better not to say "flesh of Christ," but "spiritual and glorious body."

---

4. That is, not as bread in substance, but as the shape, dimensions, and qualities of bread. (Translator's note)

5. *Immolatitius modus*: MD 70.

6. St. Thomas Aquinas, *Summa theologiae* III, q. 74, ad 1.

Nevertheless the *Catechism* says: "Communion with the flesh of Christ resurrected, 'vivified by the Holy Spirit and vivifying,' conserves, increases and renews the life of grace received in baptism" (CCC 1392). St. Ambrose observes:

> We are cognizant of the fact that grace has greater efficacy than nature.... What should be said of the blessing done by God himself where the very words of the Lord and Savior are acting? Since this sacrament which you receive is done and completed with the word of Christ... will it be incapable of changing the nature of the elements? The word of Christ... which was able to create from nothing that which did not exist: is it unable to change things which are into things they were not? In fact it is not less difficult to give things existence than to change them into other things. But why are we using arguments? Let us use the examples he gave, and let us prove the truth of the mystery with the very mystery of the Incarnation. Maybe the ordinary course of nature was followed when Jesus was born of Mary?... Well, what we set forth is the body born from the Virgin.... Therefore it is truly the sacrament of his flesh.[7]

When does the presence of Christ in the Eucharist begin?

Certain theologians consider that the consecration—by which transubstantiation is done—of the bread and wine does not come about in an instant, but gradually, and that the entire Eucharistic prayer is consecratory.

What should be said about this theory? The idea of gradual and progressive consecration is the consequence of emphasizing the value of the Eucharistic prayer in its entirety: this is an attempt to draw closer to the Eucharistic mystery, in a more complete and rich way. In certain theologians' usage, the expression "institution narrative," present at the heart of the Eucharistic prayer—or, to be precise, the consecration of the bread and wine, when at the words "This is my body, and This is (the chalice of) my blood" (CCC 1353, 1376–77) the bread ceases to be bread and the wine ceases to be

---

7. St. Ambrose, *De Mysteriis*, nn. 52–53; SC 25bis:186–87.

wine, and they become the body and blood, soul and divinity of Christ—seems to diminish an understanding of the real presence in favor of other aspects, such as a memorial of the sacrifice of Christ, his resurrection and his ascension, the role of the Holy Spirit. But if Christ were not already fully present from the moment of the consecration, the prescription of the missal's rubrics for the priest to kneel in adoration would be without meaning. About the Vatican declaration of the validity of the anaphora of Addai and Mari,[8] used in some Middle Eastern churches—an anaphora that, lacking the words of consecration, would consecrate in a "diffuse" way, without determining the precise moment—there is much still to discuss.[9] The idea of a gradual transformation of the bread and wine in the Eucharist is no more tenable than the notion that an embryo is not a human being at conception, and becomes one gradually.

Concerning the instant of the consecration, considered as sacramental time, the idea that sacramental time is totally different from physical time has been influential; but the metaphysical fact of having become temporal results precisely from the fact that the Eternal has entered the now of time. The liturgical insistence in our day on the event (that is, on the *nunc*, the now) has been to the detriment of the permanence of the sacred (*hic*, here), just as the rite itself also happens and does not last;[10] in fact the refusal of such an overflowing has led to removal of the greatest sign of the permanence of the divine, the tabernacle, in spite of St. Ambrose affirming: "What is the

8. In 2001 the Pontifical Council for the Promotion of Christian Unity wrote to the bishops of the Chaldean Catholic Church that this anaphora, whose early manuscripts dating from a few centuries after the presumed origin of the prayer lack the Institution Narrative, and which is used by the schismatic Assyrian Church of the East, can be considered valid. (Translator's note)

9. Cf. N. Bux, *La relazione tra l'epiclesi e la narrazione dell'istituzione dell'eucaristia* [*The relation between the epiclesis and the institution narrative of the Eucharist*], in U.M. Lang (ed.), *Die Anaphora von Addai und Mari. Studien zur Eucharistie und Einsetzungsworten* [*The Anaphora of Addai and Mari. Studies on the Eucharist and the Institution Narrative*] (Bonn: Verlag Nova & Vetera, 2007), 163–73.

10. Cf. J. Ratzinger, *Davanti al Protagonista* [*Before the Protagonist*] (Siena: Cantagalli, 2009), 130. "The language of faith has called this overflowing of the mere historical instant *mystery*, and has condensed in the term Paschal mystery the most intimate core of the redemptive event."

altar of Christ if not the image of the body of Christ?"[11] And so, what is the problem with having the tabernacle on the altar of celebration? There is a need to recover the balance between event and permanence, to reunite *hic et nunc*.[12]

Furthermore, even with the *Catechism* affirming that "the Eucharistic presence of Christ begins at the moment of the consecration and continues as long as the species remain the same" (CCC 1377), there are priests with the custom of administering communion only with hosts consecrated during the Mass, and not with those kept in the tabernacle.[13] Nevertheless, by dint of wanting to show in this way the sign of the presence that has just occurred, they can cause people to believe that the hosts in the tabernacle are second class, whereas it is known that the hosts cease to contain the presence only when they lose the appearance and taste of bread. Is there a difference in the Lord's presence?

These and other theories are to be found in the formulations of the liturgist Cesare Giraudo. He likes to speak of the change that occurred in the first millennium, from the patristic method to the scholastic, which latter—he simplifies—is weaker because instead of starting out from the liturgical texts, it starts out from the scholar's own head; thus writes Giraudo, even though he does not explain the reason that led them to prefer the one course over the other. Has there not been in the Church a development of sacramental and Eucharistic theology? He goes from there to a negative evaluation of the way they did theology in the Schools, forgetting that in Judaism, too, the liturgical service of the priests was found side by side with the teaching of the rabbis. If the medieval master

---

11. St. Ambrose, *De Sacramentis*, 5, 7; CSEL 73:61; PL 16:447. Consequently "The altar is the image of the body of Christ and the body of Christ is on the altar": *ibid.*, 4, 7; CSEL 73:49; PL 16:437; cf. CCC 1383.

12. The *here* and the *now*.

13. Some priests seem to consider communion with hosts consecrated at previous Masses, and reserved in the tabernacle, as a thing to be avoided at all costs, no matter how difficult it may be to count or predict in advance the number of communicants. It is possible that such attitudes are an exaggerated attempt to apply what Pope Pius XII taught in MD 118 and 121, that it is fitting to receive hosts consecrated at the same Mass. (Translator's note)

could teach to others the fruit of his speculations in his cell, it was because he had first adored the sacrament. Did St. Thomas and St. Bonaventure not teach what they had adored on their knees? One can "study" Christ, praying; and pray to him, studying. What Giraudo calls a "static" reading of the Fathers, which he sets in opposition to the "dynamic" one—but what do these terms change in Eucharistic dogma?—was nothing but their attempt to verify the correspondence of faith with the demands of reason.

And so concerning the beginning of the presence, St. Ambrose recalls:

> The Lord Jesus Christ himself proclaims: "This is my body." Before the blessing with the heavenly words the word indicates a particular kind of element of the world. After the consecration it now designates the body and the blood of Christ. He himself calls it his blood. Before the consecration he calls it with a different name. After the consecration it is said to be blood. And you say: "Amen," that is, "So it is."[14]

For this reason, in order to point out the beginning of the being present of Jesus Christ, it is praiseworthy to sound the little sanctuary bell, as explicitly provided in the general order of Mass in the Roman Missal. A little before the consecration, the server, if it is opportune, stirs the attention of the faithful by the significant ringing of the bell. In the same way the bell is rung at the showing of the consecrated host and the chalice to the people, in accord with local customs. If incense is used, the server incenses the host and the chalice after the consecration when they are shown to the people (GIRM 150). Despite the prohibition by modernist liturgists, this is the way it is done in many parts of the world, as in the papal liturgies, to the satisfaction of servers and the faithful.

Who celebrates the Eucharist

As a preliminary, a second question needs to be confronted: how do we form our rapport with God, how do we foster our relation with

14. St. Ambrose, *De Mysteriis*, n. 54: SC 25bis:188.

him? *Through,* or by means of Christ, man and God, who defines the *sacred,* who is the *most holy one* par excellence. The relationship we foster is a public and integral worship or cult (from the Latin *colere*), and so, not private and partial; it is exercised by the Mystical Body of Jesus Christ, that is, by the head and his members, and is considered a work of Christ the priest, and of his body, which is the Church (SC 7). It is the sacred liturgy of the Church, in which the fullness of the faith is contained. The *Catechism* clarifies that some of the faithful are ordained through the sacrament of order, to represent Christ as head of the body (1188). The acting subject of the liturgy, as it is usual to say, is "the whole Christ," that is, the union of head and members; nevertheless, whereas the priest sums up in himself the representation of Christ and that of the Church, the members have need of the priest who acts *in the person of Christ the head.* So, although it is the priest who is "served" by the servers so that they in a certain sense take part in the celebration, it is above all the priest who celebrates, because he participates in the function of Christ, one and only mediator (cf. LG 28). The priest, that is, "the man of the sacred,"[15] participates in such a mediation and makes possible the relation and the meeting between man and God: were this not so, the Mass could do without him. This is understood from the letter to the Hebrews: his ministerial priesthood—like the priesthood of Christ the one mediator and High Priest, who has entered once and for all into the heavenly sanctuary—has a latreutic purpose (that God reign supreme in our life), a Eucharistic purpose (font of every good and grace), a purpose of impetration (to obtain needed grace), propitiation and expiation (to complete the redemption and reparation for sins) (Heb. 9:12–14:20). The priesthood of the Son makes God the Father, angered and grieved by sins, propitious.

Bishops, priests, and lay faithful, each in his own way, participate in the one and only priesthood of Christ (cf. LG 10, 2; CCC 1538) and share the baptismal priesthood, to which the ministerial or hierarchical priesthood of the first two is ordered. Between the two

---

15. In Italian and Latin, "priest" (*sacerdote, sacerdos*) implies "sacred" (*sacro, sacrum*). (Translator's note)

priesthoods there is a distinction of essence and not only of degree: the faithful do participate actively in the Eucharistic celebration, but they do not celebrate it. With baptism one has been configured to Christ the priest, which means that we must offer ourselves in a "rational" or spiritual sacrifice agreeable to God. Giraudo, mixing things and failing to distinguish, ends up diluting ministerial-sacerdotal mediation to an intercession by faithful people. In this way mediation is annulled and the priesthood is rendered useless. If it is true that the whole Church participates in a certain way in the Eucharistic prayer, it is also true that the priest pronounces it *in the person of Christ the head,* especially the consecration, the heart of the Eucharistic prayer, on which patristic and medieval theology lingered in depth.

In the Mass the priest acts in the person of Christ, head of the body that is the Church. The fact that the Mass can be celebrated by the priest alone corresponds precisely with this personifying, which reaches its high point in the offering of self: whether we are few or many, if there is not the offering of our body in sacrifice, there is no spiritual worship (cf. Rm. 12:1). On Golgotha, was it not Mary and John who alone remained? And at Emmaus were there not just two disciples? Some have gone so far as to say that "Mass without the people" has no meaning; but if we found ourselves under persecution would not the priest have to celebrate, limiting himself to the essential words outside the context of the Mass, and celebrate by himself, so as not to be discovered? That must be said, though certain theologians are against such a possibility and the Church has not definitively resolved the question. And as persecution is the ordinary state of the Church, the exception confirms the rule; likewise for each of the faithful. The "Mass with the people" has been absolutized: but if "people" meant a mass of persons, only Sunday Masses would survive, where attendance would be high. With the presupposition of *the people,* Mass would have to be celebrated rarely, since at ferial Masses few persons are there. Not even monastic communities would survive. If the Church is a Mystical Body, it lives also in a solitary believer and in a solitary priest. Is it not the case that in order to oppose individualism, we have ended up forgetting the primacy of the person over the community? So Mass with the people must not be considered superior to the Mass where the people are not there, or where those attending are few. The liturgical Constitution establishes that *any* Mass, as such, has a public and a social nature (SC 27). Paul VI affirmed that the so-called "communitarian" Mass must not be exalted in a manner that takes away the importance of the private Mass.[16]

In this regard, the abuse found among the Neocatechumenals should be censured, that is, the abuse of systematically celebrating the Sunday Eucharist on Saturday evening, justifying this with an appeal to the Church's permission to celebrate a festival-day Mass by anticipation, while on Sunday they do not go to Mass, but celebrate the word of God at home. This practice is closer to "living in accord with the Sabbath" than "according to Sunday," and it contradicts Catholic tradition.

Finally, the truth and validity of the celebration—which is a term some wish to apply to the faithful in accord with Protestant thought, for which sacerdotal mediation is exercised also by the people—do not depend on everyone approaching for communion: today as well as in ancient times Mass is celebrated with excommunicates, penitents, and catechumens, who cannot receive communion, present at hand.[17] And so the celebrating subject is not the assembly, but the Lord.

The Lord said: "I want mercy and not sacrifices." Nevertheless it is said that Mass is a sacrifice, because he desires that man should love him as He loves, that is to say up to the point of self-gift, which *is* the sacrifice. Therefore he does not want sacrifices in the sense of things to be given to Him, but men themselves—a transformation, thanks to communion with him. "Truly this is the *mysterium fidei* that is accomplished in the Eucharist: the world that came forth

---

16. Paul VI, Encyclical Letter *Mysterium Fidei* (1965), 7.

17. The point is that persons not properly disposed (in one way or another) to receive communion have attended Mass over the centuries, without receiving communion. As regards the excommunicated, the first Code of Canon Law (1917), mostly formed from traditional practices, saw them as able to be present for the "preaching of the word of God," but not for sacramental functions. (Translator's note)

from the hands of God the Creator now returns to him redeemed by Christ."[18]

The Church, spread throughout the world, offers herself to the Father with Jesus Christ. This capacity to offer and transform is received by the priest, who represents Christ himself and is his minister insofar as he carries out this sacred service. But to the offering all Christians unite themselves: Christians who have received from baptism the grace, that is, the capacity, to transform themselves. For this reason, they, too, are in a certain sense priests, and acting in this way they attain Christian perfection.

The priest celebrates Mass with the intention of the Church: for various needs of the Church and for her members—her unity, the spread of the Gospel, for persecuted Christians; for civil society, for peace, justice, reconciliation, and because of wars and disorders; for diverse circumstances—work, hunger, refugees, exiles, migrants, prisoners, the incarcerated, the sick, the dying, earthquake, rain, for whatever need and for thanksgiving; for some particular necessities—to ask for remission of sins, the virtue of charity, concord, for the family, relatives, and friends, those who afflict us, to obtain the grace of a holy death. Mass is offered by the faithful because of devotion, in honor of the mysteries of the Trinity and the Incarnation, and the redemption achieved by the Lord; in a special way for the departed, on the eighth day after death, the thirtieth day, the anniversary.

But the offering of Mass is completed only with communion. The purpose of the offering is in fact to enter into communion with the Lord, that is, with the Father, the Son, and the Holy Spirit, and therefore to become holy. And so the Mass is the greatest and most complete act of adoration of the Lord, and it is offered in honor of the Church triumphant: of the Blessed Virgin Mary, and of the saints.

It is possible to celebrate the sacraments of initiation, ordination, matrimony, and anointing of the sick within Mass; all of these accompany man from birth until death. Nevertheless the possibility of administering these sacraments within Mass is regulated by the

18. John Paul II, Encyclical Letter *Ecclesia de Eucharistia* (2003), 8.

liturgical books; it must be on set occasions and not frequently, otherwise the faithful would not succeed in distinctly recognizing each of the sacramental rites. Furthermore the other faithful have the right to attend Mass without having to be frequently subjected to the insertion of another sacrament.

There is interdependence between the Eucharist and the other sacraments: one would wish that the faithful be inculcated with the knowledge that they flow forth from the Eucharist and flow together back into it as to their source: in fact the sacrifice of Christ is the paradigm of the life and death of man, and it accompanies every sacrament.

Who can receive the sacrament

Let us treat of holy communion or first communion—which is received at the end of the period of Christian initiation, after baptism and confirmation—and of its fruits. After the purification of baptism, in which the baptized have been adopted by God the Father as sons, receiving the white garment, made white after washing in the blood of the Lamb (cf. Rev. 7:14), and after having received the prophetic, priestly, and royal anointing with chrism, we are invited, for the first time, to the table of the Lord, which has been made ready thanks to his sacrifice. It is from him, the Lord, that at the conclusion of initiation—and it doesn't matter whether on the day itself of baptism (baptismal communion) or a day following—we receive a place at his table for the first communion, here and for eternity. Jesus has promised it: "I go to prepare a place for you" (Jn. 14:3). This is received in pledge with our having become capable, through baptism and confirmation, of being recognized as sons in him, the Son, and therefore of giving thanks to God the Father.

In the old Roman Rite, the faithful put themselves, kneeling, at the communion rail, where a long cloth, representing the table and the banquet, has been extended, and each person has a place: he or she kneels down and with recollection waits for the reception of communion. A significant gesture is the custom of hiding one's hands under the tablecloth—I have seen this done in France by little children and adults after they knelt down. This indicates the requirement of being pure in order to touch the Lord who has chosen us and called us with our faith to the table of his kingdom, of which communion is the down payment, as it were, the anticipation of the glory to come. In the new rite, cheap folklore often takes the place—as if it could—of all that: in one church, with the pews removed, a good number of tables were set up as in a restaurant, each one set for four, and the children were to be made to sit for the "meal" of their first communion. A pity that this will be the only time in their lives. Afterwards, will they understand that the Mass is a sacrificial meal consumed on one's feet?

One's place at the supper of the Lord, at the banquet of the kingdom—according to Eastern Christian theology—is given at the end of initiation: a sign of the royal priesthood received through communion. There is no exercise of the baptismal priesthood of the faithful more complete than when first communion is received, right after baptism—as the Eastern Christians do—or at the beginning of the age of reason—as for the Latins, when the child becomes capable of distinguishing the Eucharistic bread from ordinary bread. Given the precocious maturity in our day, it can happen already at the age of six. A mother told me: "The child already knows Jesus, he knows the essential truths of the *Catechism*, and above all he knows that the Eucharistic bread is the miraculous transformation of ordinary bread. Why not have him receive communion? Why let more years pass?" If we are convinced that the parents are the first catechists, and the mother desires and guarantees it, and the child understands and responds well to questions in the *Catechism*, why delay communion until he reaches nine years old? In this way we return to the custom of the 13th century, receiving communion at 13 or 14 years old—a custom that continued until St. Pius X, who established communion at the age of reason, around 7 years of age, provided the child can distinguish the Eucharistic bread from ordinary bread. With the decree *Quam Singulari* of August 10, 1910, St. Pius X moved admission to first communion to that lower age of around seven, so that Jesus could enter as soon as possible into the pure hearts of the little ones. His decision was also intended to oppose modernism: the ideology that confuses the maturity of faith with psychological maturity and is again on offer in our day, delaying by some years the steps of Christian initiation of little children, boys and girls. And to think that the reform of St. Pius X was welcomed with enthusiasm! But in not a few dioceses that model is no longer considered to work. The objective is to delay the flight that occurs after confirmation. In virtue of a sociological pastoral method—which theorizes that the older you are, the more free you are to choose—the years of catechism are prolonged; in this way we are there to observe the goodbye to the Church of many youths who remain without sacraments. As well, the catechism extended over several years has not made them more educated in the truths of faith: these youths are not able to distinguish the Eucharist from ordinary bread. Despite the multiplication of "rites of handing on": of the Bible, the Creed, the Our Father, the Ten Commandments, the Precept of the Lord or the Commandment of Love, etc.—the expression is endearing because it refers to the ancient patristic usage of the catechumenate of adults—the young remain generally in the dark and confused about the truths of faith. If there were a corresponding teaching of all this at the handing on, would that not be better? Even more serious than that, however, is that such a structuration exposes the youth, deprived for a longer time of the grace of confession, to the exponential risk of sin, even mortal, in a world where temptations are certainly not lacking. This was precisely the reason that moved St. Pius X to make that reform. But optimism about the world has deluded the pastors, except for the fact that they must then deal with the growing flood of adolescents who precociously engage in sexual experiences, often deviant and perverse.

Above all, these catechetical roadmaps place serious obstacles in the way of a right of the faithful: canon 912 of the CIC not only reaffirms that communion can be received by children who have attained "the use of reason," but clarifies that if "duly prepared," they "ought to be fed, as soon as possible, with this divine food, with sacramental confession preceding."

To understand all this is a true pastoral work; but delaying communion means distancing children from the influence of grace on their reason, although children use the computer at five years old, apply themselves to languages and music, and know how to distinguish many things. Do not adults often say, every time they speak in front of little ones, "Be careful, they understand everything"? So if they understand everything, why can they not understand who Jesus is? Is that not contradictory? Communion should be received as soon as possible, because the child is still innocent: worthy therefore to receive communion.

One can take account of the school program that progresses parallel to the catechetical program with its stages of maturity, but without identifying them; the school of catechism must not be assimilated to that of education, but to the experience of a friendship that follows Jesus as Master. One grows in the friendship. It is not necessary for the child to know the whole catechism, but the essential elements; on the other hand, if baptism is administered to newborns who do not understand, it is necessary to leave room for grace. What is important is that the child know who Jesus is, and the meaning of union with Him in the Eucharistic bread, and that he possess those notions that are fundamental for participating with the awareness proper to his age, because in growing up he will learn other things. Unfortunately, the idea has taken root that the child, and also the adult, must have a prior understanding in order to receive the sacraments. What are the results of catechesis today? Before Vatican II, the children prepared themselves for a few months with a short text of questions and answers, that is, with the celebrated *Catechism* of St. Pius X, receiving in the same year confession, communion, and often confirmation as well. Today the tendency is, paradoxically, to delay, just when the Eastern Christians are praised for having conserved the unity of sacramental initiation: the three sacraments—all together—administered to newborns and little children. A schizophrenic way of acting: on the one hand we want the exchange of gifts with the East, and on the other, we deepen the chasm. But the *Catechism of the Catholic Church* and its *Compendium* leave hope for a reversal of the tendency.

First communion is in continuity with baptismal initiation. It has come to the point of affirming that at Mass everyone must receive communion—which means everyone is without sins; on the other hand it is maintained that in order to receive communion one must be prepared, one must have gone through catechism. So we are either always ready to receive communion, even when in mortal sin, with no need for confession—and this is done, as we know—or else we are not prepared, we must be instructed? Baptism and Penance (as we shall see) serve to meet the constant requirement of purification for man. Furthermore we always need to be instructed, because we have never fully arrived at knowledge; we always need to learn, to receive catechesis in a life of catechumenate and mystagogy; it is basic to memorize the fundamental truths of the faith. But we also need the grace of God, which takes us as we are and saves us. Therefore the sacraments respond, with grace, to our weakness, because we shall never be fully worthy and we shall never be fully instructed. First of all come the sacraments of initiation that exalt the primacy of grace, which comes to meet man independently of his merits. So the two realities should not be split apart. As regards children, initiation is accomplished as soon as possible: beginning from baptism, followed by the other two sacraments: the longer the delay, the more people are subject to the polluting influence of worldly thinking that attempts to take them away from grace.

With respect to adults, not just anyone can receive communion: someone who is not baptized, or who is a catechumen and is preparing himself for initiation; someone who has sinned gravely and has not approached confession. Furthermore the Church does not permit communion for baptized persons who are divorced and cohabiting, or remarried; they do not lose their belonging to the Church, but the love between the Church and Christ, signified in the Eucharist, does not consent to such a contradiction. And then what should be said of those who are public sinners? The Eastern liturgy says: "O Son of God, make me today a participant of your mystical supper. I will not reveal your mystery to your enemies and neither will I give you the kiss of Judas" (CCC 1386). But it is known that there are priests, bishops, and cardinals who give the Eucharist to the person who not only has no intention of changing his life, but even continually professes the rightness of any subversion whatsoever of the moral and Christian order. It is not in the power of a sacred minister, even though he be cardinal or pope, to administer communion to a public sinner, that is, the sinner who has not detached himself from sin, especially if he has not abstained from attacking the Church and the faith. It is true that no sinner is irredeemable, because we can all be saved and arrive at elevated grades of sanctity—but on condition that we repent. The Christian must always and in any case love the sinner, praying for his conversion, but must hate the sin. Now when a sinner is not repentant for his sin, and even defends it, makes propaganda on its behalf, makes of it a banner, then one is bound in response to condemn it publicly and to avoid any kind of scandal by way of offering a false mercy that would inevitably become approval of sin. Or perhaps St. Paul was mistaken when he wrote: "He who eats the Body of the Lord unworthily, eats to his own condemnation" (1 Cor. 11:29)? Or perhaps the Angelic Doctor, St. Thomas Aquinas, teaching that there is no salvation for someone who profanes the Eucharist, when in *Lauda Sion* he wrote: "The good receive it, the wicked receive it, / but with unequal destiny: life or death. It is death for the wicked, life for the good: / see, from a like reception, how unlike is the effect. . . . Behold the bread of the angels, made the food of wayfarers: / true bread of sons, not to be thrown to the dogs"?

The Lord invites us to receive him in the sacrament, in order to have life within us (cf. Jn. 6:53), but for a moment so great and so holy it is necessary to prepare oneself (CCC 1385). The *Catechism* reminds us that someone conscious of having committed a grave sin must receive the sacrament of reconciliation before approaching communion (1385), observing these dispositions: faith, humility, a fast, and the bodily postures (1386–87), which are dispositions recalled also in CIC, canons 916–17 (cf. CCC 1388).

The times for receiving communion, and what its effects are

In the Our Father, the "daily" Bread is asked for: this translates the Greek *epiousion*, which literally signifies supersubstantial or, more exactly, superessential. During the delays of the projected Italian translation of the prayer, strangely, the experts have not debated this. Not a few Fathers of the Church identified this with the Eucharistic bread; in this way, there was a transition from periodic communion to frequent communion, even outside of Mass, alternating with rigorous fasts, as is still done today in the East.

Man upon earth is like the Hebrew in the desert: he eats always the same bread and then dies. If only he would see that even this is a gift not to be taken for granted! But St. Ambrose says that there is another bread: this nourishment that you receive, this "living bread come down from heaven" (Jn. 6:51), gives the sustenance of eternal life, and whoever will have eaten of it "will not die forever" (Jn. 11:26), because it is the body of Christ.[19]

Thus the postconciliar concession for receiving communion twice in the same day will not seem strange: at the daily Mass, and on the occasion of another Mass for a marriage, funeral, or other extraordinary event. The concession does not in any way mean to imply that Mass without communion is not valid. In fact, a well-known precept of the Church allows for reception of communion once a year, at least at Easter (CIC, can. 920), while presupposing obligatory participation at Mass on Sundays and Holy Days, and prescribing that communion be preceded by confession (cf. CCC 1389).[20]

The sacramental species, received in us with communion, remain for about ten minutes, but more durable are their effects. It is like the action of food: when we are hungry, we eat—in general it is like that, unless there is a pathology. Should we not always be hungry for Christ, Word made flesh? And so receiving a second communion has its meaningfulness. For priests who celebrate more than one Mass, communion is always necessary for the consummation of the Eucharistic sacrifice.

The Council of Trent had decreed that communion must be available to the faithful during Mass unless seriously inconvenient: *in singulis Missis*.[21] After Vatican II, the ritual book *De sacra communione et cultu mysterii extra missam*, published in 1973, notes that communion is normally received within Mass, but *servatis ritibus liturgicis*, it is permitted to receive it outside Mass, *iusta de causa*, for those who ask.

As it happens that we eat at times outside the principal meals, communion likewise can be received outside the Mass, with an

---

19. St. Ambrose, *De Mysteriis*, 43; SC 25 bis:178.
20. Confession of *mortal* sins not yet absolved is required. (Translator's note)
21. Denzinger, *Enchiridion Symbolorum*, 1747.

abbreviated rite. The Byzantines administer communion to children outside Mass, with the consecrated wine, after they have received baptism and the chrism anointing (*holy myron*); the Latins instead give it to children at their first communion Mass. Since antiquity the Church has exercised the possibility of administering communion outside Mass, because of the sharpened desire of the faithful to receive it often, especially if they were sick, and as a result it was necessary to carry it into the home or into poorhouses, but also to imprisoned Christians awaiting judgment if not martyrdom. Justin, around the year 150, attests that communion was brought by the deacons to those absent,[22] that is, to Christians in jail or sick. In 416, Pope Innocent I also writes about it, in the Letter to Decentius, bishop of Gubbio, in a celebrated document witnessing to liturgical rites and customs; among the other things mentioned, he says that no sick person should die without first receiving the Eucharist. Therefore, we have here a reaffirmation of the necessity of communion, outside of Mass though it be.

Noteworthy is the fact that in the Roman Ritual of 1614—officially in use again today, along with the updated version—the formula that accompanies the administration of communion to the sick is different from that for viaticum. In a certain sense, this is how the rite of communion outside Mass originated. In the new postconciliar ritual book, the formulas have been unified.

Communion outside Mass has always existed, for the aforesaid motives, and it is entirely reasonable. On weekdays, when you leave the house in a hurry to go to work, and the necessity of making sure everything was in order for the family caused you to arrive late for the first part of the Mass, why prohibit communion? The pre-conciliar custom of not considering Mass attendance valid in the case of arriving when the chalice has been uncovered (the moment when the chalice is unveiled at the beginning of the offertory)[23] has been criticized, but we have attached to the Mass a legalism of Sunday or

---

22. Cf. St. Justin, *Apologia*, I, 17, 5.

23. Moral theologians taught that laypersons did not validly fulfil the precept of attendance at Mass if they arrived after the unveiling of the chalice at the beginning of the offertory. (Translator's note)

holidays, and now, if you arrive a minute after the beginning of Mass, you risk catching a ringing rebuke from the priest. Legalism is always rising again: if it is right to invite the faithful to receive communion during Mass, that does not mean we should prevent reception of the bread of the strong, even outside Mass, on weekdays. This is because the *effects* of communion are vital: it increases union with Christ, remits venial sins, and preserves from mortal sins. The Eucharist, as the sacrament of charity, reinforces the unity of the Mystical Body, charity toward the poor, union among Christians; above all, it is the pledge of future glory.

As regards the manner of receiving communion,[24] the ordinary practice—according to the shared tradition of East and West—is to receive in the mouth, after an act of reverence, a profound bow or on one's knees. But it is not uncommon for the faithful wishing to receive it in this way to be the object of brusque and even scandalous refusals by priests who care nothing that recipients hold the sacred species in their hands. And the reception of communion standing and in the hand is only an indult, or a permission given despite the norm still prevailing in the law. Consequently it could only arouse reactions when Benedict XVI "innovated" by administering communion to the faithful on their knees and in the mouth: it was an "innovation" precisely against the indult, which permits it to be received in the hand in various nations.

In fact, not a few people hold that it was only in late antiquity or the early Middle Ages that the Churches of the East and the West began to prefer administering it directly in the mouth. But did Jesus give communion to the apostles on the hand or asking them to take it with their own hands? Visiting an exhibition of Tintoretto in Rome, I observed some "Last Suppers" in which Jesus gives communion to the apostles in the mouth. One could think that this has to do with an interpretation by the painter after the fact, a little like the posture of Jesus and the apostles at table, in the cenacle of Leonardo, which "updates" in the Western manner the Jewish custom, which was, instead, to be reclining at table. Reflecting further on this, the custom of giving communion to the faithful directly in

24. Cf. N. Bux, *Come andare a Messa*, 151–58.

the mouth can be considered not only as a Jewish tradition, and therefore apostolic, but also as going back to the Lord Jesus. The Jews and the peoples of the East in general had and today still have the custom of taking food with one's hands and placing it directly in the mouth of the lover or the friend. In the West this is done between couples in love and by the mother toward her little one, who is still inexperienced. The text of John is understood in this way: "Jesus then answered him [John]: 'It is he to whom I shall give a morsel of dipped bread.' Then, having dipped a morsel of bread, he gave it to Judas, son of Simon Iscariot. And as soon as he had taken the mouthful Satan entered into him" (13:26–27). But what should be said about the invitation of Jesus: "Take and eat. . . . Take and drink"? *Take* (in Greek, *labete;* in Latin, *accipite*) also means *receive.* If the mouthful is dipped, it cannot be taken with the hands; rather it is received directly into the mouth. It is true that Jesus consecrated bread and wine separately. But if during the "mystic supper" (as the East calls it) or Last Supper, the two consecrating gestures happened, so it seems, in different phases of the Paschal supper, nevertheless after Pentecost the apostles, aided by Jewish priests who had converted (cf. Acts 6:7), and who were, as we would say, experts in religious worship, united the gestures within the great Eucharistic prayer. The distribution of the consecrated bread and wine was then placed after the anaphora, thus originating the rite of communion. His Excellency Bishop Athanasius Schneider has deepened this question in an interesting way.[25]

At the beginning, the Christian communities were small and the faithful easily identifiable. With the extension of Christendom, precautions were taken so that the sacred species would be administered with reverence, avoiding the dispersal of fragments, which contain the Lord really and completely. Little by little, communion under both species takes one form or another, the species being given consecutively, or by intinction. Finally, in the West, ordinarily

25. Cf. A. Schneider, *Dominus est* [*It is the Lord*] (Vatican City: Libreria Editrice Vaticana, 2009); ibid., *Corpus Christi. La Santa Comunione e il rinnovamento della Chiesa* [*Corpus Christi. Holy Communion and the Renewal of the Church*] (Vatican City: Libreria Editrice Vaticana, 2013).

it is given under the sole species of bread, because Catholic doctrine, with St. Thomas as a guarantee, teaches that the Lord Jesus is
present entirely in each species (cf. CCC 1377). But appeal is made
by defenders of communion in the hand to St. Cyril of Jerusalem,
who asked the faithful to make of their hand a throne at the
moment of receiving communion.[26] I hold, treading lightly in this,
that the invitation to dispose the hands in this manner can be
understood as not for the purpose of receiving it in the hands, but
in order to extend them, also with a bow of the head, in a single act
of adoration, and in addition, to prevent the fall of fragments. In
fact, on account of the innate sense of the sacred, very strong in the
East, reverence toward the sacrament was affirmed more and more,
with the precaution of taking communion in the mouth, for multi-
ple reasons—one among them being the inability to guarantee
clean hands and, especially, the safeguarding of the fragments.

All this renders more comprehensible the statement of St. Augustine: "no one eats that flesh if he has not first adored." Benedict XVI
recalled this significantly, precisely in the well-known address on
the interpretation of Vatican II.[27] Becoming more explicit, Cyril
invites us to "not put the hands out, but in a gesture of adoration
and veneration (*tropo proskyniseos kai sevasmatos*), draw near to the
chalice of the blood of Christ."[28] In such a way that he who receives
communion makes a *proskynesis*, the prostration or bow, down to
the ground—similar to our genuflexion—extending his hands like
a throne at the same time, while from the hand of the Lord he
receives communion in the mouth. This is what appears clearly
depicted by the Purple Codex of Rossano, dated between the end of
the 5th and the beginning of the 6th century after Christ: this is a
Greek illuminated Gospel book, certainly put together in a Syriac
milieu. Therefore we should not be surprised by the fact that the
Eastern and the Western pictorial tradition, from the 5th to the 16th

26. Cf. St. Cyril of Jerusalem, *Mystagogical Catecheses*, 21.
27. See Address to the Roman Curia, December 22, 2005; cf. *Sacramentum Caritatis*, 67.
28. Cf. ibid., 5, 22.

century, has depicted Christ as giving communion to the apostles directly in the mouth. Benedict XVI, in continuity with the universal tradition of the Church, took this gesture up: why not imitate him? The faith and devotion of many toward this sacrament of the Presence, especially in a desacralizing time like our own, will gain from it.

Beyond the historical and theological discussion concerning the manner in which communion was received in antiquity, putting ourselves on our knees to receive the sacrament cannot be put in opposition with the procession that the new rite provides for.

The practice of communion in the hand brings us to reflect as well on the fragments that often fall without being caught and gathered in a paten or tray underneath. Furthermore, one should not be silent about the profanation of the sacrament committed by some Catholic groups and movements, who do not use hosts for Mass, but large loaves broken for communion; consequently the crumbs or fragments are scattered. It is forgotten that the Lord is present (cf. CCC 1377)—as St. Thomas says—in the sacrament of the Eucharist, not according to the mode of quantity, but according to the mode of substance: in a drop of consecrated wine and in a small fragment of a consecrated host there is the whole presence of the Lord; not a great deal of wine is needed in order for the Lord to be present, just as in a drop of blood, the whole substance of blood is found. As there is ignorance of Catholic Eucharistic doctrine, it is held that the small fragments are insignificant, and as a result the sacred vessels are not purified. And yet *in extremis*, when the priest realizes that the hosts or pieces of the Host are insufficient for communion, it is customary to break them into smaller pieces in order to give communion, if only a fragment! In the current crisis of faith, the question of the fragments should be clarified and reaffirmed, condemning the abuses, insofar as there is no difference between small hosts and small fragments.

How to draw near to the Most Blessed Sacrament

"If you do not succeed in speculating about high and heavenly things, then rest in the Passion of Christ, and willingly make your abode in his sacred wounds."[29] When can this "rest" begin, if not at Mass? It will be said: medieval! So let us go back to St. Ambrose in order to get closer to the origins, since this will have a greater effect. About approaching the Eucharist, he says: the crowd of neophytes advances toward the altars of Christ, saying: "I will come to the altar of God, to the God of my joy, of my jubilation":[30] the Church has desired to express this perception since the 8th century, with the prayers at the foot of the altar, at the beginning of Mass, setting the formula of the *confessio* there, speaking in the first person: the personal preparation—erroneously called "private"—without which there could not be communal participation. Is this something too late in comparison with the Church of the origins? The Eucharist is the supreme act of adoration: if one wishes to grow in faith, then he needs to participate in the Mass and accept that he will not understand everything right away. Only in this way can there be a maturing of his capacity to receive Christ truly and deeply in communion. This is the highpoint of that participation called *actuosa*: penetration of the depths of the mystery.[31] To offer, to communicate, to adore: this is "participating" in the liturgy. "Liturgy" is a word that means action or work of the Trinity and of the holy people, hierarchically ordered, that is, formed by different orders and grades (saints and the blessed, faithful alive and deceased, Pope, bishops, presbyters, deacons). This is the universal Church, formed by those who are saints and in beatitude with God (heaven); those who it is hoped have passed to the state of purification from their sins in purgatory (that is, the deceased); the faithful who are on earth. This is how the Church exists, spread through all places and gathered in unity precisely with the Eucharist. Adoration is the anticipation of the contemplation of the Lamb immolated for us, the contemplation of the heavenly Church that has vision, while with faith we recognize the divine mystery present in the liturgy.

29. *Imitation of Christ*, Book 2, 5.
30. St. Ambrose, *De Mysteriis*, n. 43; SC 25bis:178.
31. Cf. Benedict XVI, *Message to the World Eucharistic Congress*, Dublin, June 17, 2012.

Earlier I referred to the theory of the "static Eucharist" placed in opposition to the "dynamic" one: detached from Mass, the Eucharist, according to that theory, would be static because the faithful would limit themselves to contemplating it and not nourishing themselves on it; this would be a visual devotion that doesn't fulfil the truth of the Eucharist, because the Lord said "Take and eat." However, this theory does not correspond to the statement of St. Augustine cited before. The point is that for Catholics, as well as for the Orthodox, the presence in the Eucharist does not end with Mass, but remains, as already said, for as long as the species of bread and wine persist; this is very important, because it touches on the theme of the real, permanent presence of the Lord.

Adoration develops on the basis of the permanence of what goes beyond the moment of communion with the consecrated bread and wine. Until the early Middle Ages, it was customary to not let anything of the Eucharistic gifts remain, once the divine liturgy was finished; there was concern to consecrate only the bread needed for the celebration of the Mass and for viaticum, and so there was no conservation of the Eucharist for adoration. But little by little Eucharistic reservation developed, that is, a secured place where remaining sacred particles were conserved, for the days on which the liturgy was not celebrated, days of fasting, as well as for communion for the dying and the sick, and for this purpose special vessels, pyxes and cups were prepared, in which communion was conserved. From the later Middle Ages onward, there was a development of the connection between the place of reservation, which at first was a room adjacent to the sacristy, or a *sacrarium*, and the altar, until, with the contribution above all of St. Charles Borromeo, the permanence of the tabernacle, which is the living Christ, was affirmed at the center of the altar where he dies for us, in order to indicate the real presence of the Lord: the whole church had its center in the tabernacle.

Eucharistic adoration is the positive result of the Catholic deepening of an understanding of the Eucharistic mystery, a progressive deepening which reached its greatest extent in the second millennium, in a special way after the Council of Trent, in order to offer the reasons of the faith in the face of the Protestant contestation of the real presence of the Lord in the Eucharist.

If in the 1600s Mass was seen more as adoration of than thanksgiving for the sacrifice of Christ, today we are in the presence of another excess: Mass seen exclusively as a banquet, not also as a sacrifice. That is what happens when theology loses the equilibrium typical of Catholic doctrine, which holds all the parts together. The development of the liturgy is organic and not discontinuous, and it goes in step with the deepening of the consciousness of the faith that the Christian people by nature guards, as the blessed Newman so masterfully taught. Thus Eucharistic worship has ever been further developed in the Catholic world, spreading also in various Eastern Catholic Churches.

Catholic Eucharistic theology cannot turn back, but today's decentering—if it is not a deliberate putting to one side or hiding of the tabernacle—is a grave sign of an attempt to turn it back. The centrality of the tabernacle is contested, just when many Catholics do not believe in the real presence of Christ in the sacrament; on account of that, there would be a need to put the tabernacle back in the center, so people would be helped to understand that the church is the place of the presence of the Lord, not a hall to be used only when there is a gathering for the liturgy. The church is the place of the Presence, in continuity with the temple of Israel toward which the psalmist orients his steps.[32] Here I recall the first Instruction, *Inter Oecumenici,* in which it was established that the tabernacle should be put in the middle of the main altar or on a side altar, and also that it was licit to celebrate Mass on an altar where there was a small tabernacle; furthermore, as regards the celebration of the Mass facing the people, the instruction spoke of opportuneness, not obligation; as far as the place of the tabernacle is concerned, it takes up again the prescription of the conciliar Constitution (cf. n. 128).[33] The Instruction is recalled in all successive documents down to *Redemptionis Sacramentum* (n. 130). In light of this, it would be nec-

32. Cf. N. Bux, *Dove Egli dimora [Where He Abides]* (Cinisello Balsamo: San Paolo, 2005), 100–11.

33. *The Constitution on the Sacred Liturgy* at n. 128 states that laws on the placing of the tabernacle, among other things, shall be revised; it does not require that the tabernacle be removed from the main altar. (Translator's note)

essary to clarify those orientations and norms that, issued after the Council, have led many to make of the Most Blessed Sacrament a "homeless person," and almost impossible to find. Father Anastasio Ballestrero, later archbishop and cardinal, entering churches where the place of the tabernacle was not evident, used to paraphrase Mary Magdalen (cf. Jn. 20:13), saying "they have taken away my Lord and I do not know where they have put him."

Together with the centrality of the tabernacle, Eucharistic worship is nourished by the exposition of the sacrament and by Eucharistic processions with Benediction, inserted in the Roman Ritual in 1614, not to speak of the solemn forms of adoration such as the Forty Hours, which helps meditation on the mystery of Christ buried, as the hours of his staying in the tomb were about that number. Other devout practices have been emphasized, such as perpetual adoration and visits to the Blessed Sacrament. Eucharistic devotions are salutary in the measure in which they help the faithful to fully understand the Mass as the culmination and the font of the life of faith. But not infrequently, through a misunderstood emphasis on poverty, the Corpus Christi procession lacks all decorum. The Christian people appears as a dispersed remnant; the clergy, no longer used to adoring and singing together, act in a slovenly and indecorous way (hands in pockets, gym shoes, chattering and laughs exchanged with one another and with the people they know on the sidewalk; improvised photographers; banal texts, songs, and prayers with no hint of the glory of the Blessed Sacrament); essentially not a sacred order, but a profane and secularized disorder. A procession without adoration, in the style of a march with didascalia on humanitarian causes, lets the crisis of faith in the Real Presence become visible.

The Encyclical *Mysterium Fidei* of Paul VI, published in September 1965, when the last session of the Council was about to open, reaffirms Catholic doctrine in the face of the contestations that had begun concerning the permanence of the Real Presence. This Encyclical is to be considered an explication of the liturgical Constitution *Sacrosanctum Concilium,* which presented all of Catholic Eucharistic doctrine as a permanent acquisition, and was also going to be translated into practice two years later in the Instruction

Eucharisticum Mysterium. The opposing critique maintains instead that the liturgical Constitution does not treat of Eucharistic devotions, except in passing, because they were considered to be now surpassed. In short, Eucharistic devotion was now supposedly against the law, as if it were not the soul of participation in the liturgy. From that we get the recurring accusation of the liturgists that whatever is not aligned with their idea of liturgy is devotionalism. For example, the expression "Jesus is the guest of my soul" would be a symptom of the individualistic spiritual attitude, and so should never be said. It's quite strange, because participation by the faithful in the liturgy culminates in the personal offering, that is, in the sacrifice of oneself, pleasing to God, the meeting with the Lord one and triune, and his dwelling in us.

His presence is veiled, and we draw near to him—as the last stanza of the *Adoro te devote*, composed by St. Thomas Aquinas, sings—in the expectation that our thirst will be quenched: this Jesus whom we see hidden in the Most Blessed Sacrament can reveal himself to us and render us blessed with his glory.

V

Confess in Order to be Converted

Thoughts of a journalist

CHRIST pardons every man who recognizes himself to be a sinner, but Luther considered individual confession to be a human work, and perfect sorrow to be impossible on account of the radical corruption of man, while he considered imperfect sorrow to be unworthy and servile because it is dictated by fear; at the opposite extreme, Rousseau imagined man to be naturally good. These are two conceptions born from presumption. Nevertheless Luther confessed weekly throughout his lifetime. Today the practice of this sacrament oscillates from the so-called Easter precept, once a year, by a great many of the faithful, to frequent confession and spiritual direction sought by the elite.

My journalist friend Mimmo Castellaneta would like to write a book on the subject: confession or reconciliation? He has not yet written it, but he has given me some momentum. There is probably no difference between "confession" and "reconciliation"—he hazards to say—in theological terms, but substantially there is, if one takes note that the sacrament is also called penance, pardon, and conversion, all complementary names. Could we dare to say that the term reconciliation brings with it a more participatory and more active attitude of the believer toward God? Perhaps, and even certainly it does.

The principal error committed by the faithful as well as by priests consists in considering the sacrament of confession as an ATM, where, after the recalling and listing of sins, or rather the ones we consider to be sins, and the recitation of the prayer (when it is remembered), one obtains, with the washing of the soul, remission of the penalty as well. In reality that is not how it is. As when human beings have been arguing or fighting, it is not enough to say "I was wrong," but there must also be the greatest effort to change habits and attitudes so as to recover the confidence of the person who has been offended by our actions, so it would have to be as well in the relationship between man—little, a poor nothing (St. Thérèse of Lisieux)—and the Lord.

It is evident to all that over time the very concept of confession has been mechanized in such a way as to lose its original meaning: the original meaning was not a simple listing of sins, but a sincere, overwhelming interior repentance that brings the soul to be reconciled with the Creator. It is also true that a do-it-yourself confession-reconciliation, as defended by the Protestants, is abhorrent. They presume that the Christian has a direct rapport with God, and so he asks pardon from God directly. All of that is profoundly mistaken. The mediation of the priest, as minister, is not a mere accidental feature, but rather gives sacred substance to a gesture that the Church considers precisely as a sacrament. And so what is the way to follow?

With the passing of the years, the so-called fear of God has been lost, that is to say, the attitude of the faithful person who lives and thinks of himself constantly under the gaze of the Lord, more concerned about pleasing him than pleasing other men. God is therefore the judge of the actions of man, but not like a functionary seeking to catch someone at fault, but rather as a father who desires the true good of the son. The fear of God is therefore the attitude of the son who wishes to be rightly related to the love of the father, rather than the attitude of a subject who does not wish to be caught transgressing the law.

According to Catholic theology, together with Anglican theology and a part of Protestant theology, the fear of God is one of the seven gifts of the Holy Spirit: it is the capacity that is necessary in order to follow the teachings of Jesus, and to recognize that God comes to meet man with love, and that Jesus is the Savior. In the New Testament, the fear of God is often placed in relation to faith, for example, when Jesus after having calmed the storm asks his disciples, "Why are you so afraid? Do you not yet have faith?" (Mk. 4:40). Furthermore it is precisely in the teaching of Jesus, who taught his disciples to identify God as a merciful father, that the fear of God appears clearly as the fear of breaking a relationship of love, rather than punishment for not having obeyed certain prescriptions.

Does the affirmation that God is infinite mercy mean that he pardons all, and always? Christ said: "Every sin and every blasphemy of men will be pardoned, but the blasphemy against the Holy Spirit will never be remitted. Whoever speaks ill of the Son of Man will obtain pardon, but he who speaks ill of the Holy Spirit will never have it remitted, either in this age, or the next" (Mt. 12:31–32). What kind of sin is this that will not be remitted either in time or in eternity? Some doctors of the Church understood it to be the heresy of Eunomius, a heresy that denied that the Holy Spirit was God. St. Hilary judges that the sin against the Holy Spirit consists in the negation of the divinity of Jesus Christ; St. Thomas considers that every sinful act committed in conscious preference over what is known to be right is a sin against the Holy Spirit. Theologians count six crimes against the Holy Spirit: presuming one will be saved without merit or the presupposed conditions; abandoning oneself to despair; resisting the known truth; breaking fraternal charity through jealousy; obstinacy in the way of evil; final impenitence. These sins are in fact directly and maliciously contrary to the goodness of God, which is attributed to the Holy Spirit.[1] However, in the text cited above, Jesus does not speak of every sin against the Holy Spirit, but only of blasphemy against the third person of the Trinity—the blasphemy that consists in calumniating works evidently divine and miraculous, faithful, loving, and holy, which God does for the salvation of men and through which he confirms their faith and backs up the truth of his holy word. Such works, which come from the goodness and sanctity of God, are proper in a certain way to the Holy Spirit. This is the explanation of the Gospel passage given by Athanasius, Ambrose, Jerome, John Chrysostom.

The sin against the Holy Spirit will not be remitted; that is, it will be pardoned only with difficulty, and rarely. But God, who is by nature will and power, can remit and in fact does remit every kind of

---

1. The special association of certain divine attributes with one of the divine persons is technically called "appropriation." (Translator's note)

sin to the person who sincerely repents of it. This sin will not be pardoned in the future age, because whoever dies in the state of grave fault goes to hell and no longer has hope to come out. John Paul II asks himself:

> Why is the blasphemy against the Holy Spirit unforgiveable? How is this blasphemy to be understood? Thomas Aquinas responds that it has to do with a sin "unforgiveable by its nature, insofar as it excludes those elements thanks to which remission of sins comes about." According to this kind of exegesis, the blasphemy does not properly consist in an offense in word against the Holy Spirit; it rather consists in the refusal to accept the salvation which God offers to man by way of the Holy Spirit operating in virtue of the sacrifice of the Cross. Now the blasphemy against the Holy Spirit is the sin committed by the man who claims a presumed "right" to persevere in evil—in any sin whatever—and thus refuses the redemption. Man remains closed in sin as he himself makes his conversion impossible, and so also remission of sins, which he considers not essential or important for his life, becomes impossible. This is indeed a condition of spiritual ruin, because the blasphemy against the Holy Spirit does not permit the man to come out of his self-imprisonment.[2]

Therefore, one sins against the Lord with false repentance, with insufficient fear of God, and when confession is lacking or incomplete. It would be sufficient to recall what our grandmothers used to say to us when we were little: "Mind you, God is watching." All of this is a primary responsibility of priests, who should guide the flock (with tenderness, but also with firmness), and not go along with it.

It would be interesting to go through the teaching of Padre Pio and his manner of hearing confessions, and of giving out or denying absolutions. Hearing confessions kept him busy for many hours of his day. He did it with introspective vision and left no possibility of ambiguity for the penitent. It was not possible to lie to him who could see into the soul. Often, finding himself before very emotional penitents, he would himself list the sins committed by the

---

2. Encyclical *Dominum et vivificantem*, n. 46.

penitent. Padre Pio invited people to frequent the sacrament of confession, urging them to have recourse to it at least once a week. He used to say that a room, depending on how long it may have remained closed, needs a dusting out, at least once a week. In this he was very demanding: he required a real and true conversion and he was uncompromising with those who betook themselves to his confessional solely on account of their curiosity to see the friar and saint. A confrere recounted: "One day Padre Pio denied absolution to a penitent and then told him: 'If you go and confess to another, you will go to hell together with that other priest who gives you absolution,'" as if to say that without the intention of changing one's life, the sacrament is profaned, and the person who does this becomes guilty before God. Often, in fact, Padre Pio treated the faithful with apparent harshness, but it is likewise true that the spiritual distress that those rebukes afforded the souls of penitents was transformed into an interior effort to go back to him, now contrite, in order to receive definitive absolution.

And last, the penance. For someone who does not pray, the invitation to pray, by the well-known phrase: Say three Our Father's, three Hail Mary's, and three Glory Be's, or maybe a Rosary, is a real penance. But the Lord has also asked for fasting—which is not reserved for Lent—and the works of fraternal charity. Thus it is truly a penance if it constitutes a just penalty for the offenses done against God. The point is to die to ourselves. And that can be done with a work of charity (why be horrified at a possible penance of economic help to a poor person in order to expiate one's own fault?), with some personal mortification. The true Catholic cannot allow himself to be cradled in the regnant "do-goodism," which no longer makes any distinctions, and distances itself from the reality of the Gospel.

The Word is not only infinite mercy. The Gospel message is hard, difficult, and challenges us. It would be only too easy to create for ourselves a virtual system in which each of us could put in place what pleases him, and pretend that the precepts and rules of the tradition are no longer of any use. And the essential reasons for penance and reconciliation can only be found in the personal mortification, not the penance inflicted—if it can even be called that in some cases when the priest is distracted, and perhaps turns the evaluation of sins into a psychoanalytic session. Less psychology and more knowledge, at least what is in the *Catechism of the Catholic Church,* wouldn't hurt.

We must forgive. And perhaps there is nothing more revolutionary in the Gospel message than this imperative, since each of has had wrongs, great or small, done to us, and sometimes feels justified, by self-love and pride, in avenging himself. Many people ask themselves and ask me: does forgiving seventy times seven times mean we should cease being simple like a dove and wise like a serpent? No. If you trust a person with your act of believing what he says, with favors, and with friendship, and he does you some grave wrong, it is right to forgive from the heart. But if the person does not ask you for pardon, then it is in accord with the Gospel to "shake the dust from your feet," in order to have nothing more to do with him.

Thus far, the thoughts of my journalist friend, in brainstorming style: something to provoke us into understanding the sacerdotal function better, tied above all to the so-called "sacraments of healing," which are penance and the anointing of the sick, because they cure and heal. Isaiah writes: "In conversion and in calm is your salvation, in tranquility and trust is your strength" (30:15).

Are these sacraments only therapeutic? Why two of them? One for the spirit and the other for the body; in reality they affect our whole being. Where we Westerners simplify, identifying soul and spirit, the East keeps them distinct; thus they unite to these two sacraments another rite, composed of prayers to cure those who have psychic maladies: it is an "imitation sacrament" in which the Church places her intercessory power before God, a psychic therapy with the potent instrument of prayer. Like us, the East has seven sacraments and the sacramentals; nevertheless, the boundary between the two is more nuanced.

Penance first and foremost heals the spirit of man, the anointing of the sick bends over the infirmity of the body; but it is also necessary to heal the soul. The East in fact is pleased to hold to the Biblical tripartition spirit-soul-body, a tripartition that was appropriated by a good part of patristic literature. The spirit is, to put it this way, the highest part of the human being, who in this way is helped to live "according to the spirit"; below is the body that inclines to follow after material things, "according to the flesh"; the soul is midway between spirit and body, and is called to adjust the different demands so that they do not enter into conflict. Therefore it is necessary to heal the soul, over and beyond the spirit and the body, for which reason psychic therapy practiced by spiritual men, monks or priests, is also necessary. In our day when, especially in the West, depressive and psychic maladies in general have notably increased, provoking imbalance in the person, with reactive effects on the body and the spirit, such "therapy" appears useful.

When approach is made to the "sacraments of healing," one must not fail to have regard for the structure of man. The sacraments are composed of matter and form, according to the classical terminology, and so they come close to the material, physical situations, beyond the spiritual ones in the life of man, from birth until death. Man's moral actions depend not only on his spiritual health and his physical integrity but also on his psychic state. Consequently these sacraments—which in a certain sense do not contribute to establishing and determining salvation, but to maintaining and restoring it, that is, to healing man—must take account of the condition in which man finds himself.

The route of conversion

To convert or be converted means returning to the place from which we have become distant: God. When man distances himself from God, all the rest of it is but a consequence, Dostoyevsky and Solzhenitsyn have said. To take the way of return, we need a supernatural strength: Jesus began his public mission with the words: "Be converted and believe in the Gospel" (Mk. 1:15). This is what makes the penitential sacrament: it leads man back to God, man who is often left half dead along the road by the brigands of the world, and it entrusts him to the care of the ecclesial inn where the other converts are. Thus the sacrament is also an efficacious means of reconciliation, of reestablishing the communion deteriorated by sin. Sin distances man from God and penance leads him back. For the baptized member of the faithful who has fallen into sin and is therefore far from that communion, it is a matter of going back over the route, bearing a penalty—from which comes the name "penance" for the sacrament—in order to be reconciled with the Lord. Conversion of heart or interior penance is obtained keeping one's gaze fixed on the blood of Christ (cf. CCC 1432).

Often it is not admitted that the original cause of the evils of the world and of man is the negation of the innate religiosity in man. The fool thinks: "There is no God" (cf. Ps. 13:1). Tempted by the evil one, man abandons the condition of a creature and son of God. Here, then, is sin.

The *Catechism* illustrates the journey of return that leads to recognizing sin, that is, to confession, preparing oneself through an examination of conscience—not on the basis of a worldly ethic, but on the basis of Christ, helped perhaps by a passage of the Gospel, as happened to St. Anthony the abbot and to St. Francis. The sinner must see himself reflected in the Gospel passage if he wishes to recognize his sins in the light of the Holy Spirit. But, as Pius XII reminded us, in our times the sense of sin has been lost.

What is sin? Some scientists ask themselves why the man of today uses so many detergents, soaps, shampoos, and various products for hygiene. Perhaps because he gets more dirty in his body and his clothing than the ancients? No, the contrary is true. But because he is aware of something dirty on the inside, not knowing the causes, he buys and uses a variety of detergents and perfumes for making himself clean. But the "heart" cannot be cleaned in such a way, because the interior dirt is deep, intense, and diversified. St. Paul says:

> The works of the flesh are well known: fornication, impurity, libertinage, idolatry, witchcraft, animosities, discord, jealousy, refusal to agree, divisions, factions, envy, drunkenness, orgies, and the like; regarding these things I warn you in advance, as I have already said, that he who does them will not inherit the kingdom of God (Gal. 5:19–21).

These "works" are the object or subject matter of sin. Consequently the *Catechism* notes:

> Sins can be distinguished according to their object, the same as for every human act, or according to the virtues to which they are

opposed by excess or falling short, or according to the commandments to which they are opposed. They can also be subdivided according as they have to do with God, one's neighbor, or oneself; they can be distinguished into spiritual sins and carnal sins, or further, into sins of thought, word, action, or omission. The root of sin is in the heart of man, in his free will, according to the teaching of the Lord: "From the heart . . . come forth wicked designs, murders, adulteries, prostitution, thefts, false testimonies, blasphemies. These are the things that render man unclean" (Mt. 15:19–20). The heart is also the seat of charity, the principle of good works that sin wounds. (CCC 1852–53)

Therefore sin, St. Augustine says, is a word, an act, or a desire contrary to the eternal Law. It is an offense against God. One raises oneself up against God in a disobedience contrary to the obedience of Christ.

Sin is an act contrary to reason. It wounds the nature of man and attacks human solidarity. Deliberately, that is, knowingly and willingly choosing something gravely contrary to the divine law and the last end of man: that is the committing of a "mortal sin." It destroys charity in us, the charity without which eternal beatitude is impossible. If not repented, it leads us to eternal death. "Venial sin," in contrast, means a moral disorder made up for through charity, which venial sin does not take away from us.

The repetition of sins, even venial ones, generates the vices, among which the "capital sins" are distinguished from each other. They are called "capital" because they generate other sins or vices: pride, avarice, envy, anger, lust, gluttony, sloth, and acedia. There are also the sins that cry out to heaven: voluntary murder, the sin of impurity against nature (or homosexual acts), oppression of the poor, defrauding workers of their wages.

Sin is a personal act, but we have a responsibility in the sins committed by others when we *cooperate:* taking part in them directly and voluntarily; commanding them, counseling them, praising or approving them; not denouncing or preventing them when one is obligated to do so; protecting those who commit the evil. Thus sin renders men accomplices with each other and makes concupiscence—that is, the stimulus to sin—reign among them, along with violence and injustice. Sins are at the origin of the social situations and institutions contrary to the divine goodness. Structures of sin are the expression and effect of personal sins. They induce their victims to commit evil in their turn. In an analogous sense these constitute a social sin (cf. CCC 1865–69).

When I become conscious of sin, I should thank God; and so confessing sin means confessing the faith. Then one becomes aware of the urgency of turning around and returning to the filial condition from which I have cut myself off. This I can do by renouncing the various forms of evil: this is repentance. And so it starts from conscience.

What is conscience? In the Bible and in patristic literature, "the heart" is mentioned to indicate affectivity, will, and reason, or man's capacity for knowing. St. Maximus the Confessor says that their purpose is to know, desire, and love God. When the unity of the heart is ruptured, sin happens. The "heart," therefore, corresponds to "moral conscience":

> Conscience is the most secret core and sanctuary of man, where he finds himself alone with God, whose voice resounds in his own inner person (GS 16).
>
> Conscience is a judgment of reason, with which the human person recognizes the moral quality of a concrete act.
>
> For the man who has committed evil, the verdict of his conscience remains a pledge of conversion and of hope.
>
> A well-formed conscience is upright and truthful. It formulates its judgments according to reason, in conformity with the true good willed by the wisdom of the Creator. Everyone must avail himself of the means to form his conscience.
>
> Conscience can remain in ignorance or make erroneous judgments. Such ignorance and errors are not always free of guilt.
>
> The Word of God is a light for our path. We must assimilate it in faith and prayer and put it into practice. This is how moral conscience is formed. (CCC 1795–98, 1801–2)

Why confess

God became man in the Son Jesus Christ, and wills that the sin of men be pardoned in a way that *passes through* men, in order to give them the possibility of pardoning one another; it is precisely something human that becomes *the visible means of the invisible grace*, the sacrament of confession-penance-reconciliation. After the Cross, the death, and the descent into hell, on the evening of the first Easter, the day of his resurrection, the Son returns, forgives the apostles who had fled in a cowardly way, and going beyond that, delivers to them the keys, *in primis* to Peter. With the gift of the Holy Spirit he transmits to his Church the power to administer pardon to sinners, drawing from the treasury of mercy opened with the resurrection. In a word, the Risen One unites the Father's pardon to the Church's pardon, and institutes the sacrament (cf. Mt. 16:19; Jn. 20:23). Consequently it makes no sense for a Christian to say: "I confess directly to God." Rather, the Lord "hears the confession" by way of the ministers of the Church, to whom he has given the power to pardon in his name.

Finally confession is necessary because, despite the new life received in baptism and the Eucharist, the weakness of our nature with its inclination to evil (or concupiscence) has not been suppressed. We are sinners, that is, we think and act in a way contrary to the Gospel. He who says he is without sin is a liar, or blind. Therefore we must fight, with the help of grace, the battle of conversion, aiming at sanctity (cf. CCC 1427). Penitence is a laborious baptism or conversion. The Church wishes to lead man back to God after falls that follow baptism. Reconciliation with God is inseparable from reconciliation with the Church (cf. CCC 1445).

The Church's power to forgive sins and to bring back into communion the person who has distanced himself rests on the fact that the Lord has given the Church this power: it is a power that belongs absolutely to him, because God alone forgives sins, as the scribes observe in the celebrated episode of the paralytic (cf. Mk. 2:1, 12; Mt. 9:1–8). It was a blasphemy to think that a man could forgive sins. This idea is still present today when, in crime news, we hear it said that something cannot be forgiven, and people sometimes add that God alone forgives sins. It is a natural way of thinking for man, and, in effect, that is how things are: forgiving wrongs is not a natural capacity of man. In order to forgive, we need an extraordinary strength, a "supernatural" power that God himself, from the time he came upon earth, brought with him. Consequently, Jesus replies to the scribes: "that you may know that the Son of Man has power on earth to forgive sins..." So with Jesus a change has come about.

In fact the power to pardon is linked to his Incarnation. According to a beautiful image of St. Bernard, God the Father has sent to earth a bag, so to speak, full of his mercy, a bag that was torn to pieces during his Passion so that from out of it would come the price that enclosed in itself our whole ransom. It was certainly a small bag, if "a boy has been given to us" (Is. 9:6)—a boy, however, in whom "the whole fullness of divinity dwells" (Col. 2:9).[3] Therefore the sacrament of forgiveness, in particular, is linked to the presence in it of the flesh of Christ, which took upon itself our sins. Only for this reason can the Church bring man back into the communion of the ecclesial body—which is the body of Christ—after the distancing of sin, which involved self-exclusion from sacramental communion, that is, *de facto* excommunication. This comes about by way of the penitential path, the only path that makes us just before God, or rather it is he who justifies us: it is a grace (cf. CCC 1446).

Who can receive the sacrament

The awareness that the forgiveness of sins was not limited to baptism alone—the link is so close that when it is adults who are baptized, there must *not* be confession—matured with the observation that realistically the members of the Church can fall anew into grave sin after baptism, not necessarily because they commit their lives to it, but yielding to temptation. Can the possibility of that happening be excluded? Should there be no going to meet sinners excluded from communion, "recovering" them by having them go back in a certain sense to baptism, where they can begin anew the route to the Eucharist? This time it will be a route in which they must bear a penalty (*poenam tenere*), the route of penitence, beginning with the admission of being sinners, the admission made by confessing their

---

3. Cf. St. Bernard, *First Discourse for the Feast of Epiphany*, 2, PL 133:142.

sins to the priest. We understand why penance necessarily stands in a relation with the Eucharist, in the same way as baptism. The sacrament of confession gives back the grace necessary for approaching communion. In fact, in order to receive communion it is necessary to be in the grace of God, to know and think on Whom one is going to receive, to observe the prescribed fast: the Eucharist presupposes baptism as well as confession, repeated as necessary. St. John Paul II put this in high relief in his Encyclical *Redemptor Hominis*. The first thing said in the Good News was: "Be converted." "Christ who invited us to the Eucharistic table is always the same Christ who exhorts us to repent, and does not cease to say 'Be converted'" (*Redemptor Hominis* IV, 20). "Where penance disappears, the Eucharist is no longer discerned and, as the Lord's Eucharist, is destroyed."[4] Discerning the body of the Lord is a disposition of the soul in faith, and it seeks unity, not divisions. For this reason, to affirm that Penance can be untied from the Eucharist, as some theologians have maintained, does not correspond to reality, insofar as sin breaks communion with both the Lord and the Church, so that in order to return to communion, penitence is needed, a "second baptism" is needed, or—as the Fathers said—a laborious baptism. This should be reconfirmed to those who maintain that there is no need for confession in order to receive communion. Furthermore, untying Penance from the Eucharist means losing the meaning of the Eucharist, which is reconciliation. Even children, when they have to approach communion for the first time, come to sacramental confession beforehand.

The primitive Church progressively overcame the rigorism attested by the *Shepherd of Hermas*, a writing of the 2nd century, which maintained that penance was possible only once in a lifetime; that idea ended up as the characteristic of various sects. Because the penalties imposed were hard and lasted for years, many put off Penance until the end of their lives; but a sudden death did not permit them to actualize their intention, with the aggravating result of

---

4. J. Ratzinger, *The Feast of Faith: Approaches to a Theology of the Liturgy,* trans. Graham Harrison (San Francisco: Ignatius Press, 1986), 152.

remaining perpetually excluded from eternal life. The most ancient witness to a canonical (that is, regulated by norms) penitential discipline is found in Tertullian: the "second repentance," so-called because it followed the first one, or baptism. It concerned apostasy, murder, and adultery: three sins that bring one to death—and are consequently called capital[5]—and that had to be confessed secretly to the bishop.

The Fathers were moderators or dispensers of Penance. They regulated and administered it in relation to the gravity of the sins, imposing even years of penance before readmission to the Eucharist, which also constituted the remedy against venial sins and the nourishment of Christians who were weak, but also desirous of amendment and reform of their lives.[6] St. Basil attests that when sinners acknowledged a specific sin, public or secret, and decided to confess it, they went to the bishop and made their confession. The theory that the confession, in antiquity, was public, relies on its having been identified with the practice of a penance, which could be public, as we shall see, and also private; in fact the Greek term *exomologesis* (confession) indicated the entire penitential route. If the sin committed was a matter of public knowledge, the sinner performed a public penance and everyone could observe it. But the confession, as the first act along the penitential route, was secret. When the emperor Theodosius received his penance from Ambrose for the massacre of Thessalonica as a condition for re-entry into the Church, everyone knowing of the sin with which he had stained himself spoke of public penance, that is, visible penance; for a public sin, public penance.

In the East, there were various penitential grades or levels, two of them public in character: (1) *begging prayers* at the door of the

---

5. "Capital," from *caput* (head), here recalls the Roman sentence of beheading, understood metaphorically for spiritual death in this context. (Translator's note)

6. Cf. St. Ambrose, *De Sacramentis*, IV, vi, 28: PL 16:464: "I must receive it always, so it may always forgive my sins. If I sin continually, I must always have a remedy"; St. Cyril of Alexandria, *In Joh. Evang.*, IV, 2; PG 73:585: "If your sins prevent you from drawing near and if you do not stop sinning ever—who knows his own faults, says the psalmist—will you remain without participating in the sanctification which vivifies for eternity?"

church, addressed to whoever entered for the liturgy—the Greek word for that includes weeping, an outward sign of contrition; (2) *remaining prostrate* during the Eucharistic liturgy. These two external gestures, which were also done for a certain number of years, exposed the penitents, and in a certain sense humiliated them, so that they obtained the fruits of penance. The two grades of private penance consisted of: (a) listening to the first part of the Mass *seated*, together with the catechumens, and then leaving the church; (b) *standing* for the Eucharistic prayer like the faithful, but without receiving communion. If remaining seated assimilated the penitents to the catechumens, standing assimilated them to the faithful, so they would not be identified as such. The Church imposed private penance in cases of sins of lesser gravity, or to protect certain personal situations. St. Basil inflicted twenty years of penance for abortion, five in each of the grades just delineated.

Starting in the 5th century, the baptized who accepted the state of being penitents had their names inscribed in the order of penitents at the beginning of Lent. In Rome the pope imposed his hands, and after having prayed, sanctioned the reconciliation of the penitent on Holy Thursday. Canonical penance progressively declined in the West, while in the East it remained on paper. The Council of Nicaea in 325 reiterated in canon 13 the disciplinary decree that the Eucharist must not be denied as viaticum to the dying, even when they were no longer in any position to complete some work of penance, that is, when they had fallen ill before completing the penance. It was a canon not applied uniformly.

In late antiquity, the confession of sins in itself was seen as a penance, considering the humiliation of confessing one's own sins to a man, priest though he be: that development was owed above all to the spiritual men, that is, the monks. Clement of Alexandria and Origen considered the spiritual director as a physician, a therapist, a guide for discernment—from the Greek *kybernetes*—who helped the penitent stride the path of spiritual rebirth: and thus, along with the judicial aspect of Penance, the medicinal or therapeutic aspect developed. As late as the beginning of the 15th century, Simeon of Thessalonika was familiar with a kind of spiritual direction that included confession of sins to a layman endowed with a charism, but when sacramental absolution had to be given, such a layman would send the person to a priest.

The dispenser or moderator of penance, that is, every priest, is a kind of judge, and also physician, for the person before him. These two aspects were always present in the sacrament of reconciliation, even in the era of canonical penance, because it was necessary to discern the state of the Christian believer who was a sinner, and evaluate the fittingness of one penalty rather than another, whether in the case of public or private penance. In short, it was necessary to evaluate the state of health and verify that the penance would be able to heal him, and not push him down further. To a certain priest who, called to evaluate causes and remedies for sin, began by saying "in my opinion," a penitent responded: "You mean: according to the Church and her moral doctrine. I'm not interested in your opinion." In conclusion, it is misleading to consider confession as a dialogue, because one goes before a judge and doctor, not a newspaper columnist.

And so Penance, once it became secret and repeatable from the 6th–7th centuries onward, thanks also to the influx into Europe of Irish monasticism, was no longer seen as something extraordinary, and consequently it began also to include the faults not subject to the canonical penitential discipline: no longer only the capital sins (in the sense indicated above), but venial sins as well.

Some priests, thinking that they can command consciences, say that confession should be only for grave sins. In a Roman basilica where there is normally a confessor on duty, one of them seeing a considerable line of penitents, came out of the confessional and said out loud: "only those who have serious sins to confess, stay." Everyone went away, except for a nun; she stayed, probably not because she had serious sins, but because the others did not want to be identified as grave sinners. What a doctrinal and pastoral error that confessor committed!

Many people ask themselves: does the pope also confess? To whom? Certainly he is a member of the faithful and can sin, so he too must confess to a priest, whom he, like every Christian, is free to choose.

How reconciliation comes about

The sacrament happens when the priest confessor extends his hand and prays, concluding with the words: "I absolve you from your sins in the name of the Father and of the Son and of the Holy Spirit." To absolve—from the Latin—means to loosen the wickedness or the bonds entered into with evil, which paralyze us and place at the margins of the Church. This rite loosens from the tie of the sins committed, insofar as the penitent has done three things above all: (a) *contrition*, that is, he has had sincere sorrow for the sins committed, or at least fears the punishments consequent upon violation of the divine law (this is called *attrition*); (b) complete *confession* of the sins, indicating the number of times and the species of the sins, so that the priest, like a judge or doctor, can understand whether something was light or serious, an accident along the way, or a deep-seated attitude of vice—he can, with discretion, pose questions in order to help the penitent, like a doctor who has the symptoms told to him so he can identify the causes; (c) the *intention* to not fall again into sin and to make satisfaction by doing the penance imposed upon him (for example, acts of charity, prayer, fasting).

The formula of individual absolution, which accomplishes the reconciliation with God and with the Church, is an expression of the solemn promise made by Jesus to Peter: "To you I will give the keys of the kingdom of heaven" (Mt. 16–19). The door will remain closed and he who does not will to convert from his sins will not be able to enter, and he who has converted from his sins will be able to enter. This is the power of the keys conferred upon the Church, *in primis* to Peter and then to the apostles (cf. Mt. 18:18), and transmitted from them to their successors, the pope and bishops, and shared with the priests, their collaborators. As Irenaeus said, "he cannot have God for his Father, who does not have the Church for his mother": reconciliation with the Church is inseparable from reconciliation with God, because of the Incarnation of the Word, as said before. Reconciliation is recognizing that the love of God is infinitely greater than my sin; it is to ask the Son Jesus Christ to give me the strength to renew my life, the strength that enables me to use my liberty well; it is to draw grace from the Holy Spirit through confession and communion, the sacraments that make us pass from sin to reconciliation.

You, therefore, priest, make yourself available in the confessional—not in shorts, but in cassock or alb, and putting the violet stole on, remembering that you are administering a sacrament in which Jesus Christ is present and acts. Seek to understand and respect the penitent. Be one who is orienting the conscience of another, not taking its place. Be in harmony with the teaching of the Church of which you are only a minister; otherwise, do not enter the confessional. Do the gesture of imposing your hand, and pronounce the formula that has the verb in the indicative and declares the pardon that has come from God and the Church: *Ego te absolvo.* The hand lifted toward the head of the penitent—even behind the grate—is an ancient gesture, and it indicates that Jesus Christ makes the Holy Spirit descend for the remission of sins. It is an epiclesis, or a supplicating invocation of the Father, that he may send the Spirit upon the sins that entangle the penitent, and untie them.

Because the Church is guarantor of the rights of God, the sacrament expresses the juridical certitude that the priest not only calls upon the pardon of God, but declares that it has been granted. In the Extraordinary Form, he specifies: "May our Lord Jesus Christ absolve you; and I, with his authority, absolve you." The priest is he who acts *in the person of Christ*, judge, physician, and good shepherd. The formula in the declarative mood is very important from the psychological point of view, because man needs to have the certitude of having been forgiven, otherwise he remains in doubt. This aspect, which has matured in Catholic theology, is very important: the confessor transmits the truth of the pardon that has come to the sinner.

The Byzantines also have individual confession, done by the penitent in front of the iconostasis: the priest imposes the *epitrachilion* (stole) over the head, while the penitent says the prayers of contrition and receives absolution. Among them, rigorous canons concerning fasting and sexual abstinence are still in force. For example, after relations with one's own spouse, one may not receive communion; it is also by reason of those canons that married priests do not have daily Mass, and observe the days of Eucharistic fast—

Wednesday and Friday in particular—over and beyond the other days provided in the liturgical year. The Eastern formula of Penance has the verb in the subjunctive mood, that is, it begs forgiveness from God, as in the penitential act of the Latin Mass: *Misereatur* (may the Lord have mercy).

The rite of Penance in the Extraordinary Form is very similar to the Greek one, and it is lengthy enough to permit reflection on what I have done, on the gift I am receiving; this potentially also means that the condition of excommunication or interdict I incurred with sin is lifted.[7] Among other things, this helps us realize that we must not die in a state of excommunication. Excommunication ceases with death, because the jurisdiction of the Church goes up to that point; for this reason, absolution was sought before death or at least at the point of death.

In exceptional circumstances (wars, earthquakes, epidemics) provision is made for general absolution, in other words, the sacrament administered to a multitude of faithful impeded from receiving it individually. This kind of rite is traced back by some to a type of meeting held in monasteries, the so-called chapter of faults, with confession of sins by the monks individually, and absolution by the abbot. In reality, this chapter was more concerned with violations of the monastic rule than it was with moral faults or personal sins. The other source to which this rite can supposedly be traced is the involvement of the faithful in the reconciliation of public sinners, on Holy Thursday, done by the bishop in antiquity and the Middle Ages, as said before. On that occasion, the faithful who were present, including those who were not penitents, united themselves to the reconciliation of the penitents, a little like what happens today when anointing of the sick is given in communal fashion. Finally, communal reconciliation supposedly goes back to emergency confession in situations of danger; for example during wars, with the risk of

---

7. Of course only certain grave faults bring excommunication, but regardless of whether there was any excommunication, the full formula for absolution lifts excommunication and interdict conditionally ("to the extent I am able [i.e., have the faculty] and you need it [if you do]") before sins are absolved. This reflects the fact that absolution cannot be licitly and validly imparted to an excommunicated person. (Translator's note)

imminent death, on account of which general absolution is imparted. At any rate, this absolution has never been considered a sacrament.[8] The sacrament is always and only given to each person, as if by name, even when it is administered in communal form. Consequently there remains the obligation to confess, once the danger has passed.

The rite of penance,[9] in the Ordinary Form, provides for general absolution also in the case of a large crowd of penitents (cf. 31), when a sufficient number of confessors is lacking. In sanctuaries, where confessors could turn out to be too few because of so many people, an adequate number of priests to hear the confessions is provided. But in the cases of emergency, too, individual confession of mortal sins is prescribed, when the state of emergency or danger has passed (n. 34). The interlocutor of God is the individual man, because with the Incarnation the Son became an individual man. Here we have the realization of the redemption in this fundamental sacrament.

Where to confess

When there used to be a gentle light and silence reigning in the churches, there was a line at the confessional; now, despite the provision of "penitential areas," two thirds of Catholics no longer confess. Blame for Catholics no longer confessing is attributed to the new religion of self-determination, which is the opposite of psychoanalysis, which judges that man does not act freely. Who is right in assigning blame here? One reason that is not secondary in the crisis of the sacrament of confession is the abandonment of the confessional with the grate: this used to favor discretion, which is truly fundamental, between the penitent and the confessor. It seems the confessional was invented by St. Charles Borromeo. If this modality or type of official place for confessions—as is said today—came to

8. The absolution is valid if the recipients are properly disposed, but without the element of personal confession of sins, the sacramental sign is not full. (Translator's note)

9. *Ordo Penitentiae*, Typ. Pol. Vat., 1974.

be privileged, there was a reason. It is above all a symbol of the secret, or the sacramental seal, by which every minister is gravely obligated in conscience, at the cost of his life, which happened to various saints, like St. John Nepomucene. The confessor may not reveal anything he hears; even if it concerns a crime, it may not be referred to the police.

Until Vatican II, the confessional with the grate was recommended for the confession of women, while for men and the young confession face to face with the confessor was permissible. In our day, it would be appropriate to use the grate not only for confessions of the gentle sex, but also for boys: it interposes a barrier to the senses, and thus a barrier to the devil. Besides, not seeing the face of the confessor puts the penitent in the condition of being able to speak with freedom and permits the confessor to speak freely to the penitent in the name of God—unless confessor and penitent are now so conditioned by face-to-face confession that they feel unable to change it. It seems Padre Pio did not look the penitent in the face. In fact, the manner of the classic confessor was to draw his ear close to the grate, without looking, often with eyes closed, to listen and finally give absolution.

The light-hearted abolition of the confessional, in favor of "penitential areas," caused serious harm: because the confessional does not have the grate, many people do not confess (not only old people), and many as a result do not feel at ease. In our day when people have become so sensitive about their privacy, sometimes in exaggerated ways, it would be better to restore the grate.

The use of the confessional by the priest encourages many people who are in church for Mass or private prayer to confess, as can be seen in basilicas and sanctuaries, and as foreseen by the rite of Penance (13) and confirmed by John Paul.[10] It is true that it would be more opportune to do it at another time, but times for the call to conversion cannot be dictated to God. If conversion depends very much on hearing the word of God, why must it not happen during Mass or after the homily? This is certainly something to reflect upon.

10. Cf. John Paul II, Apostolic Letter *Misericordia Dei* (2002), n.2.

Confession inculcates humility, inner and outer: staying on one's knees induces attitudes for forgiveness and conversion; besides, it helps the confessor to do penance for sinners, as the holy Curé of Ars and St. Pio of Pietrelcina did.

The spiritual effects

The effects of the sacrament are diverse: reconciliation with God, which makes us recover the grace lost by sin; reconciliation with the Church; remission of the eternal penalty merited on account of mortal sins; the remission, at least in part, of the temporal penalties, which are consequences of sin; peace and serenity of conscience, and spiritual consolation; growth of spiritual strength for Christian combat; anticipation of the judgment to which we will be submitted at the end of our life (cf. CCC 1470); the peace and joy of the new life in the Spirit. To sum it all up: the growth of spiritual strength for fighting the good fight of faith, helped by the strength of God that comes from the Eucharist.

Many saints confessed often, in order to be in the grace of God as much as possible.

The "cure" so as not to fall back into evil, and to live as persons who have been saved and reconciled, is prayer. Through prayer God the Holy Spirit makes us adore, ask, intercede, thank, praise. The Christian tradition keeps and recommends three forms of prayer in particular: *vocal prayer*, because as a man I must manifest my interior sentiments; *meditation*, which seeks to understand what God desires from me; *contemplative prayer*, which is a gaze of faith fixed on Jesus, a listening to the Word of God, a silent love (cf. CCC 2700–2724).

Especially with Psalm 50: "*Miserere mei, Deus, secundum magnam misericordiam tuam*," and the *Kyrie eleison*, prayer is joined with other penitential gestures such as fasting and almsgiving.

So go to confession when you don't feel like it, because it is a sin to refuse mercy; recognize the mediation of a human being like you. Don't hide yourself behind the community: it is not constitutive of your being. Choose your confessor, even if it be in anonymity; then make the sign of the cross and say how much time has passed since your last confession. Enumerate your sins in relation to the Ten Commandments and the precepts of the Church, the theological and cardinal virtues, those very recommendable virtues of humility and poverty; then listen to the judgment and accept the "therapy" or penance to perform (prayer, a biblical selection to meditate on, a book by St. Alphonsus de' Liguori, even if for some priests he is no longer in fashion), recite the Act of Contrition, and receive the absolution, responding *Amen* and making the sign of the cross on yourself. This is why it is necessary to confess in person and not on the phone or by Internet. So the condition for being accepted by God is not being pure, but recognizing one's own sin.

The meaning indulgences have

Often in man the will to do what is good and right is weakened. Sin, beyond involving guilt, implies a penalty: confession remits the guilt, but does not obtain the remission of all temporal penalties—consequences of sin—which are counted off either here below on earth or in the other life, in purgatory. "Temporal" means they have a beginning and an end, they are not eternal like hell: there, nothing can be done. It is precisely with regard to these temporal penalties—connected with sins already forgiven as to their guilt—that the Church intervenes with indulgences, an extraordinary effect of the communion of saints: a living solidarity of Christ, and with the Church, which as it were possesses bars of gold in the cellar, constituted from the infinite merits and the mediation of Christ, Our Lady, and the saints, especially the martyrs. Merits such as these are of benefit to the faithful, living and dead. The faithful can obtain the indulgences for themselves, in the manner of absolution, and also for the souls in purgatory, in the manner of suffrages (cf. CCC 1490–1498), because the deceased are no longer subject to the jurisdiction of the Church. That is to say, the faithful accomplish good works and offer the merits of Christ to the Father, in prayer asking that he would accept them, in remission of the penalties that the souls undergoing purgation must still suffer. So prayer for the deceased (Mass of the thirtieth day, for the anniversary, or another commemoration) has its efficacy: it shortens the time of their penalty—presupposing that they are in the state of purification—if the prayer is preceded or followed by our confession and communion, by the indulgences, by the works of penitence and of charity. All this makes us and them pure and ready in the sight of God. And the deceased who are already blessed or in the state of purification repay with their intercession on our behalf before God.

Every good work performed in the state of grace—in addition to the aspect of merit, which cannot be transferred and which rightly counts for a just recompense—carries with it also a "satisfactory" aspect, by means of which it is possible to pay off the temporal debt of punishment contracted by sin. This can be made over to others as well. This making over is done, as a precious exchange of gifts, in favor of the deceased.

The power for indulgences resides in divine law and in those who have the "power of the keys" in the Church: the pope and the bishops united with him. The Church grants plenary indulgences, which remit the whole temporal penalty, and partial indulgences. We have here a commutative form of the ancient penitential discipline. The indulgence can be obtained only once a day, even if the works prescribed are done several times in one day. Among the better known plenary indulgences, we have the indulgence of the Porziuncola—the so-called Pardon of Assisi granted to St. Francis from the Blessed Virgin, which can be taken advantage of on August 2nd, the dedication day of the famous little church St. Francis repaired—and the indulgence of November 2nd, applicable only to the deceased faithful in purgatory.[11] In addition we have those of the Jubilee or the Holy Year, and in particular, the one granted to a member of the faithful at the end of life (*in articulo mortis*) who cannot be attended by a priest, provided he is rightly disposed and has recited a prayer specified for this. The use of a crucifix or a cross is recommended for the acquisition of such indulgences.[12] The plenary indulgence cannot be applied to living persons, but only to oneself or the faithful departed.

11. The plenary indulgence for the dead may be gained each day from November 1 through November 8, under the usual conditions. (Editor's note)
12. Paul VI, Apostolic Constitution *Indulgentiarum Doctrina* (1967), n. 18.

The partial indulgence remits only a part of the temporal penalty, greater in proportion to how great the fervor of the baptized person is, and how weighty the work done by him is: such an indulgence can be gained more than once a day. Thus indulgences make us experience the effect of grace, stimulate good works, increase faith, hope, and conversion. There is no place for any magical interpretation or mathematical calculation, and certainly not for scandalous trafficking, although these things are always possible in the Church, since she is made up of human beings. What Luther wrote in his *Table Talk*, criticizing Pope Leo X's indulgences for the new St. Peter's Basilica—"when the coin in the coffer rings, a soul from purgatory springs"—is perhaps a fairy tale.

The conditions for obtaining indulgences are: to be in the state of grace, that is, to have confessed and received communion, and to have prayed for the Supreme Pontiff (namely with a *Pater* and *Credo*). More than one indulgence can be obtained with the same sacramental (individual) confession; with a single sacramental communion a single plenary indulgence is acquired. The confession can also be made by those who have no mortal sin on their conscience, during eight days preceding or following the day prescribed for the good work. The plenary indulgence process includes acts of true conversion and acts of external penitence: in general, visiting a sacred place, or a pilgrimage like that of the Holy Year. Other specific indications are found in the aforementioned Constitution of Paul VI.[13]

True mercy is obtaining and granting an indulgence.

---

13. Other indulgenced acts include the recitation of the Rosary and the devout reading of Sacred Scripture for a half hour. (Editor's note)

VI

The Anointing That Blesses

The cause and the remedy of infirmity

SINCE health is always under harassment from sickness and disease, one often hears it said: health comes before everything else. It is true, provided that as Christians we think of total health: the Latin *salus*, or the salvation of the body together with the soul. As a child, from an old catechism, I learned that man's separation from God, and his rebellion, which happened in the beginning, are the first cause of sicknesses, pains, the burdensomeness of labor, and, above all, the death of the body; as it is also the cause of ignorance, malice, weakness, and concupiscence in the soul. The intellect was left darkened, so that it recognizes the truth only with difficulty and easily falls into error, and directs itself more to temporal things than things eternal. The will was left weakened and inclined to evil: it overcomes vice and practices virtue with the greatest difficulty; indeed, it often feels itself dragged toward sin, even when reason clearly understands that something is evil. In such a disturbance of man's whole nature, what did the life of man on earth become? Ignorance, poverty, diseases, wars, hunger, and vices of every kind have been the heritage of miserable humanity over the centuries. All consequences of original sin, which, for some theologians, is only a story; nevertheless, it is enough to open the book of the Apocalypse, where war, death, and hunger are represented as horses that run across history (cf. 6:1–8), until the arrival, on a white horse, of the conqueror, Jesus. He came because the sick need a doctor; thus the other sacrament of healing, which is the anointing of the sick, was added to Penance: it serves to strengthen and comfort the sick person in body, and purify the soul, making up for its distance from God, knowing well that the human being does not *have* a body but also *is* his body.

The sick should be helped to understand the meaning of suffering: participation in the restoration of creation accomplished by Christ after the corruption caused by sin. So if mention is not made of the need to endure this suffering, or to bear it in the following of Christ, then the whole truth is not being said. We must do our part to complete in our flesh that which is lacking in his Passion, as St. Paul writes (cf. Col. 1:24). Christians a few decades ago had the clear perception that suffering serves the body of the Church. We are members one of another (cf. Rm. 12:5), therefore all the good we do is beneficial to others, while the evil is harmful: here is the meaning of the offering of oneself. A truly faithful Christian still perceives that some good done by him serves as reparation for evil done by others, above all if a good person is suffering in the place of another: did not Maximilian Kolbe take the place of a man who had a family? He took his example from Jesus, who offered himself in our place and for our benefit. This is reparation or redemption. In the Veronese or Leonine sacramentary, from the 4th to 6th centuries, which is the most ancient source of the Gelasian sacramentary, we find the verbs *expiare, placare, propitiare*, today considered obsolete, together with the prayers and acts of reparation. And yet, from St. Faustina Kowalska to Pius XI (with the Encyclical *Miserentissimus Redemptor*) and to John Paul II (with the Apostolic Letter *Salvifici Doloris*), the Church has been asked to practice habitually the offering up of oneself and reparation for sins against God, especially apostasy, desecration, and profanation. It is one of the contradictions of the postconciliar period that the ecclesial dimension was rediscovered as distinct from the personal, which was well-known before, but in such a way that people think the personal dimension is surpassed. In fact, there is no opposition: each individual must suffer, taking his part in the body that is the Church—offering, making reparation, making satisfaction (*satisfactio*), which is then the real penance. This alone permits an understanding of Jesus's love. He suffered and accomplished everything, but it is not finished: I must complete what is lacking in the redemption, I must do my part. This is the true participation in Mass, and more fundamentally it is the true nature of the liturgy: to render back to God what is his own.

But let us pass on to the care and healing of the corporal infirmity that Jesus—physician of souls and bodies—personally did and commanded to his disciples. The Gospels and the Acts of the Apostles attest that his mission was accomplished doing good, driving the devil away, and curing the sick. That the Lord heals and asks us to take care of the sick indicates that the Redeemer is also the one who created and restores creation; it is God who wills to repair whatever has been damaged and to recover whatever has been lost. His death and resurrection constitute the culmination of such a work of restoration. It is sure doctrine that illness of body has for its primordial cause the separation of man from God. So illness must not be separated from the religious dimension. The Pauline invitation to unite human sufferings with those of Christ means to indicate the Lord's having taken on the burden of human infirmity to redeem it from the inside: suffering is for the sake of redemption.

A little history

The constant cure and healing of the sick by the Lord (cf. Mk. 6:13) was followed by the apostles: "He who is sick, let him call to himself the presbyters of the Church and let them pray for him, after having anointed with oil in the name of the Lord. And the prayer done in faith will save the sick man: the Lord will raise him up again, and if he has committed sins, they shall be forgiven him" (Jas. 5:14–15). In this text the Church, inspired by the Spirit, has seen a confirmation of the institution of the sacrament of the sick. For the Byzantines, the anointing of Jesus by the sinful woman (Lk. 7:36ff.) is also represented as an "anointing of the sick," because according to Simeon of Thessalonika, an excellent commentator on the Byzantine liturgy, she was a person who had been comforted and consoled by the Lord, who pardoned her numerous sins because, with the copious anointing mixed with tears, she had demonstrated her great love for him.[1]

The oil is an eloquent symbol of the care of the sick. In antiquity, especially in the East, it was used to tone up the muscles for com-

---

1. Cf. Simeon of Thessalonika, *Dialogos*, 56, PG 155:204B–205A.

bat—this refers us back to the oil used for the exorcism of the cate-chumens—and to soothe wounds, as in the parable of the Good Samaritan, who uses it together with wine as a type of disinfectant. Beyond the texts of the New Testament, in particular the passage from the letter of James, which speaks explicitly of the presbyters anointing the sick, the *Apostolic Tradition* describes the anointing of the sick: in this ritual prayer book *ante litteram*, the oil is blessed, together with other products from nature, after the conclusion of the great Eucharistic prayer. And in the Roman Canon the following formula is found: "Through Christ our Lord, you, O God, always create, sanctify, vivify, bless, and grant to the world every good thing." This attests to the fact that in the first centuries of Christianity, at the end of the great Eucharistic prayer, the faithful brought the fruits of creation to church for the blessing, which was done by the bishop or a priest; among these fruits there would be the oil that gives strength and health to those who use it.

Since the 5th century, the blessing of the oil of the sick in the Roman Rite is done on Holy Thursday, together with the blessing of the oil of catechumens and the consecration of chrism. In non-Roman rites such as the Ambrosian, the blessing of the oil is done before the anointing, like what happens with the baptismal water outside of Paschal time in the Roman Rite. In the prayers that accompany the anointing, physical effects are mentioned, while little is said about the effects on the soul or mind and the spirit; even less is said about the remission of sins, which will only gradually be numbered among the effects. The oil of the sick was itself considered a "sacrament" by Pope Innocent I, as attested by the aforementioned letter to Decentius.

Since the 8th century, concomitantly with dispositions for Penance of those who are sick, and viaticum, the anointing comes to be explicitly limited to grave illnesses, little by little becoming "extreme unction," which means "last anointing." Thus side by side with the sacraments of initiation, we have the itinerary of "departure from life," with its triad of Penance-Eucharist-Anointing.

According to the Roman Pontifical of the 12th century, the anointing had to be made on the five senses. Although still at the time of the Council of Trent the sacrament was considered as "last anointing," the Council does not define it as that, but identifies its essential elements: the receiving subject is a member of the faithful who is gravely ill; the minister is exclusively a priest; the matter is the anointing with blessed oil; the form is the prayer of the minister; the effects are: saving grace, the forgiveness of sins, the relief of the sick person.

The liturgical movement insisted that the sacrament should go back to being "anointing of the sick," and this was received and accepted by Vatican II.

How it is administered

The liturgical Constitution of Vatican II affirms:

> Extreme unction, which can also, and better, be called anointing of the sick, is not the sacrament of those who have reached the end of life; the opportune time for receiving it has come when a member of the faithful, through illness or old age, begins to be in danger of death; finally, there should be a single rite: confession-anointing-viaticum, and the number of anointings shall be reviewed, and also the prayers, so they may be adapted to the various conditions of the sick. (cf. 73–75)

The new rite of the anointing of the sick, published in 1972, is preceded by the Apostolic Constitution *Sacram Unctionem Infirmorum* of Paul VI, because the sacramental formula was modified, as for Confirmation. The new rite is articulated in five principal parts.

First, the *initial rites*, which comprise sprinkling with holy water (to recall baptism) and a generic confession of sins, or administration of the sacrament of Penance; there follow the Liturgy of the Word (that is, a biblical reading), a brief homily, and the intercessions.

Then the central *rites*, with:

(a) imposition of the hands in silence, which is the gesture done, and required of the disciples, by Jesus: "lay hands on the sick and they will be healed." In Penance, the gesture invokes healing of the spirit; in the anointing of the sick, healing of body and soul. A gesture of healing and of consolation, truly eloquent, if one thinks on the fact that a man doesn't want to touch someone who is in this situation, for fear of contagion;

(b) the blessing of the oil, when there is no oil blessed by the bishop on Holy Thursday, and if the oil does not need to be blessed, the prayer of thanksgiving. There are not many people present to participate, and generally they are family members; but the ecclesial character of a sacramental act never depends on the number of people: two or three gathered together in His name are enough, as for the Mass;

(c) the anointing has been simplified: it is given only on the forehead and on the hands, to signify thought and actions. It is accompanied by the sacramental formula: "Through this holy anointing and his most faithful and loving mercy may the Lord help you with the grace of the Holy Spirit." The sick person answers, the first time: Amen. The priest continues: "And freeing you from sins, may he save you, and in his goodness raise you up." The believer concludes this with a second Amen. Thus the physical and spiritual effects of the sacrament are brought out, as in the Letter of James. Sickness touches one's whole being, and for this reason the sacrament asks for temporal healing as well as eternal healing of soul and body.[2]

(d) the last part consists of the prayer of faith, as James exhorts— a choice can be made for the prayer most adapted to the condition of the sick person: that he may be healed, or pass out of the danger of death, or for the person who must also receive viaticum, or has already entered into his agony. The celebration of the sacrament concludes with the *Pater*, communion, and the blessing.

The rite of anointing of the sick foresees sacramental confession first, in the case where the conditions are present, especially waking

---

2. In the Roman Rite in its Extraordinary Form, as in the Byzantine sacrament of *evcheleo* (anointing-blessing), seven anointings are provided for—in ancient times seven presbyters also were prescribed—upon the five senses: eyes, ears, nostrils, lips, hands, and possibly the feet; in general, forehead and hands. "Seven" is the symbol of the catholicity of the Church, which takes part in care for the sick: she accompanies them with sacramental prayer and asks pardon for the sins committed with the corresponding sense. The aforesaid anointing intends to indicate the total regard for the body of man, so that he might be healed.

consciousness. It is easier to have someone accept the sacrament of anointing, and to celebrate it, insofar as the sick person is in a passive condition for it; but it is more difficult to have him accept the sacrament of confession: apart from the physical conditions, there must also be the will to look inside oneself a little and describe one's own sins. At times the celebrant finds himself in an awkward situation, because the sick person or the family members consent to the anointing, but give no indication regarding confession. So the celebrant remains in doubt and asks himself if the sick person wants to receive the sacrament or not, if he is capable of it, etc.; the connection between the two sacraments sometimes makes the discernment more difficult. When the anointing is done in a hospital room with many beds, there is barely any privacy, and one then ends up giving the sacraments without thinking much about them. In these cases a text written in advance, to help the sick person with what is essential for confession, would be useful.

It is also necessary to see the sacraments in their interaction: the fact that Penance, anointing, and communion are administered together says that the elements of the rite form an integral whole. The sacraments are not to be considered only in their distinction from each other, but as the divine strength of Jesus Christ who is present, who takes care of man, and thus washes him, nourishes him, heals, and pardons him; in a word, loves him. The sequence of the gestures, the pardon of sins, the anointing, and the communion, as in the sacrament of the "anointing that blesses," very specifically shows the solicitous mercy of God for man.

Who can receive it

The opinion is widespread that giving the anointing of the sick is a way to frighten the suffering person and make him think he is near to death. In order to "exorcize" such a fear, it can be useful to have a communal celebration in church, as provided in the Ordinary Form, and also within the ritual Mass for such an occasion. In the postconciliar period, such a celebration has become quite widespread, especially on the occasion of the feast of Our Lady of Lourdes, February 11th. The communal celebration of the sacrament is useful for giving relief to the sick and increasing their consolation and hope for salvation. Getting the faithful who are ill—no longer in possession of their physical strength—to attend the celebration, and, in the cases foreseen, receive the sacrament, which can be repeated on other occasions, helps them and their family members to request it when their lives will be in danger, without reducing everything to the last moment; and also, when someone shall have gotten to that point, to ask for it urgently. However, it happens that in the communitarian celebration, people who are merely old, not objectively in danger of death (cf. CCC 1514), also approach the sacrament. In a resemblance to the East—where there is a communitarian rite of anointing on Wednesday of Holy Week, in church, in which everyone ends up anointed—the sacrament of Extreme Unction risks becoming a sacrament of "continual anointing" for anyone who is sick, even with light illnesses, or for those whose illness is psychosomatic, those sick in their soul, and for every sinner. In such fashion anointing of the sick ends up in competition with the sacrament of Penance.

When one gets to the end of life, one must do what one can to receive the anointing; but that is true also for someone who must undergo a risky surgical intervention (cf. CCC 1515). The renewed rite indicates, as a condition for the possibility of administering the sacrament, the state of grave illness, or progressive illness, that is, one that leads to death, or the state of chronic illness: an illness that can no longer be made to retreat; also, an imminent and serious surgical intervention, which could put one at risk for death. In short, it must have to do with a serious danger.[3] Nevertheless, one must admit that it is not always easy to determine this objectively.

---

3. The Council of Trent defined that the sacrament is for those who are dangerously ill; the Code of Canon Law, as well as the apostolic constitution of Paul VI and the instructions for the revised rite speak of danger of death from illness or old age. In addition, the consensus of approved theological authors taught that the danger must be from internal organic deficiencies that are actually present, not externally affecting causes. CCC 1515 only states that imminent risky surgery is a "fitting time" to receive the sacrament; this leaves intact the other statements from the Magisterium on the physical conditions that must exist for this sacrament to be received validly. (Translator's note)

Who administers the sacrament

It has been maintained by some theologians that historically, from the letter of Innocent I to Decentius up to the end of the 9th century, the anointing with oil blessed by the bishop was practiced by all Christians on themselves and on family members; and so this could constitute a good reason for reintroducing administration of the sacrament by extraordinary ministers (deacon, acolyte, and delegated layperson) in our day, as for communion.

However, the ecclesial tradition of East and West considers that the sacrament pertains to bishops and presbyters (though Protestants and some Catholic theologians consider that the term "presbyters"—cf. Jas. 5:14—does not refer to the ministerial priesthood, and so the priesthood would not be a sacrament, but rather a human invention). This tradition is defined as doctrine by the Council of Trent and received in the Latin and Eastern codes of canon law (cf. CCC 1516; CCEO 739). A Note of the Congregation for the Doctrine of the Faith, of February 11, 2005, recalled: "This doctrine is *definitive tenenda* (to be held definitively)." Neither deacons nor laypeople, therefore, can exercise the said ministry, and any action whatever in this sense constitutes simulation of a sacrament.

In line with the preceding ritual books, the 1972 book as well presupposes that the minister of the sacrament is a bishop or priest. The sacrament is invalid if administered by a deacon or by a layperson. The priest, in fact, renders Christ and the Church present, in the administration of this sacrament as well as in others.

All the sacraments need to be revitalized, in the perception of the believer, by a new evangelization. Like the apostles, priests in giving the sacrament of anointing should not require the sick person to have covered a course of specific catechesis; it is enough to say to him: "if you wish, I will give you the anointing of the sick; in his infinite goodness, the Lord, if you have faith, can heal you. Let us pray together." The priest will notice the sick person turn more contented; and there will be some who truly return to health. This is a way of doing things that is fitting in our secularized situation, because it is founded on the act of faith. With this, there is no intention of diminishing the importance of catechesis of sufficient duration, but it is faith that saves, before instruction. The Church does not make salvation depend on theological or catechetical knowledge. Faith, which is the recognition of the presence of the Lord God who can heal me, is more important than all the instructions one could or would like to receive. Often it is possible to do a whole catechesis in one word, more than with ten lessons.[4] And even more, with a considerate and compassionate attitude.

The woman who was losing blood was perhaps illiterate: the evangelist says she had spent all her resources with doctors, without getting anything from it. At a certain point she heard Jesus speak and believed it was enough to touch him in order to be healed. This attitude is similar to that of so many people who don't go to church, don't frequent their parish, but when they hear about a Marian sanctuary where miracles occur, they face up to a journey to go there and ask for the grace: and it happens that they receive it, because they did this with faith. The Lord enjoys taking the most unexpected paths. Often pastoral work sins by formalism, but the people overcome everything and the grace of God comes to them outside or beyond the channels in the parish. Mercy goes beyond pastoral plans. Cardinal Ratzinger had to say that if the apostles after the Lord's ascension had met together and made a pastoral plan for grasping how to evangelize the world, you can be sure they would not have succeeded. It is necessary to allow ourselves to be guided by the Holy Spirit, who converts people as he wills.

Effects

The sacrament is above all a particular gift of grace from the Holy Spirit for the comfort, peace, and courage it infuses in the person confronting grave illness or the weakness of old age. Union with the Passion of Christ, configuring us to him, is essential.

The anointing constitutes an efficacious sign of progressive assimilation to the death of Christ, and shows how important it is

---

4. For example, the knowledge required of a penitent for valid absolution is generally held to cover only the three Divine Persons and the redemption accomplished by the Son made man. (Translator's note)

that we unite ourselves ever more to it, during our pilgrimage on earth. It is the following of Christ that begins with the mission and arrives at the end, the Cross—that is, making up for what is lacking in the suffering of Christ, in our flesh, and for the good of Christ's ecclesial body. In fact, another effect of the sacrament is grace in its ecclesial dimension, because in the communion of saints, the Church intercedes for the sick person, and this contributes to the sanctification of her members.

After the other anointings that may have been received since baptism, this last anointing prepares us for the last passage, for the last struggles, including the final agony, and for entering paradise, fortified with the Eucharist: the sacrament of the passage—or viaticum—from this world to the Father. It is therefore an anointing that consecrates man's body for the resurrection. If we believe in the resurrection of the flesh, the meaning of the anointing of a body sick or near to death would have meaning precisely in relation to faith in the resurrection; otherwise, why care for the body? The Christian believes that the body is summoned to rise again in the final judgment, reuniting with the immortal soul. Thus Penance, holy anointing, and the Eucharist—similarly to the sacraments of initiation—constitute a unity as sacraments preparing us for the eternal fatherland (cf. CCC 1525).

VII

A Holy Order for
the Consecration of the World

The Church, *casta meretrix*

WE come to two sacraments, holy orders and matrimony, which are helpful to personal salvation by way of service to others (cf. CCC 1534), generating and fostering ecclesial communion. The *Catechism* affirms that those who receive them are consecrated: with holy orders, to be put, in the name of Christ, in the office of shepherding the Church; with matrimony, since, in their capacity as Christian spouses, they are strengthened and as it were consecrated for the duties and the dignity of their state (cf. CCC 1535). The word *ordo*, which the Romans used to designate constituted social groups or bodies in the civil sense, was used by the Church to designate her own hierarchical bodies (bishops, presbyters, deacons), or the organized condition of groups of faithful (catechumens, virgins, spouses, and widows). One was integrated into them with a "rite of ordination," which could be sacramental, a consecration, as for religious, or else a blessing, as for the Church's ministers. Today the first term, "order," is reserved to the sacrament that confers the gift of the Holy Spirit and allows the recipient to exercise, through the Church, the *sacred power* originating in Christ (cf. CCC 1538). We will return to the topic. Meanwhile, we must say that this is the sacrament that best expresses the social commitment of the Church, her dedication to every man.

At this point, there comes to mind the image of the Church as *casta meretrix*, chaste harlot. The one and only Father who speaks of this image is St. Ambrose, for whom the Church is *casta*, because she is absolutely faithful to her Spouse, and *meretrix*, because in obedience to him she wills to reach everyone, in order to bring sal-

vation to all. The thinking about this little phrase is quite different
from what goes around today, when the expression is often a term
of art, highlighting the noun rather than the adjective.[1] Moreover,
the sacrament of order, through which the apostolic ministry continues in the Church, is often subcontracted. A frequent case: while
the assistant pastor is outside smoking a cigarette and the pastor
celebrating the Mass remains seated at the chair, distribution of
communion is left to the deacon and the extraordinary ministers
(who have become ordinary!). Entropy and the deformation of
these ministries have obscured the sacerdotal function: in the postconciliar era, the priest has become more and more a manager interested in a thousand things, and the deacon, often, takes the place of
the priest: in church he gives communion and baptism, preaches,
witnesses marriages, and more.

 Here is why the identity of the priest is in question: is he still seen
as a mediator of the meeting of God and man? People understand,
on various levels, what "mediation" means: the mediation of someone who settles lawsuits, or finds a house, etc.; the mediator is the
one who places himself in the middle, to be of help in attaining a
goal. The fundamental goal of man is to come to God; how does
man get to God, by himself? Can he manage that, or does he need
the help of someone else, of a mediator, to be exact? That certainly
seems to be the case, because Jesus Christ is the supreme mediator,
the only one (cf. 1 Tm. 2:5); without him, one does not get to God.
As his one and only sacrifice is rendered present by the Eucharistic
sacrifice, in the same way his one and only priesthood is rendered
present by the ministerial priesthood: in fact, Christ alone is the true
priest, while the others are his ministers (CCC 1545). So Jesus Christ
continues his work through the priesthood, which he chose to establish when he called the first disciples to follow him. Their weakness
did not stop him. On the contrary, through weakness he wants to
manifest his power; he wants to make use of his ministers to continue this work of restoring communion between man and God.

 1. In recent years, *casta meretrix* has been interpreted, sometimes in a theologically problematic way, to mean the coexistence of faithfulness and unfaithfulness in
the Church. (Translator's note)

All of the sacraments are nothing other than a continual exchange, in act, between God and man, in the effort to cause and establish an exchange: the blood of the mediator in exchange for the life of man, rescue, the redemption. Christ says: "You have fallen into sin, you are a slave of the evil one; I will rescue you with my blood, because your life has inestimable value." Here we see the redemptive function of Christ, the function in which he mediated the meeting between God and man. Man had gone off, far from the Father, and the Son leads him back by way of his function as mediator: this is the sacerdotal function. The priest is the one who, in imitation of Jesus, eternal High Priest and sole mediator, places himself at the service of the ministry of Jesus Christ: he gives him his hands, his eyes, his arms for this work of mediation. The sacerdotal function culminates in the offering of the body and blood of Christ, to whom the priest unites himself—sometimes in the place and on behalf of someone for whom we desire salvation, but who is impeded or not aware of it—for the purpose of extending the benefit of the redemption, paying the ransom. The priestly function maximally becomes an offering of one's own body in spiritual sacrifice to the living God (cf. Rm. 12). The priest is called to do, in the first place, that which all are called to do; to do it "in the person of Christ and in the name of the Church"; to do it in an exemplary way, as the choice of a way of life and a permanent condition. This man, if he is in truth assimilated to the High Priest in virtue of the sacerdotal consecration he has received, enjoys the power to act with the power of Christ himself whom he represents (MD in CCC 1548). The priest is his minister, because he takes the part of Christ.

The mediating function of the sacerdotal ministry, today rather obscured, helps us understand that the sacerdotal identity cannot be diluted in the baptismal identity of all the faithful—even though they are ordered to one another (cf. LG 10:2)—and that it is not exercised in the merely ceremonial manner by a priest who is concelebrating. This mediating function requires that the sacrifice be offered personally, because it is my person who takes his part, and because my person cannot be substituted by another, unless I am impeded. Concelebration is an expression and exercise of the unity of the priesthood in the measure it is sacramental, that is, if every priest standing at the altar offers and consecrates the holy gifts of the Mass: if one of these elements were to be renounced, the concelebration would not be sacramental, but only ceremonial. Here we see the reason why concelebration cannot be indiscriminate, taking the place of a Eucharistic sacrifice offered by each priest, but is regulated by precise norms.

The threefold division of holy orders—or fourfold, if we include the subdiaconate, reintroduced with the Extraordinary Form of the ancient Roman Rite, at least for the institutes that depend upon the Pontifical Commission Ecclesia Dei—does not modify the fact that the priesthood resides only in the two higher grades of the sacrament.[2]

One theological current would tend to affirm that the true priesthood is the bishop's priesthood, while the others would only be his collaborators. This is a theology that follows upon reading the history of Holy Orders, which has had a development, as the other sacraments have had a development. At the beginning, that is, after Pentecost, there was the apostle surrounded by the college of the presbyters; after the death of the apostle, presbyters and then the bishop here and there become important in the direction of the community: bishop (*episkopos*) is a Greek term meaning inspector or superintendent;[3] finally, especially with Ignatius of Antioch, the presbyters form a college with the bishop, who occupies the superior rank. The restoration of the prayer of ordination of the bishop, in the Ordinary Form, has highlighted in the bishop the fullness of the sacrament of order, or the high priesthood.

2. Cf. N. Bux, *Il Sacramento dell'Ordine Sacro nel Pontificale Romano (Editio Typica 1962). Una riflessione di teologia liturgica* [*The Sacrament of Holy Orders in the Roman Pontifical (Editio Typica 1962). A Reflection of Liturgical Theology*], in Vincenzo M. Nuara, ed., *Il Motu Proprio Summorum Pontificum di S.S. Benedetto XVI. Una speranza per tutta la Chiesa* [*The Motu Proprio Summorum Pontificum of His Holiness Benedict XVI. A Hope for the Whole Church*] (Verona: Fede e Cultura, 2013), 81–92.

3. In the earliest sources, the terms "bishop" and "presbyter" are not clearly distinguished in their meaning; bishops could be called presbyters, and vice-versa. Nevertheless the context can sometimes clarify, and the unanimous Tradition of the Church attributes the episcopate, as the supreme priestly grade placed over the Mystical Body, to divine institution. (Translator's note)

The power to govern

The distinctive characteristics of the priesthood are found in the conferral and exercise of the three *munera*, or tasks or offices, of teaching, sanctifying, and governing. This helps to explain the sacerdotal function and clarify the diaconal. It is obvious that a *munus* derives from a *potestas* received: "Receive the power to offer the sacrifice," the bishop says in the Extraordinary Form to the priest just ordained, handing over to him the chalice and paten (*traditio instrumentorum*). The fact that this is not the moment of ordination, but a ritual explication, does not permit us to contest—as some theologians have done—and even less, to consider as downright dangerous the idea of a transmission of power in the sacrament of order, afraid of reviving a priest who would be "the man of the sacred and of God," and who would end up with a personal *potestas* isolated from the ecclesial context. But then how does one explain what happens in the recipient of the sacrament: does the character that is transmitted change the subject, or does it leave everything as before? In reality, the sacred minister becomes involved in the life of the Lord, because there is conferred on him a mandate, a power (in Greek *exousia*)—as Jesus says in his ascension: "All power in heaven and on earth has been given to me. Go therefore and make disciples for me from all peoples" (Mt. 28:18ff)—analogously to the primacy given to Peter: "to one alone was handed over what had to be communicated to many";[4] so personal responsibility is the condition for the responsibility of all. To maintain that Vatican II exalted the ecclesial dimension of the *ordines*, and not the personal responsibility of them, means one has not said everything, because the difference between the common priesthood and the ministerial resides precisely in the *potestas* conferred: such *potestas* is for the edification of the Church, and not a personal prerogative. The person consecrated receives the power to consecrate and to absolve in relation to the community, but it is not the community that gives him this power. He is not the delegate of the community (cf. CCC 1553); that does not mean that he is independent of it. The

---

4. Cf. St. Leo the Great, *Homily* 4:3: PL 54:150–51.

priesthood, like every ministry, is for the building up of the community of the whole Church, but it would not be that if there were no possibility of a power that the others do not have. The priest has been consecrated to preach the Gospel, to lead the flock of the faithful, and to celebrate divine worship as a true priest of the New Testament (cf. LG 28; CCC 1564). The narrative of Pentecost with its list of 17 peoples, and that of the "miraculous catch" of 153 big fish (cf. Jn. 21:1–14), say that God's first thought for the Church is not the local community, but the Catholic Church, in its totality and unity. Therefore the priest is ordained as a priest for the whole Church, and through the whole Church for a particular church.[5] For this reason, the priest in the anaphora prays for, and causes the people to pray for, the pope and the local bishop at the same time.

After the Council, the impression emerged in some places that there was something more urgent than announcing the word of God and administering the sacraments. Some thought they had to construct a different kind of society before they could spend time any more on such things. The Gospel of Mark (cf. 3:13–19) is there to recall the two essential elements in the apostolic and priestly mission: they are sent to announce the Gospel and to exercise the power to drive out evil spirits. Proclamation and power, word and sacrament are the two fundamental pillars of priestly service, over and beyond the many configurations they can take.[6]

Priests must defend the rights of God, *in primis* the worship due him, which is a thing good and just, and even *"satis periculosa"* (something supremely delicate)—as the bishop says at the conclusion of ordination in the Extraordinary Form: "therefore I exhort you to learn diligently, from other priests with the knowledge, the whole rite of the Mass." Therefore, against liturgical relativism it is necessary to bring the sacred, and against subjectivism and capriciousness, the *ius divinum* (divine right or law).

The sacred power of order likewise does not mean that the minister is protected against sins, mistakes, or weakness in his acts. The

5. Cf. J. Ratzinger, *Ministers of Your Joy: Scriptural Meditations on Priestly Spirituality,* trans. Robert Nowell (Ann Arbor: Servant Publications, 1989), 63.
6. Cf. ibid., 94.

guarantee of indefectibility is given only in the administration of the sacraments, because the sacrament of order communicates a sacred power that is precisely the power of Christ. It is he who is the model of the exercise of authority, he who through love made himself last and servant of all (cf. CCC 1551).

A widespread idea holds that to speak of the sacred, in the person of the priest, is now obsolete, and that linking the priesthood with sacrifice is a pagan idea. This view forgets that Christ offered and sacrificed himself, and so put in place of the pagan victims—which were a prefiguration—the perfect sacrifice of himself. To maintain that speaking about sacrifice is pagan means tearing up the Letter to the Hebrews. And yet the prayer of consecration of the bishop, which connects him with Aaron, recalls "You have established leaders and bishops so as to never leave your sanctuary without the ministry";[7] the prayer for the presbyter recalls that "in the Old Testament various offices instituted for the liturgical service took form and shape";[8] and in the diaconal prayer the bishop solemnly affirms: "You have disposed that through the three grades of the ministry instituted by you, the new temple should grow and be built up."[9] So there is no doubt that what was sacred remains sacred, in the continuity between the Old and New Testaments: God is the same in each, revealed in Christ.

Everything that happens in the Old Testament, and everything done by the other religions, is nothing other than a symptom of man's need to offer something, or rather, to offer himself to God; it all reveals the innate religious sense. Here we see the need for sacrifice in order to come into an alliance with God. Ancient man understood that in order to cultivate his relation with God—this is what the term cult means—a thing, maybe a thing defective like the lame animals in the Old Testament as well, is not enough. The greatest of all was the offering of human sacrifice: to placate the

---

7. *Pontificale Romano. Ordinazione del vescovo, dei presbiteri e dei diaconi* [*Roman Pontificale. Ordination of the Bishop, of Presbyters, and of Deacons*] (Vatican City: Libreria Editrice Vaticana, 1992), 48.

8. Ibid., Prayer of Ordination, 98–99.

9. Ibid., 144.

goddess, Agamemnon sacrifices his daughter Iphigenia. This idea was not erroneous, but only imperfect, insofar as man's sin, which provokes the anger of God, can be adequately expiated only by God himself: here is why the Son of God came.

The passage from human sacrifice to the Eucharistic sacrifice is adumbrated in the Psalms, as Joseph Ratzinger has indicated in an exemplary way, passing from the Old Testament conception of sacrifice to the perfect spiritual sacrifice of the New.[10] The sacrifice of Christ is the sacrifice of the Word, and from this is derived the sacrificial form of the Eucharist and the form of prayer, that is, of the word. We do not offer animals or human victims; we offer ourselves, who have become a prayer, a word to the Lord. Therefore the form of the Eucharist is not an animal sacrifice or a banquet, but a prayer, the Eucharistic prayer. We offer to the Lord the Word made flesh, which becomes a Eucharistic prayer: here we see the *sacrum-facere*, the sacrifice. The paradox is that precisely those who in the name of dialogue applaud religions that continue to do animal sacrifices—which prefigure in a rudimentary, imperfect fashion what Christianity perfected and, in the Roman Canon, calls the one perfect sacrifice—do not want to hear of sacrifice in the Eucharist.

How ordination takes place

The sacerdotal mediation and function is connected to the presbyteral and episcopal grades. The other ministries, including the diaconate, are for serving and collaborating with the priestly function, but do not take its place. This distinction is important, since the introduction in the postconciliar period of the "permanent diaconate" has led to thinking that on account of the clergy shortage, the deacon can supply for the priest and do the things the priest should do. The deacon has an important auxiliary function, but he is not the priest. And on the other hand—the liturgy documents it—it is enough to see the place that belongs to him: that of constituting a

10. J. Ratzinger, *The Spirit of the Liturgy*, trans. John Saward (San Francisco: Ignatius Press, 2000), 35–50.

trait d'union between the priest and the people. This is very clear in the Eastern liturgy, where so many functions of commentary, reminder, and invitation are done by the deacon, while the priest is occupied with the dialogue with God at the altar. The deacon is the one who enters and comes out by the "royal door," the central one, to transmit actions and meanings to the assembly. The deacon, then, does not have the three *munera* that the bishop possesses and shares out to the priest who participates in them. The modification introduced into the Code of Canon Law, with respect to the typical edition of the *Catechism*, serves precisely to explain that the grade of the diaconate is not a priestly grade: the deacon does not exercise the priestly functions of confession and the Mass. This is not a matter of theological evolution, but of clarification, insofar as the deacon has never been a priest. We have in this regard an historical indication: the decree of the Council of Arles (314), which prohibited deacons from sitting in the part of the hall reserved to the priests.

The Acts of the Apostles attest the choice of seven men full of the Holy Spirit, for the service (in Greek *diaconia*) of tables in the community—through the imposition of hands (cf. 6:6). This gesture is not univocal: it does not signify priestly consecration alone, but, as in this case, a ministerial consecration; the same gesture occurs in the baptismal consecration and the chrism anointing in confirmation. In ordination to the diaconate, the candidate receives the imposition of hands from the bishop alone, and not from other priests present at the celebration—which does happen in presbyteral ordination—because, as the *Apostolic Tradition* says: "he is not ordained for the priesthood, but for service to the bishop" (n. 8), who usually assigns him to a community.

When instead a bishop has to be ordained, three ordaining bishops are necessary, as established by the Council of Nicaea in 325 (can. 4). In Rome, when it was the pope who presided for the ordination of a bishop or of priests, it was enough for him alone to impose hands, as is still the case in the Extraordinary Form. All of this expresses, on the one hand, the unity of the priesthood, and on the other, the collegial nature of the episcopal order, which is the union of the pope and the bishops, as head and members.

Pius XII, with the Apostolic Constitution *Sacramentum Ordinis* (November 30, 1947), clarifies that the essential element—or form—of the sacrament of order is constituted from the imposition of hands by the one ordaining, in silence, and from the consecratory prayer: the central actions of all three grades of order. The handing on of the instruments—the Gospel book, ring, miter, and staff in the case of the bishop; the chalice and paten for the priest; the Gospel book for the deacon—are for further explication of the rite. To this ordaining act of a bishop reference is made by the liturgical Constitution (at n. 76, it recommends revision of the ceremonies and texts of the sacrament), and this led to the 1968 edition of the Roman Pontifical.

The three ordinations—episcopal, presbyteral, and diaconal—begin, after the Gospel, with the presentation of the candidates. In the episcopal ordination, the pontifical decree (apostolic mandate) is read. In fact, for the legitimate ordination of a bishop today, a special intervention of the Bishop of Rome is required, by the fact that he is the supreme visible link of the communion of the particular Churches in the one Church, and the guarantee of their freedom (CCC 1559); the man chosen promises obedience to the Apostolic See as he carries on his ministry with sound doctrine. In the Extraordinary Form, the consecrating bishop recommends to the man chosen that his teaching be as a spiritual medicine for the people of God. In presbyteral and diaconal ordinations, it is the bishop who chooses the candidate: the priest and the deacon promise obedience to the bishop and his successors, while they extend and place their hands in the hands of the consecrating bishop: this is the entry into the heart of the sacrament with the invitation to prayer and the litany. These are followed by the central gesture of the imposition of hands by the consecrating bishop—accompanied, in an episcopal ordination, by the imposition of the Gospel book, held open and placed downward over the ordinand's head by two deacons—and the prayer of consecration, modeled on that of the *Apostolic Tradition*, which also prescribes that the ordination be done on Sunday. The imposition of hands and the consecratory prayer confer the grace of the Holy Spirit and impress the sacred character, the *potestas* spoken about earlier. The verbs *benedicere, sanctificare, conse-*

crare, present in the prayer, are substantially synonymous, but each one indicates a further depth.

The rite is continued and goes toward its conclusion with the putting on of the sacred vestments proper to each minister: an over-the-shoulder stole and dalmatic for the deacon; the stole and chasuble for the priest; the bishop instead is already wearing the chasuble. For the one just ordained, there follows the chrism anointing on the hand, or the anointing of the hands, in the case of a priest; the deacon does not receive this, to underline that his is not a priestly rank. The rite concludes with the already described handing on of the instruments, the accompanying of the newly ordained bishop to the episcopal chair, or, if it is a priest, to a place beside the bishop at his chair. Finally the exchange of the sign of peace.

In the *liber pontificalis* used in the Extraordinary Form, there are some differences, above all because of the addition of the order of subdeacon, which the East also has. Further, in the prayers of consecration and the handing on of the instruments, the necessity of purity is underlined: "since you celebrate the mystery of the death of the Lord, be careful to mortify your members from every vice and concupiscence"; and humility likewise: the sower of seed is an image of the priest, recalling that through the humility of faith and prayer, the harvest of God grows in the world (cf. Lk. 8:4–15); hiddenness is stronger than clamor and pushing something. Also the figure of John the Baptist is an example for the priest: Christ must increase, and I must decrease. In him is manifested the unity of priesthood and prophecy, sometimes presented in opposition to each other as rigid institution and innovative freedom. In reality, only that prophecy can truly come from God which proceeds from him, from the prophet's being touched first by him—something that is manifest in the priestly act, which is worship. From there follows the proclamation that transforms the world, and that always, in any case, goes beyond what we do. This is the Christian realism that gives to men the strength to conserve the patience of reason under the gaze of God. St. Augustine says that a proud minister should be put with the devil (cf. CCC 1584). Conversion, the first word of Christianity, can be proclaimed only by one who has been touched by the need for it and has thereby understood the grandeur of grace. The priest is precisely such a one. The need for purity and humility was insisted on in the priesthood of the Old Testament, but it cannot be considered less important for the Christian priesthood. The restoration of the ordination liturgy after Vatican II took up again some aspects from the history of holy orders that had become a little obscured over time; but unfortunately this requirement of purity is not present in the new rite.

Also the minor orders received a modification, from the Motu Proprio *Ministeria Quaedam* of Paul VI, also becoming instituted ministries exercised by laymen and no longer only by clerics. It is not a matter of ordination, but of institution: already in the *Traditio Apostolica* of Hippolytus, the conferral of the subdiaconate and the lectorate was distinguished from the ordination of bishop, priest, and deacon. There is no laying on of hands; in the case of the lectorate, that was the first description of an entrance into service by way of the handing on of a characteristic object, in this case the lectionary. This is an area where discussions are ongoing. The East distinguishes the *chirotonie*, the imposition of hands with which bishop and priests are consecrated, from the *chirotesie*, the designation to the minor order.

The minor orders, or the instituted ministries, do not have priestly functions; the same is true for the subdiaconate and the diaconate. The liturgy underlines this fact when, as already said, it hands on the instruments proper to the service that will be done: the lectionary for the lector, the book of exorcisms for the exorcists, the processional candles for the acolytes, chalice and paten for the subdeacon.[11] The minor orders and the subdiaconate for centuries have normally been conferred on clerics destined for the priesthood, and so these ministries are exercised only for a temporary duration. Why should they have been abolished in favor of "instituted ministries" if postconciliar norms would eventually foresee temporary "extraordinary ministers of holy communion"?

11. In the traditional rite of ordination of a subdeacon, the ordinand touches an empty chalice (and paten), because in a Solemn Mass the deacon will pour the wine into the chalice, while the subdeacon will only set the chalice and paten on the altar and pour in the water. (Translator's note)

At any rate, it is enough to see the rite of ordination and hear its prayers in order to understand its deep significance. It is true that the *lex credendi* comes down from the *lex orandi*.

Who can receive the sacrament

For some time now, Protestants "ordain" women as well as men to be pastors; in reality, since they do not recognize the divine institution of a sacrament of this kind, it is an act that is not relevant. In the last few decades, the Anglicans have joined them, but their ordinations are invalid. Catholics and Orthodox have firmly maintained that the sacrament can be received, validly, only by baptized males—because in this they recognize the will of Christ who chose the apostles from among men, as the apostles did for their collaborators. They maintain that the Lord, so attentive to the dignity of woman, could have done otherwise. The apostles could have done otherwise and instituted priestesses, resembling the Greeks and Romans; they did not do it, and for a mysterious and vital reason that we will shortly illustrate. The Church recognizes herself as bound by this choice made by the Lord himself. For this reason, the ordination of women is not possible (CCC 1577).

The position of the Catholic Church on the question of the priestly ordination of women is founded on the singularity of the Hebrew and Christian revelation, from which in turn is derived the essential character of the Catholic priesthood. To adduce, as its motivation, the consolidated usage of two thousand years of history, without explaining its theological significance, is insufficient. Nor do purely historical, cultural, and sociological motives suffice here: it is not only because Jesus is historically masculine; the basic problem is theological and ontological.

It is necessary to say that the Church's reasons do not derive solely from uninterrupted tradition. The reason can be found if one goes beyond the mere passive acceptance of a custom, if one passes from the purely historical level to the level of fittingness, that is, the ontological level of the structure of the Church, and the structure of creation. The mystery of revelation takes up the mystery of creation, the fact that God created the human being with the sexual difference: male and female he created them. The fundamental idea, therefore, is the covenant between God and Israel, expressed with the image of matrimony. In all of the biblical tradition, the daughter of Zion, the people of Israel, is always a woman, the spouse of Yahweh. In the covenant God presents himself as the husband of his people, which is always presented as woman. Woman therefore represents the Church, and Christ, who is male, is the husband of the Church. And so, when the priest celebrates the Eucharist—which is the sacrament of the New Covenant—he represents Christ, who is the husband: he acts *in the person of Christ*, it is even Christ himself who acts through him. To put a woman in the place of the husband is equivalent to an act theologically against nature. The woman priest would have to act the "husband" and be in a spousal rapport with her "wife," the ecclesial community: one will understand that the problem here is not only of an historical character. This is not a matter of starting a discussion about a custom with the hope of perhaps changing it in the future. It is the very structure of Christian revelation and of the Church that would be concerned: a revelation based on the book of Genesis, that is, on the two-sex nature of man willed by God the Creator.

It is important to note that the Church is born on Calvary, in the person of a woman, Mary. The Church is Marian before it is apostolic and Petrine, because it is born from a woman; only after Easter will the apostolic mission come. The deep reason for the Catholic position resides in the spousal bond of Jesus Christ with his Church: a bond of covenant that constitutes the theological foundation of the exclusively masculine priesthood. With the passing of centuries, the Church is always becoming more conscious of her deep structure, of her tradition. The drama of our time is that theologians no longer make reference to the sense of the tradition common to Catholics and Orthodox.

One also hears it said that the lack of a feminine priesthood in the first centuries of the Christian era was tied only to cultural motives, to the subordinate role of the woman in the society of the time. But we must not forget that women held highly important positions in the pagan religions, from Greece to Egypt, and to Mesopotamia. Israel was surrounded by peoples whose women participated actively in the celebration of worship. And Jesus was not ignorant of it: who would have prevented one who had promoted woman so much from instituting priestesses similar to the Roman vestal virgins? Among the Hebrew people, this had never happened: priests and Levites were only men. All that should make us reflect on the fact that we have to do here with a choice deeply tied to revelation itself. It is not a fact determined by socio-cultural conditions, it is even the contrary of that. Therefore, for this reason, the Apostolic Letter *Ordinatio Sacerdotalis* of John Paul II put an end to the claim that women could be priests.

Furthermore, it is not possible because no one has a "right" to receive the sacrament of order. Jesus called to himself those whom he wanted, not simply those who desired it (Mk. 3:13–19). The priesthood depends on his initiative, there is no human right to it. For him who has received this call, it means: he wants me. Christ, the Church's spouse who bequeathed the priesthood, is the source of all priesthood.[12]

Why do priests not marry?

One question remains: why can priests not marry? It is because priestly celibacy is a counsel of the Lord, which is law for the Church (cf. CCC 1599).

It happens that not a few priests occupy themselves with many things that are not proper to what they are, and neglect priestly service, *in primis* the Eucharist and Penance. Little by little, loneliness and attention to the fashions of the world—in which they, too, dwell in the midst of Christians—grow in them, and they think of this solution: the priest should get married; he, too, is a man. And so periodically someone puts priestly celibacy in question, turning to the objections that the magisterium has already responded to. Let us recall John Paul II in the Apostolic Exhortation after the Synod of 1990: "The Synod wishes to leave no doubt in anyone's mind about the firm will of the Church to maintain the law that requires freely

12. Cf. St. Thomas Aquinas, *Summa theologiae* III, q. 22, a. 4; J. Ratzinger, *Ministers of Your Joy*, 84.

chosen and perpetual celibacy for candidates to priestly ordination in the Latin rite."[13] What is the motive of such firmness? Essentially the Christian and apostolic significance of celibacy.

If Jesus had not become the affective center of his whole existence, Paul would not have labored and would not have lived for him, would not have died for him. Would he have been able to do that if he had married? He esteemed women (Damaris, Phoebe, Priscilla) and did not take his time before bringing them to know Jesus, whom he loved above everything, because he believed in the Gospel and did not spare himself to spread it. He would not have faced three adventurous journeys and a fourth one as a prisoner, if not for Jesus Christ. The attractive power of Christ, who, in order to bring the kingdom of God near, had not married, was decisive for Paul. Moreover, he was fascinated by the apostolic form of life.

And Peter? He was married. In the New Testament writings, nothing is said about his wife; perhaps she was already dead at the time when he hosted Jesus in the house of Capernaum. He was taken care of by his mother-in-law, a hardworking woman, and the apostle had to ask Jesus, who had come to his house, to free her from a fever, otherwise ... they don't eat (cf. Mk. 1:30). It has also been considered that Peter had left his wife in order to follow the Lord (cf. Lk. 18:28). Peter also faced one or two trips to Rome; how would he, the fisherman, have been able to imagine abandoning Galilee without a great love for Christ? He had sworn to him: You know it, you know that I love you. With Christ, virginity of the heart occurs before that of the flesh: "He who loves father and mother ... more than me is not worthy of me" (Lk. 14:26 and parallels; 18:29 and parallels; Mt. 19:12). In all these sayings, the wife of Peter is never mentioned. In this way the other apostles, if they had left everything, both persons and things, in order to follow him—a radicalness of following incomprehensible in Judaism—did it through a greater love for the Lord. The attractiveness of the grace of Jesus Christ, drawing many hearts, was of such a kind that it was no longer fitting to marry.

Recent research demonstrates that celibacy goes back to a much

13. John Paul II, Apostolic Exhoration *Pastores Dabo Vobis* (1992), 29.

earlier period than the habitually quoted sources of canon law permit us to recognize. The Fathers, interpreting Scripture, considered that those apostles who had been married undertook the practice of celibacy.[14]

Without these premises, no Christian law would be meaningful. The law of celibacy is only the form of that Christic and apostolic content, and in that sense it has force. This form delineated itself quite early and little by little became normative, being attested especially in the state of life of the bishops, because presbyters (priests) at the beginning did not have pastoral assignments as individuals.

Through the priest, Jesus Christ makes all things new, transforms the world, and makes the Church grow. Celibacy is the novelty from the other world, where there is neither wife nor husband, which comes into this world where it is found in the fishers of men, that is, the men who participate in the mission of new life that Christ came to inaugurate. If one speaks of eternal life, which in Christ has burst into time—the famous eschatology, a Greek word much in fashion in the postconciliar period—then behold, celibacy is a sign of it. If every ecclesiastical law did not serve to promote the Christian newness, then it would not save men, and consequently would be good for nothing. Because of the radicalness of the kingdom, the demand set forth by Christ could go so far as to require a rupture of familial and matrimonial bonds: this would not have been less scandalous than other requests of his. Of course such a demand made the apostles "incapable" of attaching their affection to persons and things of the earth (cf. Mt. 19:12). The normal priest experiences this: detachment from affections according to the flesh, in order to choose the form of life of the apostles; from his relation with Christ, he goes to the relation with his brother priests, in order to reach all those who await the Gospel.

In this way celibacy is the greater love, by which a man gives his life for his friends; it is the same as "it is no longer I who live, but Christ lives in me" (Gal. 2:20).

14. Cf. C. Cochini, *Apostolic Origins of Priestly Celibacy*, trans. Nelly Marans (San Francisco: Ignatius Press, 1990); S. Heid, *Celibacy in the Early Church*, trans. Michael J. Miller (San Francisco: Ignatius Press, 2000).

If someone objects that it is an ecclesiastical law, that in the East only bishops are celibate while priests can marry, and that the link between celibacy and the priesthood is not necessary, then he overlooks the fact that the very state of celibacy of the bishops, preserved in East and West, contradicts such an opinion. And neither is it true that Eastern Christian priests can marry; this is never permitted. On the contrary, it is permitted to ordain already married men as priests; a priest who is left a widower cannot remarry. So the candidate moves within this canonical framework in the Eastern churches; in the West, analogously, the candidate knows that his request presupposes the gift of chastity in celibacy. This clarification shows that celibacy is a form of imitation of the life of Christ and of the apostles, considered most fitting for him who wishes to follow the Lord.

The idea of celibacy as "ecclesiastical law" needs to be deepened, and in a certain sense overcome: it is, first and foremost, a counsel of the Lord, as Paul would say (cf. 1 Cor. 7)—an evangelical counsel that the apostolic Church experienced as necessary for the efficacy of its mission, in imitation of Christ. As the Gospel mission is entrusted *in primis* to the successors of the apostles, the bishops, and to their collaborators, the celibate or virginal state in history came to be considered ever more fitting for the priests, who live from celebrating the Eucharist and Penance, but also for deacons, ministers, and the lay faithful who have freely associated themselves with them (cf. Mk. 3:14) Celibacy turns out to be connected with the exercise of that intimate sacramental brotherhood marvelously linking priests among themselves.[15] It cannot be a sign of Christ if it is lived in a solitary manner: this is the answer to someone who objects that the celibate priest experiences the loneliness characteristic of the fleshly level of human existence. No, the celibate does not suspend living in communion, because beginning from communion with the Lord, and passing by way of communion with his confreres, he comes to the faithful generated in the faith that the priest has: celibacy does not leave time for worldly loneliness. The

15. Cf. Decree on the Ministry and Life of Priests *Presbyterorum Ordinis* (1965), 8.

priest who wants to conquer loneliness with marriage cheapens matrimony and has not understood celibacy, which is a fecund loneliness that comes from the Spirit, and which is the state of being alone with God, even when one is surrounded by communion.

Priestly celibacy does not exist without the *apostolica vivendi forma*: the way of life of the apostles. Authentic friendship has its source in Christ: "I have called you friends" (Jn. 15:15).[16] The apostles bet everything on this friendship; in this way Paul met Timothy, who became his great companion in mission, and friend, and then Luke. In two thousand years this type of companionship has been reproduced many times, from Benedict to Francis and Dominic, from Teresa of Calcutta to Don Giussani.[17] This friendship is at the origin of the *We* of the Church and of the Gospel. But the reason of all reasons for celibacy is one only: he who has been called to be a priest of Jesus must seek to live like him.[18] He is the source of the joy that begins here below and is fulfilled in heaven. A love and a joy, first of all human, lived with a human heart, and then supernatural by being lived with the divine heart of Christ. Celibacy is an obedience and a poverty that helps us to be perfect like the heavenly Father; a choice that is a sign and stimulus of charity (LG 42).

With reason, Benedict XVI was able to affirm with the Synod fathers that the fact that Christ himself, priest for eternity, lived his mission up to the sacrifice of the Cross in the state of virginity constitutes the sure point of reference for understanding the meaning of the Latin Church's will and intention in this regard.[19]

The effects of the sacrament

The indelible character and the grace of the Holy Spirit are the two principal effects. We have already seen that the character impressed in the ordination of bishop, presbyter, and deacon remains always,

---

16. M. Marini, *Il celibato sacerdotale. Apostolica vivendi forma* [*Priestly Celibacy: The Apostolic Form of Life*] (Siena: Cantagalli, 2005), 63.

17. Founder of the movement *Comunione e Liberazione*. (Translator's note)

18. Marini, *Il celibato sacerdotale*, 86.

19. Benedict XVI, Post-Synodal Apostolic Exhortation *Sacramentum Caritatis* (2007), 24.

is indelible (cf. CCC 1583). Here is the reason why there does not exist an "ex-priest," except in the sense of having been dispensed from priestly obligations and functions, through his having been forbidden to exercise them. He still can consecrate the body and blood of Christ, because ontologically he remains a priest always and can no longer become, in a strict sense, a layman.

Priestly identity, like every Christian identity, has its source in the most holy Trinity, which reveals itself and communicates itself to men in Christ, constituting, in Christ and by way of the Holy Spirit, the Church, as seed and beginning of the Kingdom. Peter writes: "Holding fast to him, the living stone ... for the building up of a spiritual edifice" (1 Pt. 2:4–9). To make family members out of strangers: that means a "spiritual" family, that is to say a mode of belonging that is more vital than relation by blood, because it is in communion with Christ (cf. Jn. 1:13)—a continual construction, a place for the meeting with Christ, a place for learning the virtues of the Church. The priest must lead men and keep them in the communion of the Church, even though by origin, upbringing, temperament, and living conditions they are strangers to each other. He must render men capable of reconciling, forgiving and forgetting offenses, and of being generous. He must help them to bear with one another in their diversity and have mutual patience; to know how to cultivate, in the proper measure, trust and wisdom, discretion, sincerity, and many other virtues. He must above all be able to assist men in their physical suffering, as well as in their disappointments, in mortifications and fears, which are spared to no one. The priest must, in the first place, have the capacity to accept pain and overcome it—an essential condition for human fulfilment; otherwise shipwreck of one's existence is inevitable. These things are learned together. And since irritation against everyone and everything corrupts the foundation of the soul, reducing it to a dead land, it is necessary to train oneself in the art of renunciation, of overcoming oneself, of internal freedom from our appetites (once called "ascesis," today training or self-control). In the bishop's exhortation before the conferral of ordination in the Extraordinary Form, the reminder of the link between worship and ethics, a reminder to live what one celebrates, rings out: "In your ways of acting in life, maintain the integrity of a holy and chaste life. Recognize what you do. Imitate what you handle. May the fragrance of your life be a consolation in the Church of Christ."

Christ is the Word become flesh. The priest believes not only in the Bible, but also in the sacraments: therefore he preaches them and administers them, but before all else personally adores the Lord who is present. The sacrament of Penance must be like the glowing coal of purification (cf. Is. 6:6); it must be the force of the reconciliation that brings us continuously from conflict with the Lord to union with him. The liturgy must be silence and solemnity, mystery that envelops us and takes possession of us: a mystery to enter into. Worship must be connected to culture (music, literature, figurative art, love of nature): a culture without cult [worship] loses its soul, and a cult without culture loses its dignity. Priests must know how to be servants of others' joy (cf. 2 Cor. 1:24). To become and be a priest means a constant approach toward identification of my I with the I of Christ, the divine-human *I am*. The identification is never definitively accomplished, but if we seek it, then we will find ourselves on the right path: the path toward God and toward man, the path of love. In this way culture is joined to charity, and charity develops into mission. Grandeur such as this requires permanent conversion. For Gregory of Nazianzen, the priest is divinized and divinizes; for the Curé of Ars, he continues the work of redemption, and is the love of the heart of Jesus (cf. CCC 1589).

The other effect of the sacrament is the grace of the Holy Spirit, from whom, according to St. Basil, all that is sacred comes. There are those who do not wish to use the expression "consecration" for ordination; thus it has been thought that the term "ordain" is preferable, because it is more ancient in this context than "consecrate." This seems like an archeological operation, insofar as to ordain implies to consecrate. The *Catechism* affirms, as said before, that the sacrament of holy orders, which confers a gift of the Holy Spirit, permits the ordained minister to exercise a *sacred power* coming from Christ through the Church.

Ordination is also called "consecratio"—*consecration*—since it is a separation and an investiture by Christ himself for his Church.

The imposition of hands of the bishop, together with the consecratory prayer, constitutes the visible sign of such a consecration. (CCC 1538)

The problem of *potestas* comes back, because the word consecrate better manifests power. The word ordain is less weighty, it indicates what may be simply the installation of a person as member of an *ordo*, as for a journalist or a doctor.[20] But if the doctor is not first "consecrated," that is, does not get his degree and qualifications, how will he get himself admitted to the order of doctors? The two terms are nevertheless not absolutely synonymous; the term consecrate seems burdensome, because it recalls the sacred. Everything that recalls the sacred causes annoyance today. In reality, the sacred indicates a mysterious presence. The word sacred indicates something I cannot touch, but that I desire to touch. People want to touch saints' relics, or at least draw near as much as possible, because they want to receive a share of the miracle-working power that the body of the saint has. So, what cannot be touched, but that we want to touch, that is the sacred. The woman with the flow of blood thought: "if I succeed in touching him . . . I shall be healed." Jesus confirms it, when, to the disciples saying "But everyone is touching you, what do you mean?," he responds: "No! I felt a power go out of me." The sacred is the power of the divine that comes from the presence of the Lord, otherwise it remains generic. Sacred things receive their power from the presence of him who is the Holy One.

The priesthood is a great, humble sign of the presence of the sacred in the world, also by outward dress. What a pity that some priests have abandoned the cassock and even the clerical suit! In this way they contribute to the eclipse of God from the world, which remains impoverished.

There is so much of the world that is not sacred and does not let itself be consecrated. What can be done? I conclude with Joseph Ratzinger:

20. "Order of journalists" and "order of doctors" are Italian expressions for the professional associations in the respective fields. (Translator's note)

If it is true that the Old Testament forms one body with the New, then the defamation of the sacred and the sham exaltation of the profane must be overcome. Naturally Christianity is a ferment, the sacred is not something definitive and completed, but something dynamic. The priest is subject to the command: "go into the world and make men my disciples" (Mt. 28:19). But this dynamism of the mission, this interior openness and amplitude of the Gospel, cannot be exchanged for the formula: Go into the world and become the world yourselves! Go into the world and become like it in its worldly state! It is just the contrary of that. It is the holy mystery of God, the mustard seed of the Gospel, which does not mix with the world, but is destined to penetrate into all the world. For that reason we must recover the courage of the sacred, the courage of the distinctiveness of what is Christian; not in order to put up fences around it, but in order to transform, to be truly dynamic.[21]

Here we see, for example, the meaning of clerical and religious garb, liturgical vestments, and the distinction between the *presbyterium* or sanctuary and the nave of the faithful.

---

21. J. Ratzinger, *Ministers of Your Joy,* 123; here translated from the Italian edition, *Servitori della vostra gioa,* 127.

VIII

Marriage Elevated to a Sacrament

The revealed truth about marriage

SOME time ago, I read a reader's comment in a newspaper: "Let's hope that the time will come when those who don't believe will have other ways at their disposal for celebrating the hinge moments of life (birth, maturity, death), without needing to have recourse to religious functions, taking away their true meaning. In this way, those who request sacraments will do it because they appreciate them for what they are; they will be protected from losing their true meaning, and there will be no anger with the Church when it lays claim to a minimum of consistency from people's children, parents, and godparents. This is my dream. But I know that one can't take anything for granted, as shown by the case of marriage, which can be celebrated today with a civil ceremony. For which reason it should be permissible to expect that someone who chooses the religious ceremony will do it because he believes in it. And yet despite everything, how many marriages celebrated in church get turned into fashion bazaars? And what kind of understanding is shown by brides who present themselves at the altar with necklines down to their navel, as if they were going to the first night of an opera? So let us try to understand the nature of marriage."

According to the doctrine of the Church, marriage is radically different from the other six sacraments. They exist only in the supernatural order, while marriage is of natural right: if both parties are baptized, it also becomes, of itself, a sacrament of the New Law, with no further requirements in order to be a sacrament, and always presupposing that both spouses have been baptized (cf. CIC, can. 1055, s. 2).

That being presupposed, the family in the Church is born from a sacrament that unites the spouses in Christ and "consecrates" them together (cf. CCC 1535), in order to orient the daily path of their family to the Father. The Christian family is a project of communion in Christ Jesus and a living cell of the Church. The design and intervention of God regarding the family and marriage is found on several occasions. The two accounts of the creation of man and woman (cf. Gen. 1:26–28; 2:18, 20–24) culminate in the proclamation of the institution of marriage. In the first text, man created in the image of God fully expresses the resemblance he has with God in the human couple and in the community of love formed by man and woman in marriage: the oneness of the couple, its indissolubility, and the commitment to mutual fidelity. The Old Testament calls attention to the ideal of monogamous and indissoluble marriage, despite various cases of polygamy and divorce.

The revelation of God about this sacrament reaches its highpoint in Jesus. He is the Son of God born from woman (cf. Gal. 4:4), and who grows up in the context of a family. Jesus proclaims the religious character of matrimony and its indissolubility: God himself unites man and woman. Their free choice becomes, in matrimony, a consecration that transcends them and surpasses them. Jesus gives a foundation and a new meaning to matrimony: the eternal covenant in his blood (cf. Mt. 26–28). He is the spouse of the Church and the spouses participate in his power to love. Their love, responsible fecundity, and humility, their attitude of mutual service and their mutual fidelity, are signs of Christ's love, present in them and in the Church. Their love—consecrated by the sacrament of matrimony—is a love fully human, and not a mere transport of instinct and sentiment; it is a choice of their free will, destined to become stronger and to grow in their lives. It is a total love: Christian spouses share everything, without reservations or egotistical calculations. It is a love faithful and exclusive until death. It is a fruitful love that does not expend itself in the communion between the spouses, but instead procreates new lives. Paul proclaims such things when he writes to the Christians of the church of Ephesus (cf. 5:2, 25–33). The love of Jesus, which gives itself to the Church up to the total sacrifice of self, constitutes the living rule that Christian spouses must imitate.

Every sacrament is an ecclesial act. Matrimony, in being celebrated before the community, becomes a commitment assumed in the sight of the Church. The freedom with which the choice was made, with the commitment to fidelity and responsible procreation, are the defining aspects of this Christian sacrament.

Historical evolution of the rite

According to St. Ignatius of Antioch, disciple of the apostles, who died in AD 107, Christians get married like other people, but they do so with the approval of the bishop: "so that the marriage may be conformed to the Lord and not to passionate desire."[1] Were it otherwise, how would Christian marriage differ from the natural union? And why did I want to emphasize this? The bishop must approve precisely in order to verify whether the marriage is some project of mine, or the recognition of an encounter with the mystery. This awareness was already present at the origins of the Church, which kept alive the memory of the presence of the Lord at the wedding in Cana of Galilee. Simply his presence transforms the love of the spouses from natural to supernatural, like water into wine—a sign that prefigures the Last Supper.

In the West, the principle developed that a marriage is made by the consent (*consensus facit nuptias*), whereby the liturgical action seems secondary; while in the East, the liturgical action is essential, because the one who consecrates the marriage is the priest. The most ancient Roman sacramentaries attest a nuptial blessing and a Eucharistic celebration for a marriage. But according to the Western tradition, matrimony is founded solely on the will to contract it, expressed publicly. In the East as in the West, it pertained to the bishop or priest to give the blessing to the spouses; they probably did the crowning themselves, with crowns of metal or flowers. This typical rite, which gives Byzantine marriage its name, is now preceded by the rite of engagement, at one time celebrated separately.

---

1. St. Ignatius of Antioch, *Letter to Polycarp*, 5, 2.

In the Middle Ages, the celebration before the church door, *in facie ecclesiae,* takes root: Raphael, in his *Espousal of the Virgin,* represented the rite in that fashion. It is true that in Jewish custom, marriage comes to be celebrated under a baldacchino, recalling the tent or dwelling of the Lord. It is helpful to look in a comparative way at the Jewish tradition and rites—prefiguration of the sacraments in the Roman Rite—and at the Eastern rites, because they allow us to better understand the Latin tradition.[2]

Another characteristic gesture of the rite is the consigning of the marriage contract, followed by the blessing of the ring—only the bride's ring—to be worn on the left hand, and the rite is concluded with the prayer of blessing of the bride, near the door.

The Protestants deny the sacramentality of matrimony, as they do that of the other sacraments[3]; but the Council of Trent reaffirmed it, holding to the principle that it is the consent of the spouses that constitutes it, and that it is therefore obligatory to observe the form, as established by the decree *Tametsi* of the same Council: a) questioning about the will or intention to marry; b) the consent. Eastern Christians consider, to this day, that matrimony as a sacrament is conferred by the ministering priest and not by the spouses. Without being defined doctrine, it is the consolidated tradition among Catholics instead that the spouses are the ministers of the sacrament (cf. CCC 1623).[4]

Vatican II called for the revision of the rite of matrimony, so that the grace of the sacrament would be more clearly signified and the

2. Cf. N. Bux–M. Loconsole, *I Misteri degli Orientali* [*The Mysteries of the Orientals*] (Siena, Cantagalli, 2006), 111–35.

3. Protestant theologies which do apply the term "sacraments" to two of them, baptism and "the Lord's Supper," nevertheless decline to accept some aspects of the Church's faith regarding the sacraments. (Translator's note)

4. Despite the greater importance attributed to the priestly blessing in the East, the sacrament divinely instituted nevertheless has the same essential form "substantially" in both rites: signification, in *some* way, of marital consent. The Byzantine priestly blessing, which expresses the acceptance and prayer of the Church regarding the marriage, implicitly signifies the consent which establishes the marriage "contract." (Translator's note)

duties of spouses inculcated (SC 77). The rite is foreseen within Mass, inserted after the Gospel and the homily. It begins with the minister's questions to the spouses about their intention to celebrate Christian marriage (so, a kind of *scrutinium*, as in the catechumenate); it proceeds with the blessing of the rings, the reciting of the formula of marriage (to be chosen from among some options), and the confirmation by the celebrant, in the form of a blessing, with the quotation from the Gospel: "what God has joined together, let no man put asunder" (Mt. 19:6b).

The pagan customs that entered the Christian rite quite early, such as the nuptial *velatio* (veiling) and the *ekdosis* or handing over of the bride by the father to the husband, make it understandable that already in the post-Tridentine ritual, and in those that followed Vatican II, variations have been permitted in accord with national or regional customs. The most striking example is the blessing of the bride (and of the husband, in the Ordinary Form) by the minister after the consent, rather than immediately after the *Pater*, as in the Roman Missal.

Who the minister of matrimony is

In the Extraordinary Form of the rite of matrimony, newly restored to use, we find the celebrated formula *"Ego coniungo vos in matrimonium"*—which highlights the role of the priest—apparently in contradiction with the thesis that it is the consent that makes the marriage, and the ministers of the sacrament are the spouses. In fact, on the Catholic side, the thesis that the priest is the minister in a marriage had a protagonist in Melchior Cano, Spanish Catholic theologian and bishop (d. 1560) who at the Council of Trent had maintained such a position, though it was not successful.

As the East, but also the Catholics maintain, the matrimonial pact between the baptized has been elevated to the dignity of a sacrament (CIC, can. 1055; CCC 1601). The matrimonial bond was inscribed in creation as it first existed differently from its present natural condition; creation was then corrupted by original sin. Here we see that in the sacramental celebration of matrimony a passage takes place, a passage for which the crowning in the Byzantine rite is the symbol: a supernatural transformation accomplished precisely by the sacrament. For this reason, according to the East, the only ministry that can accomplish this transformation is the priest's: the spouses cannot do it.

In the Byzantine rite, as in the Roman, the blessing of the spouses, in Greek *epiclesis*, that is, invocation, is pronounced by the priest. The marriage rite, in the Ordinary Form, would seem to wish to highlight that there is an epiclesis in the sacrament of matrimony too, as in all the sacraments, with the invocation of the Holy Spirit, and even of the Trinity; in the *editio typica*, there are three formulas of benediction of the spouses. The juridical aspect of matrimony, developed in the West, does not exclude the sacramental aspect, but rather strengthens it, insofar as the sacramental aspect itself belongs to the *ius divinum* of which the sacrament is an expression. Consequently it is right to retain and deepen the idea that matrimony is perfected by way of the priest's blessing. The liturgical theologian Achille Triacca in his treatment of the subject speaks of it as a transforming action of the Holy Spirit.[5] The consent, necessary for the validity of sacramental marriage, implies that it be given before the minister of the Church. To this we add that normally marriage is celebrated within Mass (cf. CCC 1621) and the spouses are invited to go to confession and receive communion: the sacrament is fruitful, or it is not, depending on whether those contracting it are or are not in the state of grace.

It happens that some baptized people come to matrimony without having received confirmation, especially when confirmation has been deferred until after first communion. Why can a person not marry without being confirmed? Canon law requires that confirmation be received before matrimony, so as to perfect initiation, noting nevertheless, "if it is possible without grave inconvenience" (can. 1065, section 1); that means it is necessary to receive it after adequate preparation, which would have to be part of the pre-matrimonial preparation. In general, those who are engaged but not

5. Cf. A. Triacca, *Spiritus Sancti virtutis infusio* [*Infusion of the Power of the Holy Spirit*], in *Notitiae* 26 (1990), 365–90.

confirmed provide for their reception of confirmation in this context of marriage.

Perhaps there is a need to institute a rite of engagement, like the *arrhabon* or commitment among Eastern Christians.[6]

To administer a sacrament means to cause some happening in life to be read in the light of faith, and to desire that the salvific action of God transform the human action by way of prayer, the memorial, and the epiclesis. Therefore the sacraments consecrate the times of the life of a man, from birth till death. But how could they consecrate if they were limited simply to human gestures? It is true that a man and a woman met and chose each other in view of marriage, but in this meeting they must catch a glimpse, not of mere chance, but of God's salvific action taking place here and now, opening into the future.

The complementarity between the consent of the spouses and the priestly blessing so that the sacrament of matrimony will be there became, in the second half of the last century, the object of a debate between theologians and canonists, such as Jilek and Corecco. The latter, who later became bishop of Lugano, took up again the thesis of Melchior Cano's ecclesiology and sacramental theology, according to which the ministers of the sacrament considered as an efficacious sign of grace are not the spouses, but the priest. Such a position does not stand in contradiction with the doctrine of consent, insofar as the blessing of the priest, in his function as a sacred minister of the Church, contributes to forming the marriage into a sacrament or sacred sign, and in the canonical forum it reinforces for the baptized person the inseparability of matrimonial contract and sacrament—this on the basis of the *ius divinum* and not of juridical positivism.

At this point, the sacramental formula: *"Ego coniungo vos in matrimonium"*—rather than the 1969 *editio typica*'s new phrase, "I receive you as my wife/husband," which assimilates the family to a

---

6. In the Extraordinary Form of the Roman Rite, the traditional rite of betrothal is already returning under the influence of *Summorum Pontificum*. (Editor's note)

guesthouse—is eloquent.[7] At least the earlier formula "I take you"[8] recalls the Gospel of John, in the passage where it says of Our Lady: "he [John] took her into his home," which in the Greek text "*eis ta idia sou*" means: he took her into his own.

Who can receive the sacrament

Matrimony introduces those who receive it into an "order" in the Church, and constitutes a state of life, creates rights and duties between the spouses and toward the children: for this reason it is necessary for there to be certainty about a marriage. To this end, the Church requires that it be celebrated in its ecclesiastical form, with the sacrament; from that flows the obligation to have at least two witnesses present (CIC, can. 1108). The witnesses visibly attest, with their presence, that the marriage is an ecclesial reality (cf. CCC 1630).

By divine and natural right or law, marriage is effected by the consent of the parties (cf. CIC 1057); but since it is a social institution, it is of interest to society. That society to which the spouses are subject can establish conditions for its validity, even if there is a limit to what those stipulations can be, so as not to prejudice the fundamental human right to marry. In this way civil society, for the non-baptized, and the society of the Church, for the baptized, enter in. It is in the interest of the one and the other that the marriage that has taken place be publicly recognizable, for which reason the society can condition its validity on a certain public form of celebration. The Church, starting from the Council of Trent, conditioned the validity of marriage to a particular form of celebration: before a qualified witness and two common witnesses—that is the canonical form (cf. canons 1108ff.). The function of canonical form

---

7. The author is contrasting the clarity of the traditional words of the priest, *Ego coniungo vos in matrimonium*, with the Italian translation for the spouses' consent in the modern rite—the verb chosen in the Italian can easily signify "welcome," hence his reference to an institution of hospitality. In English the verb for the consent is the traditional "take." (Translator's note)

8. Cf. also CCC 1627.

is not to add the quality of a sacrament to the marriage, but only to ensure the juridical and social certainty that there has been a marriage: the quality of sacramentality is already inherent in a marriage by the fact that those exchanging consent are two baptized parties, a baptized man and a baptized woman. The two common witnesses are not in any way comparable to the godparents in baptism, because their function is only to attest that the exchange of consent took place between the parties, and always in the interest of juridical certainty. The two common witnesses do not in fact need to be pointed out beforehand, and there is no need for them to be conscious of their role. It is enough that at the moment of exchange of consent two persons (in addition to the qualified witness, who is the Church's minister) actually see and hear the parties as they exchange consent, so as to be able to testify, if necessary, that the exchange of consent occurred. In view of the extremely limited and purely human character of their function, it does not follow a priori that they must be baptized, but that they be reliable *de jure* (cf. can. 96) in people's estimation, as for civil society; they certainly do not have a sacramental function.

Already in the 1970s the International Theological Commission challenged this doctrine on the marriages of all the baptized and the consequent law, pointing to what the commission considered as a problem: how can marriages celebrated by baptized persons who don't believe be sacramental? Pope Benedict XVI wished to present once again a similar topic in his last allocution to the Roman Rota (January 26, 2013), inviting reflection on it. A change of doctrine in this respect could not occur without calling into question the doctrinal maxim promulgated again by canon 1057, section 2, namely that matrimony between baptized parties cannot exist without *eo ipso* being a sacrament. For, if it is said that the marriage of baptized persons without faith (even if only one baptized party lacks faith—marriage is a two-way street) is not a sacrament, it will inevitably be necessary to say that a merely natural marriage between baptized parties is possible—which would also mean contradicting the doctrine of many centuries: obviously people cannot be deprived of the natural human right to marriage only because they have become unbelievers. Basically, this would involve a genetic mutation of the whole doctrine on marriage. As long as this has not in reality taken place, Pope Francis, too, in fact has to hold to the doctrine and laws in peaceful possession in the Church, even if in an interview with journalists he seems to have foreseen some significant change of the doctrine, and consequently a change in the laws on matrimony.

We now come to some frequently asked questions. Can a baptized person marry someone not baptized? It being presupposed that whoever is baptized is always part of the Church, unless he is excommunicated, he can contract the marriage in church with a non-baptized person who nevertheless shares the natural foundations of Christian marriage (fidelity, indissolubility, fruitfulness), respects the faith of the spouse, and consents to the children being educated in the faith. In such a case one can choose the rite without Mass.

A baptized person who has suffered a divorce, but has not remarried—can he go to confession and receive communion? Certainly. But one who has remarried, producing a second union, which he considers stable and closer to the faith than the previous one, can, with prior consultation with the priest, undertake a path that will lead him to spiritual communion[9] and to the declaration of the first marriage's nullity, especially if he should have doubts about its validity, due to lack of maturity or of freedom, etc. The ecclesiastical tribunal serves precisely to judge of the validity of the bond.

Not infrequently it happens—it is a sign of self-made religion—that someone intending to marry civilly comes to the priest to ask for the blessing of the rings. That makes no sense, because the blessing is a rite that presupposes the sacrament, insofar as the ring expresses the bond just consecrated.

---

9. "Spiritual communion" is being used in a wide sense here, which can include persons who pray for the grace of moral conversion, but have not yet renounced the grave sin of adulterous or non-marital relations, before their marital situation is rectified. In St. Thomas Aquinas's usage, "eating of the sacrament spiritually" presupposes that the person is *now* in the state of grace, which implies that he *presently* has no habitual or actual intention to do anything gravely sinful. (Translator's note)

And now a question that touches on front page news: why can only a man and a woman marry, and not homosexuals? The Congregation for the Doctrine of the Faith published in 2003 the document *Considerations Regarding Proposals to Give Legal Recognition to Unions between Homosexual Persons.* It starts by stating the fact of what the human person is, as male and female, and how the being-together of man and woman can receive a juridical form, since today that is no longer considered to be a single notion. Epistemological and moral relativism have also eroded philosophical and theological anthropology, and new opinions have delineated themselves, which lead to a dissolution of the image of man, the consequences of which can be extremely grave. Indeed they can already be perceived in the slide in public debate from *de facto* couples to artificial fertilization and to "marriage" between homosexuals with the possibility of adopting children.

In the evaluation of erroneous opinions like these, Catholic doctrine first of all affirms the unconditional character of human dignity and of human rights that come before any political jurisdiction whatever and point, in terms of their origin, to the Creator,[10] and so to the permanent value of the Decalogue. In this sense, analysis of the relation between the freedom and the nature of man turns out to be important, as demonstrated by John Paul II:

> It is necessary to understand the true meaning of the natural law; it refers to the nature which belongs exclusively and originally to man, to the nature of the human person, who is the person himself in the unity of soul and body, of his spiritual and biological inclinations, and of all the other specific characteristics necessary for pursuing his end.[11]

In the second place—since faith in revelation has changed, insofar as relativism leads to not perceiving the natural order as a font of rationality—the Church today, paradoxically, is called to defend

---

10. Cf. J. Ratzinger, "The Spiritual Roots of Europe: Yesterday, Today, and Tomorrow" in M. Pera and J. Ratzinger, *Without Roots: the West, Relativism, Christianity, Islam* (New York: Basic Books, 2006).

11. John Paul II, Encyclical *Veritatis Splendor* (1993), 50.

reason *before* faith. Consequently, she defends the bond between reason and faith, for the purpose of healing the deadly separation between thought and ethics, even as she is likewise called to highlight the rational aspect of human nature, as John Paul II did in his commentary on the encyclical *Humanae Vitae* of Paul VI.

And so on this issue, it should be enough to get supporters of the "naturalness" of homosexuality to ask themselves the question: Why do men and women exist in the world, rather than all men or all women? In the face of this evident clarity, homosexuality appears as an impossible attempt to sanction an identification of human nature with one sex or the other, to the point of annulling that obvious difference, while being always ready to bring difference back in, when it is time to demand the right to *difference*, for the purpose of getting a juridical recognition for "gay civil unions."[12]

In the face of the reality that not a few Catholics have adopted an individualistic, liberal idea of conscience, and rather refuse the idea of conscience in communion, which sees the Christian and the Church as a single body, and given the gravity of the subject matter and the urgency of the present moment, it is necessary to shed light on, among other things: (a) the manipulations of the percentages for the phenomenon of homosexuality; (b) the alleged fact that the homosexual tendency is innate or constitutes a "third gender,"[13] as if it were a natural or normal condition of the person; (c) all the other aspects that are not sufficiently appreciated, directing attention above all to demonstrating the fundamental fact that human dignity resides in the sovereign capacity of man to decide his own actions and to posit free acts, not in homosexual or heterosexual orientation; (d) whether homosexual orientation is, in itself,

12. Cf. Sébastien [sic], *Ne deviens pas gay, tu finiras triste* [*Don't become gay, you will end up sad*] (Paris: Éditions du Seuil, 2001). This book is a forceful witness by an ex-member of the gay community, who rebels against the very idea of a pact of solidarity or civil union, an idea he judges hypocritical and damaging for the possible children to be adopted by homosexual couples.

13. Cf. Congregation for the Doctrine of the Faith, *Letter to the Bishops of the Catholic Church on the Collaboration of Men and Women in the Church and in the World* (2004), 2.

a psychological (neurological, etc.) anomaly.[14] The phenomenon has a complex psychogenesis and socio-genesis, which could go so far as to give rise to hormonal and functional alterations, although this is not yet demonstrated, and seems improbable. In general terms, the question should be confronted in a perspective of therapy and change. If the right commitment and motivations are present, then there exist good therapeutic prospects.

The strategy on the part of Catholics should begin by calling attention to the relevant articles in the *Catechism* (cf. 2357–59 and 2396, with a clarification by the Latin *editio typica* of 1997); then, the strategy should underline the importance of the grace of God that positively influences the liberty and acts of a person, to the end of reinforcing him in virtue. Grace, in helping to resist homosexual temptations, will not remain bereft of effects. Furthermore the strategy must unhook the ideas about homosexuality from other convictions that are right and present in society, for example respect, equality, and avoidance of unjust discrimination. Finally, the strategy should point out serious scientific studies on homosexuality that are open to the prospect of change and conversion, while criticizing and warning against those that are distorted. The truth about homosexuality should be said with charity, breaking with the indifference on the topic.

Lastly, let us give indications for the case, by now widespread, of mixed marriage (between a Catholic and a baptized non-Catholic) and marriage with disparity of cult (between a Catholic and a non-baptized person). The first case requires particular attention from those contracting the marriage and from the Church's pastors, because the division of Christians has not been overcome, and the

---

14. The *Diagnostic Manual* of the American Psychiatric Association was modified (cf. P. Cameron—K. Cameron—T. Landess, *Errors by the American Psychiatric Association, the American Psychological Association, and the National Education Association in Representing Homosexuality in Amicus Briefs about Amendment 2 to the U.S. Supreme Court*, in *Psychological Reports* 79 [1996], 383–404). Various psychological and sociological research studies have been promoted, though they ignore and falsify the data, while valid results have been censored. See also G.J.M. Van Den Aardweg, *The Battle for Normality: A Guide For (Self-)Therapy For Homosexuality* (San Francisco: Ignatius Press, 1997).

divergences about the concept of marriage and the education of children can constitute a source of tension and temptations to relativism and religious indifference. This is why express permission from the ecclesiastical authority is necessary. Even more attention and care are required in the second case, because marriage presupposes that the parties know and do not exclude the ends and essential properties of marriage, such as indissolubility or the unicity of the couple, etc. (for example, in the event of a Muslim spouse). In this case, an express dispensation from the impediment is required. Whether for a mixed marriage or for disparity of cult, in both of which the presence of a non-Catholic minister is allowed, the Catholic party must confirm his commitments to conserve his own faith and to assure the baptism and upbringing of the children in the Catholic Church. These commitments must be made known to the non-Catholic partner as well (cf. CIC, can. 1125). Still, for a Catholic, as not a few will acknowledge, having a spouse who shares the faith in addition to married love shows itself over time to be vastly preferable.

The effects befitting the covenant with God

In the present secularized context, the question arises: Why, if one has been abandoned by one's spouse, is it not possible to make a new life? The reason is this: from a valid celebration of marriage there arises between the spouses a bond, perpetual and exclusive by its nature (CCC 1638). The bond is the seal that God places upon the consent, himself first of all guaranteeing fidelity (cf. Mk. 9:10). The stability of marriage is given by its having been constructed on the rock that is God; from the fidelity of God comes the fidelity of the spouses. The part they must do is to bear the yoke (*coniugum*) or bond together, with a free human act, and "consummating" the marriage: the yoke is gentle, if they are united to Christ.[15]

---

15. *Three to Get Married* is the title of a famous book by the theologian and bishop Fulton Sheen (New York: Appleton-Century-Crofts, 1951, reprinted many times since).

The marriage bond is consecrated to God and cannot be loosened by man. Not even the Church has power over it.

To the bond is added the grace, proper to the sacrament, which perfects the love of the spouses and reinforces their indissoluble unity—a unity called to sanctify itself in married life through mutual help and welcoming and bringing up the children. Jesus is the font of this grace; with his presence between the spouses, joined with the family in prayer, he gives the strength to follow him, to take up one's own cross, forgiving and bearing with one another, or bearing the weight together. In this way they learn to be subject to one another in reverence for Christ (Eph. 5:21) and have a foretaste of that supernatural love, tender and fruitful, which will have its completion in heaven.

These goods of marriage—which come from the sacrament of matrimony and make the spouses happy through Christ, who, as Irenaeus says, is the teacher of unity—are the object of the envy and traps of the evil one. He who is the accuser and divider par excellence tempts the man and the woman concerning the dignity of marriage, created and redeemed by Christ: from adultery to divorce, from incest to free cohabitation and concubinage (the so-called *de facto* couples), as far as polygamy and premarital sexual relations—offenses that wound on the natural level, and wound even more when the two are united in the sacramental bond. If and when cohabitation of the spouses becomes impossible, physical separation of the spouses is a remedy allowed by the Church (cf. CCC 1649), in the hope of the reconciliation that is always possible with a path of prayer, penance, and charity, and the help of good Christian friends.

If two baptized spouses catch wind of the fact that their consent was vitiated from the start by violence or external constraint, by natural or ecclesiastical impediments such as impotence for sexual intercourse, or psychic disorder—in essence, that their consent was not freely expressed—and they publicly claim this, they can go back before the Church, in the Church tribunal, and state the question of the possible nullity of their marriage: an inexact expression, insofar as the Church does not have the power to annul a valid marriage, but only to declare, after attentive examination and scrupulous expert opinions, that it never existed, despite the external celebration, on account of the aforesaid vitiating factors. Only in this way are the parties free to marry, respecting, however, the natural obligations of the previous union (children, support, etc.) (cf. CCC 1629). It is not true that the so-called annulment is gotten easily, or that only the rich and famous can have it quickly: this is suggested by the adversaries of the Church, in order to make divorce more desirable to the baptized, as a quicker procedure, and also because it spends less time examining the causes and has no purpose of attempting reconciliation. The baptized who have remarried civilly after a divorce find themselves in a situation that contradicts the divine law. For this reason, as long as it lasts, they cannot approach communion and cannot exercise certain ecclesial responsibilities. They can reconcile themselves with the sacrament of Penance only if they repent and undertake to live in complete abstinence from sexual relations (cf. CCC 1650). Nevertheless they continue to belong to the Church, while they are invited and helped to keep their faith by way of acts of charity and penance, and to educate their children in a Christian way, to pray and frequent Mass, and to implore daily the grace of God (cf. *Familiaris Consortio*, in CCC 1651).

Chastity in marriage and virginity for the kingdom of heaven

Sacrifice for a great ideal, before it is a Christian experience, is a profoundly human experience, corresponding to the stature of being a person. Traces of such experience can also be found in parallel traditions, whether in the Semitic world, or in the Hellenistic. With different motivations and ends—from purity, to the idea of the saint, or from sacrifice, to expiation—it is nevertheless possible to affirm that chastity, as a temporary or definitive existential attitude, can be traced in a multiplicity of historical experiences.

Chastity is not first of all a prerogative of priests and monks, as commonly believed: it is a virtue that concerns everyone, even spouses. "Chastity" is a Latin word, from the Greek root *katharòs*, whole, pure, immaculate, virgin, uncontaminated. Does not virtuous integrity of that sort express, perhaps, the innate desire of every human being? How can it be possessed, or recovered when it has been lost? "Chastity" has the same root as castigation, which is precisely the action of correcting, restraining, strictly warning, in order to improve and perfect man, to bring him back to integrity and purity. He who has not willed to be the master but has left his own instincts without restraint will have for castigation the punishment man inflicts on himself, separating himself from God.

Jesus has very strong words on acts against purity; Peter and Paul say that the impure will not inherit the kingdom of heaven and will not see God.

The Church knows the experience of perfect continence for the kingdom of heaven. It is not born, in the first place, from a will to sacrifice or to make expiation, but from the recognition of Christ as the fullness of life and from an all-consuming interpersonal relationship with him. Such an attitude is born, as well, from a radical identification with the Master, who, considering even the Hebrew cultural climate of his time, made choices completely different from what was normal. In fact, St. Paul recalls that instead of the current normality, the reality (*to sôma*) is Christ (Col. 2:17); he uses the term body here, in the sense of a concrete reality, as opposed to a shadow. The true body that the risen Christ has put on constitutes the beginning of the new world, the seed of the future reality that has entered the world in this way.

Jesus said: "There are eunuchs who were born that way from the womb of their mother, and there are eunuchs who were made eunuchs by men, and there are eunuchs who have made themselves eunuchs for the Kingdom of Heaven. Let him who can understand, understand!" (Mt. 19:12). This threefold indication about the existence of eunuchs (a term that indicates the non-use of sexual functions) can be seen as an ever greater use of freedom: in the first case there is no freedom; in the second, there is a bad use of freedom by others; only in the third case is it the man himself who uses his own personal freedom as a manifestation of the following of Christ. The *chios* of the verse indicates incontrovertibly how much chastity, before being a human conquest, is a gift of God not granted to all, but only to some whom he chooses, and consequently only some can fully understand the extent of its meaning.

The Christian has the awareness of being, in the world, a continuation of the presence of his Lord and lives with trepidation and enthusiasm the task of testimony to him: such testimony has asked of the Christian—in the past, but also today—the sacrifice of physical life itself, in order to not betray, or simply to affirm, a state of belonging to another. As the instinct for survival is sacrificed in the experience of martyrdom, in order to testify to the victory of Christ, so the strongest instinct of man, after the survival instinct—the sexual instinct—is voluntarily sacrificed for the sake of testimony to the Lord of life. People's reaction, widespread as it is, to this type of testimony is the most obvious confirmation that it is maintaining all of its characteristic effectiveness, and the characteristic effect of provoking thought about the faith, or at least a search for the reasons for this free choice.

In the causes of canonization of saints, examination of the virtue of chastity and of purity is a condition that cannot be neglected. Why? Charity is the form of all the virtues, says the *Catechism*; under its influence, chastity appears as a school of the gift of the person. Chastity makes the one who practices it a witness, for his neighbor, of the fidelity and tenderness of God (CCC 2346). The *Catechism* dedicates no less than 35 paragraphs to chastity: chastity and purity are virtues given by the Holy Spirit, in baptism; they should be conserved and increased, because they are at the foundation of true friendship: they render friendship not possessive, but free. Chastity concerns the engaged and the married: it increases charity and mutual love; it leads to self-mastery and helps one to dominate, to contain, and—together with other supports, *in primis*, sacramental grace—to overcome all the affective fragility of man at any time. Chastity must grow continually, so that it leads to the acquisition of full self-mastery.

Our world seems deaf to the value of chastity, but what is the alternative? Scripture affirms that man either dominates his own passions, obtaining peace, or he lets himself be enslaved by them and becomes unhappy (cf. Sir. 1:22). The virtue of chastity is strictly dependent on the cardinal virtue of temperance, which aims at having reason give the lead to the passions and appetites of the human senses (CCC 2341). For priests and laypeople, for parents and educators, there is material for reflection, for examining themselves, and for taking up again and announcing the beauty of chastity, on any occasion: homily, spiritual direction, confession, lectures, catechesis, and above all, from the "rooftops" of television and the media. It pertains first of all to priests to be heralds, with mercy and truth, of the salvific value of chastity: source of order, whether internal or external, personal or social. Those who administer the sacraments of healing, Penance and anointing, have been put in a position where they may always remind people of the importance of offenses against chastity and the value of good observance in this area. "Be perfect as your Father is perfect" (Mt. 5:48); this is the high standard of the following of Christ. The Lord requires from every Christian and every man that he seek the way of truth and of life, and that he not exclude the area of affectivity from the joyful and sure path of faith. In this way we will discover that chastity is not a death for man. Chastity is a new way of possessing all things.

Let us take the example of the life of the spouses Maria Corsini and Luigi Beltrame Quattrocchi, beatified by John Paul II. They practiced the virtue of obedience, above all in spousal submission in marriage, together with obedience to the Pope in the Church: a free obedience, done from love before all else. Obedience sets out from God and ends in him, as a pure act of faith; for this reason, faith is a criterion of judgment that does not go along with a worldly or a simply human mentality. By way of the sacramental life and prayer, one walks toward God's presence and assimilates his will: this was the life-program of the two spouses. The permanent choice of one's spiritual father is a clear expression of renunciation of oneself: analogously, the relationship of being a couple, lived—as has been said—in spousal submission, becomes a contest of reciprocal obedience in charity.

The two spouses, though not coming from poor families, made themselves poor, above all interiorly, so that they seemed immersed in a total renunciation, detached from earthly goods, and rich only with Jesus. That led them to use and appreciate every created thing without dissipation; with the joy proper to the saints they conjoined their dignity with poverty, in a marriage that had its reference point in God. From all this there flowed forth chastity, a virtue exercised to a heroic degree as a passage from the "I" to the "Thou," the good of whom is desired more than one's own good. As spouses they knew how to maintain sanctity and respect for the body. In this way the two *beati* came to consider purity as a social virtue, possible for every individual. In addition, they lived the reality of their family as the goal of their common aspiration, transmitting to their children the same sense of purity, in the fear of God, lived in the community of the family as a domestic sanctuary and church. And so Maria Corsini and Luigi Beltrame Quattrocchi were, also in chastity, models of Christian spouses.

If laypeople give an example like that in the exercise of the evangelical counsels, how much more should the clergy be able to give, and actually give, the same example![16] The *querelle* concerning marriage for priests, never appeased, is renewed today, perhaps as an occasion, or even as a help, for avoiding cases of pedophilia and homosexuality. Apart from the fact that we would with such a decision be returning to the much vituperated idea of marriage as *remedium concupiscentiae*,[17] let us point out that it is an end run around the evangelical counsel of the Lord: "If you wish to be perfect, leave everything you have . . . and follow me" (Mt. 19:21); that is to say, the "form of life" that the Lord Jesus proposed to the disciples who followed him, to the point of their lives becoming obedient, poor, and chaste.

16. Chastity with the exercise of conjugal relations within a marriage is a virtue, but it is not, properly speaking, the evangelical *counsel* of chastity, which means total abstinence from sexual and conjugal relations. (Translator's note)

17. "Remedy for concupiscence." This is often understood to mean that sexual relations within marriage remedy wide-ranging desires by providing them one legitimate "outlet." But the expression should more properly be understood as the fact that since marriage is a *contract* for a noble purpose, conjugal intercourse can come under the virtue of justice, because with the marriage bond, intercourse is the mutual rendering of what has been given to the other as his or her *right*. (Translator's note)

IX

The Extension
of Sacramental Meaning

The divine power that reaches man

"The whole crowd was trying to touch him, because from him there went forth a power which cured everyone" (Lk. 6:19). Jesus himself is aware of it: "Someone touched me, because I felt a power coming out from me" (Lk. 8:46; cf. Mk. 5:30).

A little statue of the Madonna containing water from Lourdes is a rather widespread sacred souvenir, but it is not only that: it is an object that can produce spiritual effects, thanks to the daily working of the Church. In fact, the seven sacraments, which represent Christ's will to consecrate the world with the symbolism of the biblical number, contain and produce other signs. They are not efficacious in the same way, but they are equally holy, like imitations of them: they impetrate and obtain effects that predispose man to more, extending the divine power of sanctification in the seven sacraments to all the circumstances of existence. The Church calls them "sacramentals," because she herself instituted them; their efficacy derives from the action of the Church that performs them, and in the degree in which she is holy and works in intimate union with her own Head (cf. MD 23). So they are signs that confer grace, through the intercession of the Church (cf. SC 60), because in any case they touch on the presence of Christ in her. In this way, the seven sacraments on the one hand constitute the *opera omnia* of the Lord Jesus, and on the other hand give rise to the ongoing work of the Church, likewise ever united with Christ.

The Eastern Christians did not avoid the fascination of the number seven, and they made it their own. Nevertheless their sacramental universe remains more varied in its shades in comparison with the rigorous Latin definitions; they do not like sharp distinctions between the sacraments and the sacramentals with regard to their salvific efficacy. Simeon of Thessalonika recalls: "Where in fact there is the name and invoking of God, the most holy Trinity who has created everything and is the only God, there everything is holy, and by way of grace, works, sanctifies, and saves everything."[1] Orthodox and Catholics agree on this, even if the latter separate the sacraments from the sacramentals, in view of the fact that the former certainly transmit the divine power of Christ (*ex opere operato*), that same power that came out from him and healed all those who were seeking to touch him (cf. Lk. 6:19); while the latter transmit the power of the Church praying (*ex opere operantis ecclesiae*), a work in progress, let us say, until the end of the world.

The sacramentals are usually distinguished as: blessings, exorcisms, religious professions, funerals.

Some blessings constitute persons and objects in a state they did not have before, like the consecration of virgins or of a church and liturgical furnishings: these are constitutive blessings. The other blessings, which concern persons and things that remain in their state (foods, the sick, etc.), are the invocative blessings. The objects and persons that were profane before the blessing become sacred once consecrated and blessed. Every blessing brings back a piece of the world (person or object), far from God, into relation with God, in whom everything lives; and in this way death is conquered. The point is to consecrate what is profane and bring it to the sacred, conscious as we are that the world is far from God and closes itself to him because of sin, which leads to death. Here we see the importance of the blessings. As with the sacraments, the efficacy of the sacramentals does not depend on the moral state of the minister; what is important is that they be correctly administered, according to the prescriptions of the Church.

As already recalled, the Church has always gazed upon the realities of the universe created by God, and of the things made by man, as things for which God deserves to be praised, as is done at the end

---

1. Simeon of Thessalonika, *Dialogos* 128; PG 155:336D.

of the Roman Canon: "You, O God, create and sanctify always, vivify, bless, and give to the world every good." The *Apostolic Tradition* (cf. 21) attests that on the occasion of baptism, milk, honey, and water were blessed. As the sacraments sanctify the principal events of human life, blessings sanctify material things, exhorting us to use them rightly, and for the praise of God (cf. SC 61). The lay faithful, too, called to consecrate the world, can do some blessings within a narrow range, such as family meals, or the children by the parents, etc. (cf. SC 79 and the *Book of Blessings* of 1984); on the other hand, the blessings having to do with the public spaces of the Church are reserved to her ministers.

As a spiritual and sacred act, the blessing, in Hebrew *berakah*, praises the presence of God and asks that his power descend upon the person or the object, to sanctify it; presence and descent can be traced back, respectively, to Christ and to the Holy Spirit. This is like the sacraments, with their pattern of anamnesis and epiclesis. The blessing nourishes and expresses the faith, by way of the sign of the cross and the sprinkling with holy water.

Among the blessings of persons, one that stands out is the blessing of the mother who has given birth and of her child. It can be traced back to the Jewish purification, as was done by the Virgin Mary, after the fortieth day from the birth; thanks to it, the mother could again participate in public worship. This blessing is present in the Byzantine baptismal rite; in the old Roman ritual the theme of giving thanks for the gift of the child is united to it. In the new ritual, every reference to purification has disappeared; furthermore, it is presupposed that the mother will participate at the baptism together with the father and, at its conclusion, receive the blessing foreseen for both of them. In earlier times, mothers were not in any condition to participate at the baptism, because it was administered as soon as possible.

In the ritual book there are blessings of objects and persons, such as the blessing of candles on February 2, of ashes, of palms, of the sick and of the pilgrims in sanctuaries, and yet others meriting mention, for example the blessing of a marriage engagement, of the mother before the birth, of wedding rings, wedding jubilees, etc., or of tombs. Other special blessings have been put in the Pontifical, the liturgical book for a bishop: blessings of the sacred oils, or liturgical furnishings, of the altar, and of the church.

Consecration of an abbot, of religious, and of virgins

Also among blessings is that of religious profession, which concerns those groups of persons, men (whether priests or not) and women (sisters) who leave aside the possibility of having their own family in order to constitute a community, in order to love the Lord with greater immediacy and to serve their brethren better. They are called men and women religious, because they bind themselves[2] officially with a bond of covenant with the Lord, in complete fidelity, in the vows of chastity, obedience, and poverty.[3]

In the ancient period, profession was made *super altare*; when the practice of professing vows publicly began, the choice was made to lay the vow document on the altar with the relics, in the monastic community's chapel. In the medieval period, another manner of expressing the total gift of self to Christ in the monastic orders was to put one's hands in the hands of the superior; in the modern age, in the orders and congregations, the practice of swearing the vow before the Sacrament was adopted: if this was during Mass, then before communion, and if outside of Mass, then before the monstrance. The renewed rite was published in 1970: while no public celebration is foreseen for the entrance into the novitiate, the ritual of temporary and perpetual profession, and likewise for the consecration of an abbot or abbess, proceeds analogously to that of priestly ordination. After the Gospel, the call of the candidates takes place, and then the superior's allocution, the questioning of the candidate, the litany of the saints, the placing of the profession document on the altar and the signature; further on, the solemn prayer of blessing and the handing on of the ring, of the choir garment,

2. In Latin and Italian, "religion" and "to bind" have the same root, and a classic Latin interpretation says the word "religion" means being bound to God in some way. (Translator's note)

3. Cf. Decree on the Adaptation and Renewal of Religious Life *Perfectae Caritatis* (1965), 1.

and the book of the hours, it concludes with the kiss of peace. In particular, in the consecration of the abbot, since the introduction in the 9th century of the *Pontificale* (the liturgical book for the bishop's parts in ceremonies), the handing on of the order's book of rules, the pastoral staff, and sometimes the miter is done—these last elements, however, not for an abbess.

Also considered a sacramental is the consecration of virgins, presided over by the bishop, a rite that in the female orders is traditionally associated with perpetual profession. Some theologians discuss how it may include women who do not enter the cloister or the convent, but remain in the world in a secular condition, although placing themselves at the service of the Church, as happened in the ancient period. The analogy with the nuptial liturgy, in order to express union with Christ, is given by the use of certain symbols, such as the veil and the ring.

In short, the blessings or consecrations of religious call all Christians back to the value of death to the world and the hiddenness of the life with Christ in God, as the Apostle wrote (cf. Col. 3:3), a life that comes about in the silence and the calm of monasteries, convents, and religious houses. St. Bruno observes:

> In the silence and solitude of strong men, it is granted to recollect themselves as much as they desire, to happily nourish themselves from the fruits of paradise. There is acquired that eye whose clear gaze wounds the Spouse with love, and whose transparent purity allows for the vision of God. There one abandons oneself to a laborious repose and one is quiet in calm action. There God grants the mercy desired for the work of the struggle, that is, the peace that the world does not know, and the joy of the Holy Spirit. . . . This is the better part that Mary chose and that will not be taken away from her.[4]

Blessing of the church . . . and profanation

Though much emphasized as regards the effects and the changes it calls forth in the place that has been chosen for the purpose, the

4. St. Bruno, *To Radulphus*, 6.

dedication of a building to Christian worship is very quickly forgotten these days: in fact, one is frequently present at the profanation of everything that was offered to the Lord with such a rite. The blessing of a church is very important; it is distinguished from other blessings and resembles the Christian initiation of a person: it is also called dedication or consecration. The church building or temple of the Lord—so called because the Lord dwells there in the Blessed Sacrament and welcomes the mystery of the body of Christ, which is the people of God—is treated as though it were a person: possession is taken of it by its "measurement" by the bishop, who traces Latin and Greek letters on a cross made with ash on the pavement, as if to protect the sacred place from the evil one. The lustration of the altar and the walls of the church with holy water, as if a baptism were taking place, follows. After the homily, the Credo, and the litany of the saints, the relics are placed under the altar; the prayer of consecration is recited, and the altar is anointed with chrism; then the incense is brought to the altar, to incense it from top to bottom, to symbolize the sweet odor of Christ that rises from the altar, the presence of the Holy Spirit, and the prayer of the community, which rises permanently from that sacred place. The rite culminates with Mass, the first one to be celebrated on this altar after it has been clothed with altar-linens and the candles have been lighted.

One could make a detour into the history of religions, especially Judaism, which still celebrates Hanukkah, the feast of the dedication of the temple after its profanation by the pagans, but let us limit ourselves to Christianity. The disciples of the Lord who gathered for the divine mysteries created a holy space that, little by little, thanks to the assiduousness with which Christians met, came to imply, first, the use of appropriate surroundings in private houses, generally placed at their disposal by wealthy converts, and then, above all after the Peace of Constantine, the construction of buildings for worship, for "the holy things of the holy ones."[5] In this way

---

5. In the Greek liturgy, the phrase "Holy things for the holy ones" refers to the Eucharistic gifts about to be given by the priest to the baptized faithful who are worthy to receive them. (Translator's note)

the term "church," which indicated the community convoked by the Lord, became, significantly, a term for the holy place itself.

From the beginnings, the Christian community decided to reserve this place exclusively to the worship of God, and underlined this decision through a "solemn" action—to be recalled every year—that recalls the grace of God above all. The rite of dedication of a church comes from the East, where it began to be celebrated in the 4th century, with the placing of the relics of martyrs underneath the altar; then it was brought to the non-Roman West and eventually accepted into the Roman Pontifical. In the Ordinary Form of 1977, the Mass of dedication underlines the will of the ecclesial community to dedicate the new building to divine worship, in an exclusive and perpetual way. In particular, the presence of the sacrament and the altar do not permit any other use; in fact they are there to recall to us that the church is the sign of the heavenly sanctuary where Jesus Christ has penetrated, in order to appear before the sight of God on our behalf (Heb. 9:24).

A rite so redolent of meaning, with its venerable gestures and texts, offers Christians the opportunity to reflect on themselves as the Mystical Body consecrated to the Lord, on the authenticity of their worship, and on the seriousness of the commitment they have undertaken before God: that means the new and eternal covenant. Liturgists would say that for the sake of the truth of the sign, a church cannot be employed for purposes other than worship, on pain of gravely offending the Lord to whom it has been offered. Besides, its dedication is rightly commemorated every year on the anniversary day, especially within the church that was consecrated. It is therefore a grave error that, in practice, the consecration we have just described is emptied of meaning in our day by the actions of priests themselves, with the holding of events incompatible with the sacred place: concerts, performances, ballets, meetings of every type, which at one time were done outside or "in front of the temple," as the Latin word *pro-fanum* recalls; the phenomenon of using churches for concerts of not only sacred but also profane music seems unstoppable. Acts that are not sacred, and normally done elsewhere, bring with them a profanation of the church. In the advertising for the aforementioned concerts called "Sacred Nights," this phrase also slid into the copy: "music, prayer, and performances in churches"—an aping of the "White Nights" that are by now widespread in the secularized cities of Europe.

Just as the Christian in his initiation consecrates himself to God after the exorcism, so the holy place is consecrated to God with the dedication, after having been removed from the influence of the evil one, who must remain outside the temple with all his actions. Welcome cannot be given to profane actions of this type, or to any others, in the place where the divine mysteries are celebrated. How is it possible that bishops and priests have forgotten that such a place as that, so often built with sacrifice by the faithful, has been "dedicated"—a word that recalls the act with which something very personal is offered to someone who is loved. To dedicate something means that it is no longer mine, but his. If I were to take it back, that would be a betrayal. It is a grave matter, because we take from God that which is his, what we ourselves had sworn we would give him. The rite itself of dedication shows that it is a kind of oath or vow, that is, a sacred act. What need is there for such solemnity, if afterwards the sacred place is employed for profane uses? It would be necessary to recall that with the rite of dedication of the church we say to the Lord: "This space was ours, now we give it to you, so that it may be yours, and that only the worship owed to you shall be done in it." Often, in mosaics and medieval frescoes, figures of the bishop and of the sponsoring lay faithful offer a little model of the sacred edifice to the Lord, to the Virgin, or to the titular saint.

Liturgists exalt the rite of dedication, but in contradiction with that, they go silent and speak not a word in the face of the transformation of churches into multi-purpose halls. This is worse than what was done by totalitarian atheist regimes, which had transformed these places into theaters, gymnasiums, and stores. It is a very serious phenomenon, because it means, first, that the sense of the church as a place offered to God, for the worship owed him, has been lost; we have consecrated something, and then we take it back in order to do purely human things there. In the second place, we favor in this way the eclipse of the divine presence, because in the church we practice activities proper to a theater or an auditorium, such as speaking, eating, applauding, and other attitudes typical of places of entertainment. When a church becomes a theater where people laugh, applaud, and shout, it then becomes difficult to demand, for the same place, the proper attitudes for worship: listening, recollection, silence, adoration, because the conviction that one is standing in a versatile locale has taken root. That conviction leads to obscuring the principal and characteristic function of a church, which is adoration, and to prohibiting kneeling for prayer, either when the liturgy is being celebrated in the church, or outside the liturgy. But in reality, the church remains a place of presence and prayer, and of silence, even when there is no liturgy being celebrated. Personal prayer, without which there is no liturgy or public prayer, would also gain from that. Instead, a kind of desolation has replaced what is said in Psalm 84: "How lovely are your dwelling places, Lord of Hosts. My soul languishes and yearns for the altars of the Lord. My heart and my flesh exult in the living God. Blessed is he who lives in your house: always he sings your praises! Blessed is the man who trusts in you, O Lord."

In the *Rule* of St. Benedict, it is written:

> The oratory [given that name from a Latin term for prayer] should be what its name says, and so nothing else should be done or put there. At the end of every liturgical celebration all go out in perfect silence and with great respect for God, so that if anyone should wish to remain for prayer privately, he may not be impeded in that by the indiscretion of others. But if at another time as well someone desires to pray on his own, let him certainly go in and pray, not out loud, but with tears and inner fervor. Therefore, as we have said, he who does not intend to dedicate himself to prayer should refrain from staying in church after the liturgical celebrations, so as to avoid disturbing others with his presence.[6]

There is no place more apt than a church for bringing people who so desire—and there are many of them!—to an encounter with God. The Church must not be considered as "the liturgical space"[7]

---

6. St. Benedict, *Rule*, chapter 52.
7. The Italian equivalent is "aula liturgica," "hall for liturgy." (Translator's note)

and nothing more than that! Is it possible that there are no available places for concerts, theatrical performances, and other such things? Then we should not be surprised that the sense of the sacred, the sense of the divine presence, has been lost. Few today know what sacred and holy mean. The "theology of secularization" considers that everything is sacred and that there is nothing profane, and so it wishes us to believe that the dedication of a church is not a consecration; it can also be used for profane activities. Dedication, however, is an ancient term. Carrying out a dedication with a chrism anointing makes sacred what was not sacred before: it is a consecration. Everything that is sacred comes from the Holy Spirit.

Someone will object that Christians have no need for a temple in order to worship. It is true that spiritual worship is enough—but a spiritual worship that does not cut us off from the body and material things. So, someone will continue to say, let us no longer build sacred places, and let us meet in the open, hot and cold weather permitting. But if we continue in that vein, we need to be coherent. Are not Christians the living stones of the spiritual edifice, as St. Peter says (cf. 1 Pt. 2:5)? Or do the words of St. Paul to the Corinthians, "Do you not know that you are the temple of God, and that the spirit of God dwells in you? If someone destroys the temple of God, God will destroy him. Because the temple of God, which you are, is holy" (1 Cor. 3:16–17) not refer to us? And is this truth not mystically adumbrated, according to the Preface of the Dedication of a Church, in the sign that a temple is?

In order to drive out the evil one

"Exorcism is directed at the expulsion of demons or to the liberation from demonic possession through the spiritual authority that Jesus entrusted to his Church" (CCC 1673).

With the Motu Proprio *Ministeria Quaedam* of Paul VI, the minor order of exorcist has been considered abolished, together with the order of porter, that is, the ancient ministry of checking entries and departures at the church doors. The cleric on his way to the priesthood who received the order of exorcist was enabled to help the priest in the exorcising ministry. In a certain sense, such orders have not been simply abolished, for the Motu Proprio refers to some of the functions of those orders, functions that can be retained where they are judged necessary. For example, the order of porter is exercised *de facto* today by all those who in some way exercise a function of keeping order in church, such as members of the faithful charged with being vigilant so that the participation of the faithful in the rites, especially the processional movements (entrance, offertory, and communion), may take place in good order or not be disturbed by strangers. Also, the office of a priest appointed exorcist has been renewed in almost all the dioceses, with the task of putting into practice Jesus's order to drive out demons (cf. Mt. 10:8).

Together with the healing of the sick, driving out demons constitutes one of the fundamental aims of the mission of the Savior, who came into the world to confront the power of Satan. The devil exists and the Church must follow the example of her Master, receiving the power and the assignment to exorcise, as attested by the New Testament and other writings, such as the *Apostolic Tradition* (cf. chapters 20 and 21), which refers to exorcisms on persons and over the oil of catechumens, also called for that reason oil of exorcism, which receives its power on account of the invocation of God by the priest. After that, exorcisms were done on everything that was to be used in divine worship, so that it would all be exempt from the power of the demons, and thus also on demonically obsessed or possessed persons. The totality of the rites and formulae, given shape over centuries, are found in the ritual book of 1614, under the title "Major Exorcism," to which was added a short exorcism composed under Pope Leo XIII.[8]

The renewed rite shows signs of the postconciliar crisis, which went so far as to cast doubt on the existence of the devil and to favor identifying the possessed, who were healed by Jesus, with the mentally ill. The exorcism before the baptism of children, which is a sim-

---

8. This short exorcism text, added to the *Rituale Romanum* by Leo XIII, and reserved to authorized priests, is not to be confused with the simple Prayer to St. Michael, also published by Leo XIII, and commonly recited by priest and people at the end of a Low Mass in the Extraordinary Form. (Translator's note)

ple exorcism,[9] has been changed into a prayer of liberation; in the baptism of adults, into an invocation geared toward reinforcing the spiritual life, and only secondarily, to being freed from the power of the devil. There is thus a discontinuity between the renewed ritual and the ritual in the Extraordinary Form of the Roman Rite, above all if one observes that in the latter there is a direct address to the evil spirit, ordering him to come out in God's name, while in the first, an invocation of Christ or of the Father. Thus not a few exorcists denounce the weakness of such formulas for obtaining the principal effect of the exorcism, which is deliverance from the evil one. Why would one ever change the addressee of what is said, if Jesus, first of all, addressed himself directly to the evil spirits, intimating to them as he drove them away: "Be silent and come out of this man" (Mk. 1:25)?

While the Code of Canon Law, at canon 1172, treats of the exorcism on the possessed, which can be carried out with special permission of the bishop, and gives the norms for doing the exorcism with prudence, the *Catechism* keeps a mention of the solemn or "major exorcism," which the Congregation for Divine Worship has had to prepare anew for the exorcists charged with the ministry by their bishops (cf. CCC 1673). In the major exorcism, it is publicly asked for that a person or thing be protected against the influence of the evil one and taken out from under his dominion. Before doing the exorcism on someone, it is important to verify that it is not a case of sickness, psychological in this case.

A gift of the Spirit: popular piety

Original forms of sacramentals include the veneration of relics, visits to sanctuaries, pilgrimages, processions, the *via crucis* or Stations of the Cross, the Rosary, medals, etc.: we are treating of expressions of the religious sense of the Christian people, a prolongation of the liturgical life of the Church. For that reason, one speaks of "popular

9. "Simple," as opposed to exorcism on a person seen to be possessed; for the latter case a priest needs the faculty granted by the bishop according to canon law. (Translator's note)

piety" or "religious piety." Despite the clarification by Paul VI (cf. *Evangelii Nuntiandi*, n. 48), the two expressions continue to be used interchangeably (cf. CCC 1674); in reality, the first expression is appropriate to Christianity, while the second refers to religion in general.[10] That being presupposed, one should not think that popular piety is foreign to the liturgy, which is the principal manifestation of the people of God; on the contrary. Therefore the misunderstanding that the liturgy is not "popular"—a rather considerable affirmation to make, on account of the emphasis placed, since Vatican II, on the *people's* participation as a criterion for celebration—must be overcome.[11] For the Christian, "participate" first of all means being conscious of one's belonging to the ecclesial Body of Christ. Without this consciousness, there is no active participation. Perhaps it is here that the gulf between liturgy and popular piety, which came to be at a certain historical period and then continued, should be situated. In this way there have been evident conflicts and divisions in the people of God, for example opposing to ancient forms of gathering and worship such as confraternities, considered conservative and surpassed, the new forms of association, considered innovative and free from any defect—as if a form by itself would be enough to safeguard a content.

At the origins of Christianity—as attested by the *Apostolic Tradition*—liturgy and popular piety were identified, were not opposed to each other either conceptually or pastorally; rather, they ran together harmoniously for the celebration of one single mystery of Christ, thought of in a unitary way, to sustain the supernatural and moral life of the Lord's disciples. That would be a valid program still today. Because the purpose, from the 4th century on, was evangelization, the relation between these two things is one not only of spontaneous convergence, but also of conscious adaptation and inculturation: the local Churches in fact did not disdain to take on pagan ceremonial forms. It must be observed that it was precisely in this era that the various Eastern and Western liturgical families were

---

10. Cf. Congregation for Divine Worship and the Discipline of the Sacraments, *Directory on Popular Piety and the Liturgy* (2001), 9–10.

11. Ibid., n. 11.

born, in a manner parallel to the rapport between Tradition and Scripture: the latter was born in a certain sense from the former, as the liturgy was born from the *pietas* of the people. The liturgies—especially the ancient Eastern liturgies—brought about a symbiosis between the speech of mystery and the speech of the people, successfully opposing, over the centuries, the various ideologies and heresies (think of 17th-century rationalism and Jansenism). When that exchange gradually ceased to take place, popular piety was progressively detached from the liturgy of the Church and had to react on its own, up to paroxysms sometimes, against the penetration of heretical ideologies into divine worship.[12] Dualism and the crisis of Christian worship resulted, the most garish reflection of which can be seen in the developments that took place in religious imagery. This was a dualism that from the 17th century on accentuated the disconnection between the "religion of the learned," potentially close to the liturgy, and the "religion of the simple believers," close by its nature to popular piety. This temptation to dualism is still alive today, when an effort is made to privilege a Church "of catechesis," by nature elitist, over against a Church "of ceremony," which is nevertheless the one that sees people coming to it in much greater numbers. Certain Puritanical rigidities have caused and do cause a decay of the liturgy into indecipherable symbolism, which ends up accentuating the disconnection from the people and their so-called devotionalism.[13] So we should be attentive to the lesson of history: the liturgical reform of Vatican II itself recalls that disregard or disesteem for popular piety betrays an inadequate valuing of some

12. A notable example: the Jansenistic Synod of Pistoia legislated against aspects of popular piety that touched on the liturgy or the churches. Among its 85 theological and disciplinary decisions condemned by Pius VI in 1794, according as they would be understood in ways more or less contrary to the mind of the Church, we find synodal prohibitions of flowers on the altar, and of veils on statues. Pius VI upheld these customs as examples of legitimate piety in the Church. Laypeople reacted as well: when statues were stripped of veils, and sacred images from suppressed houses of religious were removed from churches by reformist clergy, imposing crowds invaded, to restore veils to the statues. (Translator's note)

13. In the Italian context today, rigidities and indecipherable symbolism are exemplified by the proliferating new churches of "contemporary" design, often characterized by bare cement and brutal shape and line. (Translator's note)

facts of the Church's life, and seems to express ideological prejudices more than the doctrine of the faith.[14] Such tendencies constitute an attitude that takes no account of the fact that popular piety is also an ecclesial reality promoted and sustained by the Spirit, and that the Magisterium exercises its function of authentication and guarantee on it.[15] It is important to affirm this, as it is analogous to what is affirmed in the conciliar Constitution *Dei Verbum* on the two sources of revelation inspired by only one Spirit. It must not be forgotten that saints have drawn from popular piety, because the Holy Spirit works in it. Besides, piety is one of his seven gifts. Is there sentimentalism in popular piety? But why ask the question—is it really the case that a certain "liturgism" is not also affected by sentimentalism? In order not to fall into *sentimentalism*, sentiment, a noble component of the human spirit, should not be excluded. The genuine concept of Christian liturgy includes the popular dimension.

It can therefore be said that the source of popular piety is the presence of the Spirit in the Church; its point of reference, the mystery of Christ the Savior; its goal, the glory of God and the salvation of men; its historical occasion the happy meeting between the work of evangelization and culture.[16] In this way people who lack understanding of it, or who neglect or despise it, should be helped to adopt a more positive attitude toward it and take greater account of its values, which constitute a true patrimony of interior attitudes and virtues. The transmission, from generation to generation, of the gestures of piety is nothing other than the unfolding of the tradition; indeed in various cases the fusion is so profound that the proper elements of the Christian faith have become an integral part of the cultural identity of a people. One of the more evident examples is given by the *ex votos* with which the saints are venerated and thanked: votive tablets or anatomical shapes indicating the episodes and events in which someone came into contact with the saints' intercession and received a grace, a life-giving gift, or a healing, or escaped a danger. Popular piety is a fundamental element of the

---

14. Cf. SC 13. (Translator's note)
15. *Directory on Popular Piety and the Liturgy,* 50.
16. Ibid., 51.

identity of a people; it does not come into being like a fungus, but flows from such subjects of identity as the family and associations of the faithful, in particular the confraternities.

If the Holy Spirit is at the origin of every genuine manifestation of liturgical worship and of authentic popular piety, then in order to evaluate and renew popular piety, it is undoubtedly necessary to promote, among the faithful, the filial attitude and the same sentiments as those of Christ, which the saints translated into their lives in their way and in their time. And since popular piety brings with it a Trinitarian stamp, there is something to work with, to enlighten the faithful concerning the characteristic feature of Christian prayer, which is Trinitarian, not disconnected from the contemplation of the suffering humanity of the Savior, or from his glorification, and pointed toward the Eucharist. Furthermore, since the Holy Spirit confers on the faithful the "sacerdotal" capacity to offer themselves, it is necessary to help them draw from the word of God. It is precisely a reminder of their "sacerdotal" capacity, between prayer and Scripture, that will prevent any slip into sentimentalism or Biblicism, that is to say, a merely intellectual exercise. Only in this way, as has been said, does the culture of the faith flow forth from cult (worship). Liturgy and popular piety, synonymous at their origin, must turn and converge on the single purpose for which they exist: communion with the Lord, which is the goal of the people's piety, as it is for the individual, in order to reach sanctity.

Catholics know well that the ultimate purpose of veneration of the saints is the glory of God and the sanctification of man, through a life fully in conformity with the divine will, and the imitation of the virtues of those who were eminent disciples of the Lord. Venerating a saint takes nothing away from adoration of the Lord; rather, it increases it. The fact is that among us Catholics a certain Protestantization has caught on, which substitutes the Lutheran *aut . . . aut* for the Catholic *et . . . et*;[17] on the contrary, honoring the saints is inclusive of giving honor to God, not exclusive—as the Orthodox attest with us. There is a link between the feasts of the saints and the celebration of the mystery of Christ, because the feasts of the mem-

17. "Either . . . or"; "Both . . . and."

bers of the Body, the saints, are in the final analysis feasts of the Head, Christ. In regard to charisms, which are talked about so much, it is precisely the charism of saints that has enriched the life of the Church: their very relics, placed under the altar, indicate the saints' contribution to the building up of the body of Christ.

Christian funerals, or neo-pagan?

"I await the resurrection of the dead and the life of the world to come," and in the Apostles' Creed, "the resurrection of the body and life everlasting": this is the last of the truths of the faith that the Christian professes. What does it mean? As it happened for Jesus Christ, so it will happen for us: not only our souls but also our mortal bodies will overcome death. Therefore, the Christian believes not only in the immortality of the soul, as Plato did, but also in the immortality of the body, which will begin with the resurrection. What does it mean to rise again? The body, which—because of the separation of the soul that occurred at death—is subject to corruption, will be reunited to the soul. Who will rise again? All human beings: those who did what was right and good, to receive the eternal recompense, that is, an eternally blessed state (paradise), and those who have done evil, to receive the eternal condemnation (hell). How is it possible? As it happens in nature with a seed, which corrupts in the earth but gives rise to a new plant, so our body, which corrupts with death, will be transformed into a "spiritual body"[18] by reuniting with the soul. Does the resurrection happen right after death? No, but at the end of the world, or the last day of history, which only God the Father knows.

In the meantime, whenever we confess and are given communion, Jesus Christ transforms us little by little into himself, the Risen One, through the work of the Holy Spirit, thus making us participate in his own humanity hypostatically united to the person of the

---

18. This expression, from St. Paul (1 Cor. 15), is not intended to deny the corporeality or material reality of the risen body, but to emphasize its perfect subjection to and harmony with the rational soul. It is a body permeated with the human spirit and in no way resisting that spirit. (Editor's note)

Word and his immortal life, with faith, hope, and charity. Through this we are already risen with Christ, who said: "I am the resurrection and the life. He who believes in me, even if he dies, will live: and whoever lives and believes in me will never die" (Jn. 11:25–26). How does one get to this resurrection? With baptism we are already "dead with Christ," because the water, which came down over us, is like the tomb of Christ, in whom we have renounced sin. With death, the soul is separated from the body. It seems natural; in reality it is a consequence of original sin.[19] But to the faithful in Christ, "life is not taken away, but transformed," as the liturgy says.[20] This Christian meaning of death, as a Paschal event, or passage to eternal life, is received at baptism.

What is eternal life? Precisely that life that begins when we are baptized in the faith of Jesus Christ; it reaches its plenitude after death, when the soul appears for the particular judgment before him, receiving as retribution either eternal beatitude or eternal damnation, or else the pain of purification (purgatory), which deprives the soul for a time of the vision of God. This retribution will be manifested to all in the final and universal judgment; at that time, every purification will finish, and there will be new heavens and a new earth (2 Pt. 3:13) for man and the universe. St. Leo the Great says:

> It is right that the blessedness of the vision of God is promised to the pure of heart. The darkened eye could not in fact sustain the splendor of the true light: that which will be delight for pure souls shall be cause of torment for those stained from sin. Therefore let us avoid the dark cloud of earthly emptiness, and let the eyes of the soul be washed from all filth of sin, so that our limpid gaze may be fed from the sublime vision of God. It was precisely so we would work to merit this sublime vision that the Lord said: "Blessed are the peacemakers, because they shall be called children of God" (Mt. 5:9). This beatitude, brethren, does not refer to just

19. Death is the natural consequence of the physics and chemistry of the universe and the human body itself, but before sin man was specially preserved from death by his Creator. (Translator's note)
20. In the Preface for the Dead.

any kind of mutual understanding or agreement, but to the agreement the Apostle speaks of: "Be at peace with God" (cf. Rm. 5:1), and concerning which the prophet says: "There is great peace for him who loves your law, he finds no obstacle in his path" (Ps. 118:165). Neither the closest bonds of friendship nor the most perfect resemblance in character can claim to possess this peace if they are not in harmony with the will of God. Outside this sublime peace we find only conniving and associations for criminal enterprises, wicked alliances, and pacts with vice. The love of the impious world cannot be reconciled with the love of God. . . . In fact the love of God and the love of neighbor will render them deserving of the great reward. They will no longer feel any adversity, they will no longer fear any obstacles or tricks, but, when the battle and all tribulations are over, they will rest in the most tranquil peace of God.[21]

This long preface explains what the light of Christ's Passover is, and expressions such as "let perpetual light shine upon them" and "may they rest in peace," which are used in the liturgy for the deceased. For this part of the liturgy, the Church has taken account—St. Augustine is an illustrious witness—of customs and cultures, once corrected and completed, which feed the vast and rich popular piety surrounding the deceased. In spite of that, however, we are faced today with grave deformations of Christian funerals. In a "letter to the editor" of a newspaper, there was the following: "At a recent funeral for a noted theater actress, it got to the point that relatives and friends (everyone from the so-called 'world of culture'!) considered it right to commemorate, from the ambo, the activities of the deceased woman that were in sharp contrast with the teaching of the Church, and also to protest the fact that the priest was opposed to this." There are also the various cases of suicide: unless it was the outcome of a grave malady that put someone out of his mind, or unless a confessor or someone else who knew the person in the last moments could give witness to a conversion, how can there be celebration of the sacred liturgy of the Church, which is an act of public worship, for someone who has notoriously

---

21. St. Leo the Great, *Discourse on the Beatitudes*, 95, 8–9: PL 54:465–66.

disregarded, or even lived constantly outside, the grace of God and the Church's communion? Without meaning to prejudge the mercy of God, it used to be said: he is *un disgraziato*, that is, outside the grace of God.[22]

St. John Chrysostom invited his listeners to distinguish between pagan despair and Christian hope.[23] Therefore, let us seek to clarify. Funerals, which are as old as the world, mean, according to the Latin root, "funeral procession": but a funeral is not only that for a Christian; rather it is a complex rite, which begins at the moment of death, at home or in the hospital, where vigil is kept in prayer by the family members, and it concludes with the burial at the cemetery. So funerals cannot be considered as limited to the liturgy in church; rather, they include the accompaniment of the coffin by the cortege, from the house to the church, and to the cemetery, where this is still laudably done. Why should we consider that to be lugubrious or from another age? Would it not help people in the secularized society to understand that death is sacred, as life is?

The risen Jesus is the firstborn of all those risen from the dead (Col. 1:8), because he has taken down the last screen of that tunnel that every man tries to excavate, uselessly, in order to pass over to the other side, into eternal life. Consequently, death is marked by mourning, which from its Latin root means "crying." Only faith in the resurrection opens the heart to hope, which is able to soothe the pain and the weeping: *Surrexit Christus spes mea!* Therefore Christian funerals—measuring up to the solemnity of death—consist of both sadness and hope, but often they are reduced to something more like a performance: applause when the coffin passes by, celebration of the true or merely presumed merits of the deceased, in place of prayer of suffrage for his soul. And to think that in place of funeral laments, Christians put psalms, readings, and prayers in their place, as Jerome attests, and sought to abolish distinctions and preferential treatment for some in funeral practices, as the Liturgy

22. According to the etymology of the word in Italian; commonly it has more the sense of "miserable." (Translator's note)

23. Cf. St. John Chrysostom, *Sermon on St. Berenice and St. Prodoce*, PG 50:634.

Constitution still recommends (cf. SC 32)! Here, as well, the sense of the sacred has been lost. The conclusion of the celebrated *'A livella*, by Totò, comes to mind: "These farces are done only by the living: we're serious... we belong to death!"[24] Certainly in the homily one can soberly recall the life of the deceased, especially his Christian virtues, but without seeking to beatify him early with the usual "he's surely in heaven," since the Church has not competence over the eternal judgment of God. Above all it is necessary to read the mystery of death in the light of the risen Christ, and to help people turn their minds to the kingdom of heaven. It is a moment of Gospel proclamation, insofar as faithful who rarely attend Mass, or friends of the deceased who are not Christian, are often present to participate. At the prayer of the faithful, it is possible for relatives and friends of the deceased to read intentions if they are brief, and first submitted to the priest to correct and organize, as may be needed; eulogies should be given in front of the entrance to the church or at the cemetery, or in exceptional cases at the end of the celebration in church—and only after the celebrant has gone out.

For all the faithful departed, there exists a right to a funeral in church (cf. CIC, can. 1176, s. 19). The word "faithful" is underlined, that is, those who have not been legitimately deprived of this right (cf. can. 1184) on account of irregular situations (changing to another religion, diffusion of heresies, causing divisions in the Church, choosing cremation for reasons contrary to the faith), or on account of other manifest situations of sin (those living in concubinage, "remarried" divorced, etc.).[25] In short, it is not possible to grant a religious funeral when the following three conditions are verified: (1) the irregular situation is publicly manifest; (2) such a

---

24. *'A livella* is a poem in Neapolitan by modern Italy's beloved actor, Antonio De Curtis, "Totò" (d. 1967). The line quoted, said by a commoner's ghost to a nobleman's ghost who feels dishonored because the commoner is buried next to him, concerns the pomp and honors of this life. (Translator's note)

25. Situations of sin: the Church traditionally considers that external offenses punishable by canon law are to be presumed morally imputable to the persons committing them, if the persons have been warned (or are equivalently knowledgeable), unless the contrary is evident. Cf. CIC (1983), canon 1321, section 3. (Translator's note)

sinner has not given some sign of repentance before death; (3) the celebration of the funeral in church is a source of public scandal for the faithful—that is, pushes them in the direction of committing sin, in this case, to consider an irregular situation as something normal. In a case of uncertainty, and as the Byzantines normally do, it is possible to celebrate the rite of the Word, without Mass, and then the leave-taking.

We come to burial. In the contemporary ecological uproar, respect for nature is demanded for minerals, vegetative life, and animals, but not so much for man from conception until death; thus for the body of the deceased the violent action of fire—cremation, which from the Latin root means burning—is admitted, instead of the natural decomposition of the mineral elements from which the body is made, the decomposition by which it returns to the mother earth. It is true that the Church allows it, provided there is no intention to express hostility against the Church, or to exclude faith in the resurrection, but one should ask himself if in our day such faith still exists: statistically it seems to be at minimal levels, and not without confused ideas. Has there not been a surrender to the neo-pagan mentality? Why not recommend burial, whether in the earth or in a tomb, after the example of the Lord who wished to be buried like a grain of wheat that, once fallen into the earth, dies and bears the fruit of eternal life? It is sown corruptible, and it rises incorruptible, the Apostle says; we lay it down like seed in the earth, but the body will rise again in glory (cf. 1 Cor. 15:42–44). It is an offering—this time of the body—which, preceded and followed by the ritual blessings of a funeral, finds it complement in the Eucharistic sacrifice. The grain of wheat permits us to illustrate the truth of the resurrection: the plant that is born is in continuity, but it is also a new thing.

In the case of cremation, the ashes are to be conserved in a cemetery or another sacred place; only with the laying down of the urn there does the funeral rite conclude. Burying the dead is a corporal work of mercy, therefore the scattering of the ashes goes against the identity of the deceased human being and reduces him to "utopia," that is, something nowhere, and with nothing to remember it by. In contrast to that, the Holy Spirit stays near tombs to watch over them, in expectation of the resurrection, according to St. Paulinus of Nola; I like to see that as the meaning of the light always kept burning there.

Visiting some of the necropolises of antiquity, the Vatican necropolis, for example, one observes the gradual changeover in mentality that was caused by Christianity: from the "city of the dead" (in Greek, *nekropolis*), which one enters via cremation or burial, not believing that the body can rise again, the concept changed to "the place of rest" (this also being a Greek term, *koimētērion*), as though it were only a prelude to the eternal rebirth. But now we've turned backward, back to the "necropolis," with the aggravating circumstance of the disappearance of signs of respect for the place itself, so that the time of death as well is no longer considered sacred, as life is sacred. Likewise, the thing needed by the "differently living"—grant me the expression, instead of "deceased"—is help for approaching the face of God as soon and as much as possible. The soul has a thirst for God, whether it knows it or not, and in the manner of Augustine is restless as long as it does not rest in him. This the ancients intuited, in fact they used the word "refreshment" for their convivial rituals on behalf of the deceased. Christians took over the funeral banquet of the third, seventh, thirtieth, and fortieth day, but they completed it with the Eucharist of suffrage for the deceased, as a support and favor to the candidates for eternal life, as the term suffrage indicates. This is the greatest thing there is for helping those who live beyond this world to see God. Therefore, when the liturgical calendar permits it, Masses for the faithful departed should be promoted, with all the sacred signs that characterize them: from the color of the vestments, black or violet,[26] to the November 2 commemoration and the observance of the eighth day. Furthermore, it is well to do the tolling of the church bells to announce the death of a parishioner and to help the faithful to write up the funeral notice

---

26. The modern Roman rite allows for black, violet, or white vestments at funerals; the traditional Roman Rite uses only black. White is a less fitting color because it celebrates the known triumph of Easter and of certain classes of saints, while at a funeral we are still uncertain of and praying for the deceased's participation in that triumph; violet, too, is less fitting because it is the color of penitence (as in Advent and Lent) rather than mourning and prayer specifically for the dead. (Editor's note)

with expressive Christian phrases or Biblical verses, with the Cross or the image of Jesus who has saved us from death, rather than the image of a saint, like Padre Pio, however much loved. In this way the Church will nourish hope in the resurrection beyond death, and go against the effects of desacralization, which seeks to hide death from view, because it is afraid of it.

The ritual of funerals, in the typical edition of 1969, offers three basic models, with "stations" at the house of the deceased, in the church, and at the cemetery. With the funeral Mass always presupposed, a religious funeral consists in lifting the prayer of intercession to God the Father for the first time, with the "commending of the soul"—in the ancient period this was the last prayer at the moment of departure and the first one of suffrage; this prayer is formed from the chant of psalms and the celebrated medieval antiphons that accompany the absolution at the coffin, called a "leave-taking" in the Ordinary Form: the antiphons are *Subvenite, In paradisum, Chorus angelorum* (in the vernacular though these can all be); additionally in the Extraordinary Form, the *Libera* and *Dies Irae*. The coffin is sprinkled with holy water and incensed in order to express the fact that the body has been the temple of the Lord: "Do you not know that you are the temple of God and that the Spirit of God dwells in you?" (1 Cor. 3:16). Mother Church has borne in her earthly womb the Christian whom she now puts in the hands of the Father and, in the exact sense, bids him Godspeed.[27] With the variety of customs already seen in funeral rites today, a priest out of his pastoral zeal and generous welcome should surely be able to accommodate requests for funerals in the Extraordinary Form.

The leave-taking from a deceased person who is baptized—who dies in Christ—is only temporary: the soul goes into exile from the body (cf. 2 Cor. 5:8) in order to dwell with the Lord; the bond of the communion of saints persists, that is, the circulation of the merits of Christ, of the Virgin, and of the faithful, living and departed.

---

27. In Italian, *addio*, "good-bye," etymologically means "to God." (Translator's note)

The Extension of Sacramental Meaning

Without Jesus Christ's mediation before the judgment of God, our supplications would be worth nothing: here we see the meaning of the Mass of suffrage, in order to express the efficacious communion of the Church with the deceased person, that is, to ask for purification from sins and their consequences in purgatory, from which admission is granted to the Lord's table in the Kingdom. Therefore prayer for the deceased (Mass of the thirtieth day, anniversary, or other kinds of commemoration) has its efficacy, in the sense that it abbreviates the time of their penalty—in the hypothesis that they are in the state of purification—especially if preceded or followed by confession and communion, corresponding indulgences, works of penance and charity. All of this renders us and them pure and ready in the sight of God. And the deceased who have arrived at blessedness or are still in the state of purification repay with their intercession for us before God.

The relatives and friends of the deceased are "comforted" with spiritual words (cf. 1 Th. 4:18), words of hope in eternal life. In this way they learn to live—not with stratagems other than these words—in communion with the deceased person, communing in the first place with the body of Christ, of whom the deceased is a living member, and with the deceased through this. Therefore, praying for the deceased and with the deceased, friends and relatives shall one day be reunited forever.

At the traditional Easter vigil, in the litany, there is an invocation with "From a sudden death, liberate us"; in the Hail Mary one asks: "Pray for us sinners ... at the hour of our death"; St. Joseph is invoked in order to obtain a good death; and with St. Francis we raise the hymn: "Praised be you, my Lord, for our sister, bodily death, from which no living man can escape; woe to those who will die in mortal sins, blessed are those whom you will find in your holy will, because the second death will do them no harm." It is necessary to be ready for death, to avoid the surprise of death when in mortal sin. Confession and communion are necessary for this reason, too. In the expectation of the coming of the Lord, it is necessary to entrust oneself to his mercy, so that in spite of our sin it may draw forth from us all possible good, since we are called and are faithful, as the word *Amen* indicates: "I believe, I have faith."

In this way the Christian's itinerary is concluded, by passing through the sacraments and the sacramentals (cf. CCC 1680), and arriving at the day of death, the day of birth into heaven, because it is the fulfilling complement to the new birth begun with baptism, the definitive "resemblance" to the "image of the Son" conferred by the anointing of the Holy Spirit and participation in the banquet of the Kingdom, anticipated in the Eucharist, even if, in order to don the nuptial robe, he still has need of further purifications (CCC 1682).

CPSIA information can be obtained
at www.ICGtesting.com
Printed in the USA
FSHW011551220920
73986FS